The Life & Legacy of Elizabeth Miller Watkins

The Life & Legacy of Elizabeth Miller Watkins

A PIONEERING PHILANTHROPIST

Mary Dresser Burchill and
Norma Decker Hoagland

UNIVERSITY PRESS OF KANSAS

For Elizabeth, Joe, and Brower

~

Published by the University Press of Kansas (Lawrence, Kansas 66045), which was
organized by the Kansas Board of Regents and is operated and funded by Emporia
State University, Fort Hays State University, Kansas State University, Pittsburg State
University, the University of Kansas, and Wichita State University.

Library of Congress Cataloging-in-Publication Data
Names: Burchill, Mary D., author. | Hoagland, Norma, author.
Title: The life and legacy of Elizabeth Miller Watkins : a pioneering
philanthropist / Mary Dresser Burchill and Norma Decker Hoagland.
Description: Lawrence : University Press of Kansas, [2023] | Includes
bibliographical references and index.
Identifiers: LCCN 2022042403 (print) | LCCN 2022042404 (ebook)
ISBN 9780700634231 (paperback)
ISBN 9780700634248 (ebook)
Subjects: LCSH: Watkins, Elizabeth Miller, –1939 | Women
philanthropists—Kansas—Biography.
Classification: LCC HV28.W38 B87 2023 (print) | LCC HV28.W38 (ebook) |
DDC 361.7/4092 [B]—dc23/eng/20221230
LC record available at https://lccn.loc.gov/2022042403.
LC ebook record available at https://lccn.loc.gov/2022042404.

British Library Cataloguing-in-Publication Data is available.

Printed in the United States of America

10 9 8 7 6 5 4 3 2 1

The paper used in this publication is acid free and meets the minimum requirements
of the American National Standard for Permanence of Paper for Printed Library
Materials Z39.48-1992.

My greatest object is to realize the most I can from lands and invest it to the glory of God in my lifetime and leave just as little as possible to be fought over when I am no more.
ELIZABETH JOSEPHINE MILLER WATKINS

Contents

Contents

Acknowledgments

Elizabeth found her way into our minds and hearts as we researched, at first individually and then together. She has been waiting for us to tell her story. Perhaps she's been tapping her foot at how long it has taken us. It's worth the wait. She has inspired us in so many ways and, we hope, will do the same for our readers. It's a wonderful and unique story that we are proud to share.

~

We begin by thanking Elizabeth for revealing a bit of herself in her business letters and her scrapbook. Our thanks go to Professor Malin for saving the Watkins papers and to the catalogers at Spencer Research Library for putting those papers into a usable order. Thank you to the Kenneth Spencer Research Library and their exceptional staff for being such a pleasure to work with and sustaining an environment so welcoming to researchers. The Watkins Museum of History deserves our great thanks. Steve Nowak, Brittany Keegan, and Monica Davis have each been a cheerful source of help and enthusiasm. We express our thanks to University Press of Kansas. They have been good stewards of history. Joyce Harrison and Kelly Chrisman Jacques have been patient advisors, and Janet Yoe skillfully copy edited our manuscript.

When this journey began the Watkins name was a familiar one, but Elizabeth became a very real, incredible woman as we began to understand her and her world. What she accomplished deserved to be set down for everyone to know. Research of this sort is never complete. There is still more to dig out, but we are satisfied that we have made a creditable start.

Thanks to all the women who have constantly asked about the project and encouraged both of us. When Norma began this journey as a "Watkins Woman" living in Watkins Hall from 1969 to 1971, she knew nothing about Elizabeth. As a member of Kitchen 8, the alumnae group for those scholarship halls, she began to learn about Elizabeth and compiled the book

Watkins and Miller Halls. At that time, she met Mary, who had extensively researched and been drawn to Elizabeth's life. Both of us are grateful for each other and the fun we have had together; and we are pleased to give readers a look into Elizabeth's life as an inspiration.

To our husbands, Brower and Joe, heartfelt thanks for their constant encouragement and good advice. It has been a long endeavor and so satisfying.

Introduction

The papers were nearly lost during World War II. America had finally become involved in the worldwide conflict and her citizens were enthusiastically doing their part. War bonds, rationing, coupons, paper drives.

One morning in January 1942, Professor James Malin of the University of Kansas (KU) was driving with his young daughter, Jane, past the Lawrence City Hall. In its previous life, this building had been the home of the Watkins Bank and the Watkins Land and Mortgage Company. A beautiful and carefully constructed building, it stands at Eleventh and Massachusetts Street, the main street through downtown Lawrence, Kansas. At the back of the building, Malin noticed boxes of paper being heaved out the third-floor windows. So, the report of the Red Cross paper drive was true. He had read about it in the *Lawrence Journal-World* last Saturday evening. Papers rained down. A historian, his natural curiosity got the better of him.

He and Jane looked through a few boxes, looked at each other, and began to load whatever they could into the trunk of their car. Professor Malin called KU chancellor Deane Malott. Malott called Dick Williams, Elizabeth Watkins's former business manager. Truckloads of the Watkins business records and letters were already at the junkyard, being made into six-hundred-pound bales for loading onto railway cars, in response to the WWII paper drive. An agreement was reached. Malin, his daughter Jane, and a friend, Charles Realey, worked for several days, loading those boxes of history into a university truck; they were then "dumped in the ramp area of the (university) Library," to wait for years before being sorted and organized.

Those boxes held the transactional "bones" and the history of the Watkins Land and Mortgage Company and the Watkins National Bank. Those papers contained the thread of the story of the fortune Jabez Bunting Watkins created largely from his own effort and resolve. He didn't do it entirely alone. Also between those fluttering pages was the thread of the story of his much younger wife, Elizabeth Josephine Miller Watkins, who worked for him, learned from him, and ultimately helped him accumulate that fortune. Together they forged an unusual life and developed a unique theory of intelligent philanthropy.

The information and the facts related here come largely from letters that Elizabeth wrote, and made copies of for her own records, over her seventy-six years. She left no diary. Most of the letters are business, not personal, ones, which makes the work of a biographer more difficult. But those business letters often include a line or two about her life, her current activities, joys, and sorrows, that give us insight into her life. These remaining letters are now sorted and housed in the Kenneth Spencer Research Library on the campus of the University of Kansas. The letters, not listed individually in the text, are all found in the same collection of archival boxes, which, lined up, measure 627 linear feet. Other sources are documented in the text or are listed in the bibliography.

This telling of Elizabeth's story shows how her upbringing and her years working for and alongside Jabez Watkins shaped her business acumen and ethics. Their work together prepared her to oversee and use the fortune the two had accumulated according to their carefully thought out philanthropic approach. They planned to benefit young people seeking an education, the University of Kansas, and the city of Lawrence. Elizabeth's incredible impact on students, the university, and the city is evident in the public record.

Numerous facts are included that may seem irrelevant to the core of the story, for example, descriptions of the fancy automobiles and household details of the period that preoccupied both Jabez and Elizabeth. As Susan Cheever said in *Louisa May Alcott*, "In its own way, biography is more imaginative than the novel and more intimate than memoir. Every biographer reads letters, journals, contemporary accounts, and other biographies to discover the story of their subject's life. A dream would be to find a diary. Then they illustrate the story they have imagined using the facts that fit."

The intent is to reveal more of Elizabeth's life than has heretofore been easily accessible to those associated with the university, Lawrencians, and the thousands of young people who are grateful for her help in getting an education. Her story needs to be told, for her impact was and is enormous; it cannot be overestimated, and must never be forgotten.

∾

" . . . any story told about what has happened in the past can never be certain, there is always yearning in the piecing together of information. There are truths lost to time and desire."
Marisa Silver, *Mary Coin* (New York: Blue Rider, 2013)

CHAPTER

Early Years

The year 1861 saw two important births: Elizabeth was born January 21 and Kansas achieved statehood on January 29. Although Elizabeth was born in Ohio, the new state of Kansas would hold her future in a most meaningful way.

A girl born in 1861 was born with limitations. With a life expectancy of just over forty-six years, she could expect to spend those years ruled by her father and then her husband, if she chose to marry. Women were not expected to earn their own living and very rarely had careers. It was nearly impossible for a girl to become a doctor, a banker, or an accountant. Teaching was an acceptable way for an unmarried woman to earn her living, or perhaps she could be a midwife or a dressmaker. However, once married, she was expected to limit herself to the home. Elizabeth would challenge those norms. She would push her personal limits and society's expectations to pursue the life she wanted. What led to that desire? How did she come to want such a different life?

Elizabeth's father, Valentine Gideon Miller, was an 1852 graduate of Cincinnati Medical College. Her mother, Ella Gardner Miller, was a homemaker. They married in Elgin, Ohio, Ella's hometown, which was just south of New Paris, in Preble County, near the Ohio and Indiana borders. New Paris was where Elizabeth was born and where her father established his medical practice.

Elizabeth, named for her Grandmother Gardner, was the youngest of three children; her brother Edward Benson Miller was born October 1, 1853, and Frank Clifton Miller was born February 13, 1856. She was called

Elizabeth Josephine Miller, at about age eleven when her
family moved to Lawrence, Kansas, from New Paris,
Ohio. (Douglas County Historical Society, Watkins
Museum of History)

Lizzie until later in life, when she chose to go by Elizabeth. To her future
husband, Jabez, she was always Lizzie or Miss Miller.

Her father's medical practice in New Paris was adequate, and the family
lived a life that was comfortable but by no means fancy, until the start of
the Civil War in 1861, the year Elizabeth was born. Families all over America were impacted by this war of state against state and, at times, brother
against brother. President Lincoln called for volunteers, and Elizabeth's

The Battle of Perryville, Kentucky, fought October 8, 1862

Battle of Perryville, one of the Civil War battles in which Elizabeth's father served as a surgeon for the Union Army. (*Harper's Weekly*, November 1, 1862)

father joined the Union Army as a surgeon on November 1, 1861, when she was ten months old, an event that would shadow her childhood and color her life forever.

Medical personnel usually did not fight during the Civil War, but they worked long hours and in every kind of weather. Valentine served in the Sixth Division, 20th Brigade, 64th Ohio under Colonel Charles G. Harker. At the end of the Kentucky campaign of 1862, his regiment was at the Battle of Perryville. After that battle, the Union controlled the Bluegrass state until the end of the war. The route to Perryville had been physically challenging. Drought made it hard to find water, almost impossible to find good water. Added to that, great clouds of dust were raised as the troops walked. Robert Broadwater's *The Battle of Perryville* tells of a soldier who gladly drank "from a pond where men and mules drank fifteen feet apart. Across the pond soldiers washed their socks and feet and at the end of the pond floated a dead mule." Thirst, disease, and exhaustion started to decimate the Union Army. Valentine lived under these same conditions, and, after each battle, he treated the wounded under those same conditions.

Like many soldiers, during and after the war, he became ill with dysentery, a gastrointestinal disease that caused diarrhea.

Dr. Miller was discharged and sent home to recover in May 1863, when Elizabeth had turned two. Barely a year later, when yet another call for volunteers came, Valentine again felt the pull of duty and signed up. On May 4, 1864, the 156th Ohio Volunteer Infantry was one of the hundred-day regiments to be mustered at Camp Dennison, which was near Cincinnati, close to the Ohio River. Valentine joined these men from little Preble County, which had already sent a number of sons, brothers, and fathers to the war. In *History of Preble County, Ohio,* R. E. Lowry reports that the 650 men marched various places and ended at Flock's Mill in Maryland, where they performed garrison duty, meaning they were to protect Flock's Mill. They were mustered out September 1, 1864. One of the officers listed in this unit was Surgeon V. G. Miller.

Elizabeth was just over three years old when her father came home to stay. In all, the two tours of duty had kept him away from New Paris for about nineteen months. Next to coping with the absence of their father, the hardest adjustment for those months would have been the lack of income. In *A Civil War Treasury,* Albert Nofi writes that the pay of a surgeon in the Union Army was equivalent to that of a colonel, $212.00 per month. Pay was scheduled to arrive every two months, but that could stretch to four or even six months. However irregular the time periods, some of the pay was sent to families, but they were left to dwell with uncertainty.

The cost of living fluctuated throughout the war as supply and demand drove up prices. Several sources from Printer's Row Publication Blog give representative prices from the time: dress fabric, $.10 per yard (four yards would make a dress); firewood, $7.00 per cord (128 cubic feet); beef, $.09 per pound; eggs, $.20 per dozen, coffee beans, $1.20 per pound (coffee beans were roasted and ground at home). Most households had a garden to supplement their diet.

During the war, life for the women left behind went on much as usual, but it was lonelier and harder without their partners. Taking sole responsibility for the family would have been a mental as well as a financial burden. Women continued their regular work of caring for the children, housekeeping, sewing, and gardening. Although Ella's life may not have changed a lot, she had to do more of the work and she was under more stress without her husband at home and without a regular income. But she put food on the table and clothes on their backs, and she kept a roof over their heads, all while raising a baby girl and boys aged six and nine. The boys certainly would have helped with chores; youngsters learned to work early in the 1860s.

While Valentine served in the Civil War, it is likely that Ella joined a ladies' aid society. A social outlet for lonely wives, these groups sewed and knitted to provide clothing and bedding for the soldiers. If they were near the active battle lines, members would prepare food and do laundry for the soldiers and would even care for the wounded, although they were untrained as nurses.

Elizabeth would have been at her mother's side as Ella worked hard to keep the family together and cared for. The amount of work required to run a household at that time was immense. All was done by hand; there were no modern appliances to help with the chores. Adding to the burden was the underlying fear that father might not return from the war. This difficult time made a clear impression on a very young Elizabeth.

Frank and Edward and, later, Elizabeth would have attended a nearby school in New Paris. It was housed in a two-story brick extension that had, in the early 1860s, been added onto a large frame house on East Cherry Street, which had been built in 1840. The Millers, in the 1870 census, lived at dwelling no. 275, a few blocks from the school. Class rosters have not been found, but several class pictures in *A Pictorial History of the One-Room Schools of Preble County, Ohio* include girls. It seems clear that Elizabeth attended school there and was taught the basics of reading, writing, and arithmetic, as described in Pamela Riney-Kehrberg's *The Routledge History of Rural America*. Schools were by subscription, funded by tuition fees; however, only county residents paid the fee. The Miller family lived in town, so they would not have been required to pay. As educated adults, Valentine and Ella would have ensured that their children got as good an education as was possible.

After Valentine returned from the war in 1864, he resumed his medical practice but never regained full health because of his dysentery; Ella and the family spent years caring for him. There were 1,528,000 cases of gastrointestinal disease in the Union Army. According to Stanley Burns in *The Burns Archives*, for every soldier who died in battle, two died of disease.

Recovery was possible in some cases with proper care, but the shadow of this illness would follow Miller for the rest of his life. He practiced medicine as his health permitted and, although the family's standard of living may have been lower than it had been before the war, they no doubt were still comfortable.

The death of Valentine's father on September 5, 1864, brought a turning point for the Miller family. After the estate was settled, Valentine sold his portion of the inheritance and realized a profit. This money gave the Miller family some financial security and the option to seize a new opportunity that was to follow.

Ephraim Miller, superintendent of schools in Lawrence, Kansas, was Valentine's cousin; their fathers were brothers, a relationship confirmed by census records. In 1872, Ephraim wrote Valentine to tell him that there was a need for good doctors in Lawrence, which, at the time, had twenty-one doctors to serve a population of eighty-three hundred. Elizabeth's father thought that his opportunities would be better in Kansas, so the family decided to move.

Valentine had done some buying and selling of land; his net worth according to the 1870 census was $2,300, which included his inheritance from his father. In 2020, this would be the equivalent of $45,262, enough that they could probably afford to travel by train. So, they packed up their belongings and moved to Lawrence in the fall of 1872. The state of Kansas was the family's future.

~

Much has been written about Jabez Bunting Watkins and his remarkable success in accumulating vast wealth. That is understandable. Kansas's own captain of industry, he was called the wealthiest man west of the Mississippi River. History often judges people by their visible achievements and their wealth. Buildings are easier to see than the character of the donor. Extremely wealthy people can be very private and leave no diary or personal papers. A lucky rescue has provided us with JB Watkins's business papers, to read and interpret. He was a very complex character, truly an economic visionary. Self-made, confident, hard-working, and intelligent, he was marked by the events of a hard childhood. He grew up in Virginia during the Civil War, with the battles so near he could hear them.

Jabez, or JB, as he frequently signed his letters, sacrificed much to go to school in his early years. He writes that he rode eighty miles on horseback at the age of seven to live with his sister so he could go to school. When he was nineteen, he left home again and went north to attend college. He put himself through law school, graduating in 1869 from the University of Michigan. Within twenty years' time, he would amass vast holdings and great wealth. Education was a touchstone in the life of this ambitious and driven young man. The same was true of Elizabeth, even though she lacked a formal secondary education. This was one of the first common bonds between JB and Elizabeth. They both encouraged and supported education for all young people, as is evident from their numerous gifts to students during their adult lives and the fact that, after their deaths, the fortune they left is dedicated to education.

An examination of JB's beginnings helps explain this man more fully. Jabez himself tells the story of his early years. In the Kenneth Spencer Research Library, in that huge collection of Watkins Papers, are handwritten pages of his autobiography, begun but never finished.

I was born the 25th of June 1845 in Indiana County, Pennsylvania, six miles south of Punxsutawney. The grandparents of my mother were from Germany. My father was born in Wales and was a farmer and coal miner. He usually mined coal in the spring and autumn. Through the mining of coal he was able to buy the winter shoes for the children. It was a happy day in the Watkins household when father came home on horseback with shoes in each end of a bag. I remember before I was six years old father did not bring the shoes until after there had been heavy frosts. In the morning I went to the meadow in my bear [sic] feet to bring in the cows. The tall grass was white and stiff with frost. I would drive up a cow and spring into the unfrosty place where she had lain and warm my feet. This was replicated until there were no more cows to drive up, then I would urge the cows home rapidly with the frost clinging to my bear feet and ankles. Our clothing was homespun woven by mother upon the loom which she had in the house. At the age of

A young Jabez Bunting Watkins,
at about the time he moved to
Lawrence, Kansas. (Douglas
County Historical Society,
Watkins Museum of History)

seven I rode on horseback from home to Sinking Valley, Blair County, a
distance of eighty miles and for two years lived with my sister and half
brothers helping upon the farm, driving the cattle to and from pasture,
and going to school. It was during this period that my father died in
his fifty third year, having been born in 1800. At the age of nine years I
returned home, again riding eighty miles on horseback. Two of my half
brothers, Dave and Abe, went with me. On reaching home I quickly entered the house unnoticed, closed the door and stood against it. Then
my mother observed me and said "and whose nice little boy is this."
Sister Ellen said "that is Jabez." Mother took me in her arms and cried,
she said "because I did not know my own boy."

In 1855, our family, with household effects moved in a wagon to Sinking Valley. Then for five years I did all kinds of work upon the farm in
the summer and during the winters attended to the horses and cattle
and went to school. The spring of 1860 we migrated with household
goods, five horses and a score of cattle, three hundred miles to Fairfax
County, Virginia, eight miles from Washington. On the way we crossed
South Mountain, where the famous battle was fought during the Civil

War. In Virginia we had to carve farms out of the woods and extensively fertalize [*sic*] the land. Our duties were to make and haul into Washington cordwood and charcoal and bring back oyster shells which we burned into lime for fertilizer with a four-horse team. The load in was two cords of wood or one hundred bushels of charcoal and out with six tons of oyster shells. I helped to unload a hundred bushels of charcoal into the basement of the St. James Hotel, corner of 6th St. and Pennsylvania Avenue. To burn the cord wood into charcoal we hired the slave Tom, from his master, during the day. At times I assisted with the charcoal pit, and nights in Tom's Cabin the slave taught me to make baskets from hickory splints also how to make the splints out of hickory. My usual work was upon the farm. I would rise at 4am, feed six to eight horses, a score or more of cattle, groom the horses and harness four of them, then get breakfast. After breakfast I would hitch the four horses to the wagon and in the woods help to load on the wagon two cords of wood. Then I would go with the hired men into the fields, and all day cultivate the land, build fences, scatter lime, mow grass, cradle or bind grain or chop wood. After quitting time for the men I would again feed the cattle and horses, help to unload six tons of oyster shells, then unharness the four horses that had made the round trip to Washington—sixteen miles. For this service I was paid $7, $10 or $12 respectively per month according to my age. At times by the light of the moon I would, to add to my savings, cut cordwood at 50 cents per cord. When I attended school in Virginia my teacher was the sister of Jackson who killed Ellsworth. In Washington I saw Abraham Lincoln soon after he had passed through Baltimore in disguise. When he delivered his first inaugural address I stood not far from him, and standing near me were two men discussing how easy it would be to shoot Lincoln. At a gate to the east Capitol grounds I saw Lincoln and Seward in a carriage turned away by a soldier guard because they did not have a pass.*

---

* Colonel Elmer E. Ellsworth, the first Union officer killed in the Civil War, was a personal friend of President Lincoln's and had worked as a law clerk for Lincoln in Springfield, Illinois. While Ellsworth was removing a Confederate flag from the roof of an inn in Alexandria, Virginia, he was shot by James Jackson, a zealous defender of slavery. Jackson was killed by Ellsworth's troops during the attack. "Remember Ellsworth" became a Union battle cry early in the war.

JB made notes of other remembrances he wanted to include but never finished the autobiography. From what he did write, he indicated that hard work throughout his early years had prepared him to succeed in his later life. He was a determined young man, confident in his abilities, and persuasive. Charismatic may not be too strong a term for this dynamic young businessman.

More about JB's early life can be found in William Connelley's 1918 *A Standard History of Kansas and Kansans*. Connelley, then secretary of the Kansas State Historical Society in Topeka, compiled JB's biography for the book. He wrote:

> At the age of fifteen, Mr. Watkins accompanied his mother and other members of the family from Pennsylvania to Fairfax County, Virginia. He lived in that county during the stressful days of the Civil War. His home was a cabin of two rooms and an attic. The home was in the county that was so desperately fought for by the armies of the North and the South. Residents of the Watkins house could hear the roar of the cannons in both battles of Bull Run. Soon after the first of those battles four of the Watkin's horses were taken away by Confederates, but Jabez, with the aid of a hired man, recovered them. As a boy, Watkins saw much of war times, though he was not an active participant. . . . During Colonel Ellsworth's funeral, young Watkins witnessed the procession and for a few minutes leaned on the wheel of President Lincoln's carriage. Jabez had many opportunities to see the great war president and heard him deliver his inaugural address in 1861. He was also in the rotunda of the capitol at Washington when the vote was taken for the impeachment of Andrew Johnson, February 24, 1868. At the age of nineteen in 1864, Mr. Watkins went north to the University of Michigan to attend school and in 1869 he completed the law course. In the meantime, he had taught school for half a dozen terms in Virginia, Pennsylvania, Illinois, and Wisconsin. From 1870 to 1873 he practiced law in Champaign, Illinois. As a lawyer, his expertise was in the examination of lands and real estate titles.

These early life experiences led JB Watkins to become ambitious and driven. Quite naturally, when he saw an opportunity to go west to evaluate land, promote mortgages, invest, and find entrepreneurial possibilities, he made the most of it.

JB amassed his fortune in the 1880s with the same speed as other "robber barons," such as John Jacob Astor (real estate and fur) of New York City and Andrew Carnegie (steel) of Pittsburg. JB Watkins (real estate and banking) of Lawrence, Kansas, was a captain of industry by 1891. He would spend the rest of his life trying to hold on to the wealth he had already accumulated.

Yes, JB was a visionary, but he did not grow his massive estate alone. When he made the decision to come to Lawrence, little did he know he would find a helpmate. He would hire a young girl whose work ethic, intelligence, loyalty, and ambition would make her an invaluable asset in realizing his plans.

CHAPTER 2

Coming to Lawrence

When Dr. Valentine Miller's family arrived in Lawrence in 1872, they likely traveled by train, probably on the Burlington railway route. The Findlay, Ohio, *Jeffersonian* of June 21, 1872, reported that the Burlington train ran to three great regions in the West: "1st to Omaha connecting to the great Pacific Roads, 2nd to Lincoln, the capital of Nebraska, and all that beautiful region south of the Platte, and 3rd to St. Joseph, Kansas City and all Kansas points."

The Miller family would have arrived on the north side of the Kansas River. A horse-drawn vehicle would have carried them over the river on a bridge that, though a bit unstable, was the only way across. The population of Lawrence, reported as 8,320 in 1870, was probably a bit larger by the time they arrived in the fall of 1872. Still a frontier town, it was enjoying prosperity and was rebuilding after the bloody turmoil of the Civil War. As the city worked to shed the ghost of Quantrill's Raid, it was showing promising signs of cultural growth.* This is what the Miller family would have seen in their new hometown.

The city had seven newspapers with varied publication schedules, nine churches, and various benevolent societies. Incorporated companies such as the Gas Works, Kansas Roofing, Douglas County Agricultural and Mechanical Association, and the Board of Trade were all in Lawrence by 1872, along with five banks, four railroads, and ten schools. The Lawrence Street Railway Co. furnished (horse-drawn) transportation in the town.

---

* Quantrill's Raid of August 21, 1863, made national news. Many men, women, and children were killed and much of the town was left in ruins.

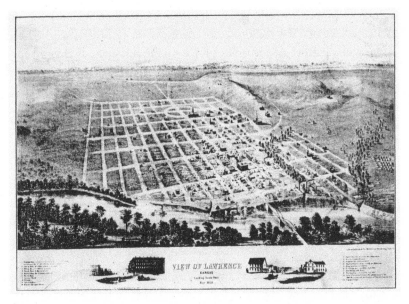

Drawing of Lawrence, circa 1858. (E. F. Caldwell, *A Souvenir History of Lawrence, Kansas, 1898*)

Sidewalks, mostly made of boards, and unpaved streets, where cows and pigs tended to wander, made for hazardous walking and traveling conditions, to say nothing of the aroma. A favorite grazing area for these animals was South Park at the south end of downtown.

Lawrence boasted two theaters. Frazer's Hall, south of the Eldridge House Hotel on Massachusetts Street, held operas and hosted speakers, including Ralph Waldo Emerson. On the northeast corner of Seventh (Winthrop) and Massachusetts, the second-floor Liberty Hall seated a hundred. Among speakers who appeared there were Horace Greeley, Henry Ward Beecher, Anna Dickinson, and Dudley Haskell. It was a shared building; with Poole's pork packing business in the basement and his retail shop on the first floor, it was possible there were strong odors in the summer months.

Bismarck Grove in north Lawrence was the premier gathering place for chautauquas and other celebrations, but it did not gain prominence until 1876. Sports of the time consisted of baseball and some football. Picnics on the Kaw (Kansas) River usually included swimming.

Imagine eleven-year-old Elizabeth's excitement when she moved from a small village of a few hundred to a town of over eight thousand. There were so many more opportunities for her. She undoubtedly looked forward to continuing her education. Lawrence had an active library and access to books; there were many cultural activities for a growing mind, such as presentations and speeches given by prominent people of the day. Various lecture tours came through Lawrence, including addresses by suffragettes. In a larger city, there were more young girls for Elizabeth to befriend and numerous shops for her to explore. One establishment that the Millers surely visited was the Wiedemann Confectionary; Elizabeth patronized the store her entire life. (Among the rescued Watkins papers are numerous receipts from this shop. Elizabeth had a sweet tooth!) Established in 1866, it supplied wonderful candies, taffy, and ice cream made with milk from local cows.

Weather statistics from 1873 are fairly typical for a Kansas year: the high was 104° and the low was 26° below. Snowfall was 26.50 inches and rainfall 32.94 inches; there were forty-eight days above 90° and nine below 0°. There was a drought in 1873 to 1874 and a grasshopper invasion; as a result, the area population decreased somewhat that year.

Although work opportunities in Lawrence may have been better, Valentine's health had not improved. He started a small practice and worked as he was able. For a while, the family lived over the E. F. Goodrich grocery store at 154 Massachusetts. It is likely that during this time they would have met a young banker, lawyer, and mortgage agent named Jabez Bunting Watkins. He had come to Lawrence in 1873 from Champaign, Illinois, to be involved in land matters in Kansas. The handsome young man was no doubt friendly toward the family. Everyone met along Massachusetts Street, the main street. The Millers would have become known and accepted quickly by the townspeople; Ephraim Miller, Valentine's cousin and superintendent of schools, was their entrée into good society.

The University of Kansas held its first commencement in June 1873 with four graduates. That year, the year JB came to Lawrence, Elizabeth was a freshman at the prep school that was part of the new university. The school was created to serve the many students who were not academically ready for university. Elizabeth was only twelve years old then, the youngest age admitted, and she made good progress in her classes. One of her

EAST SIDE—MASSACHUSETTS ST.—LOOKING SOUTH.

WEST SIDE—MASSACHUSETTS ST.—LOOKING SOUTH.

WEST SIDE—MASSACHUSETTS ST.—LOOKING NORTH.

EAST SIDE— MASSACHUSETTS ST.—LOOKING NORTH.

VIEWS OF LAWRENCE, KANSAS, 1898.

Four views of Massachusetts Street, the main street through downtown Lawrence, in 1898. (E. F. Caldwell, *A Souvenir History of Lawrence, Kansas, 1898*)

classmates, Carrie Watson, went on to become the university librarian; the university library was named for her in 1921, as noted in Clifford Charles Griffin's *University of Kansas, a History*.

The Miller family did not stay at 154 Massachusetts Street long. They moved to a house at the corner of Tennessee and Quincy (Eleventh Street). Jabez Watkins lived at Hancock (Twelfth Street) and Connecticut, and his first business was at the corner of Winthrop (Seventh Street) and Massachusetts.*

From 1876 to 1877, Elizabeth's father also served as the Douglas County coroner. The income was a welcome supplement to his earnings as a physician. He was paid $5 each time he was called out and extra if an inquest was necessary or if written depositions were needed. Elizabeth's father was a great role model; in the evenings, as he told about his day, she learned about the troubles of those in the community and the work he did to help

---

* Streets in 1872 all had names: Pinckney became Sixth Street; Winthrop, Seventh; Henry, Eighth; Warren, Ninth; Berkeley, Tenth; Quincy, Eleventh; and Hancock, Twelfth.

Collegiate Department.

Abbreviations.—Cl. for classical; Sc. for scientific; M. L. for modern literature; E. for engineering.

Names.	Courses.	Residence.

SENIORS.

Ida L. Blood,	........Sc.....	*Lawrence.*
E. B. Noyes,	.........E.....	*Wakarusa.*
Hannah Oliver,	.......Cl......	*Lawrence.*

JUNIORS.

E. H. Bancroft,	.......Cl......	*Emporia.*
Alice G. Boughton,	....M.L....*Moraria, N. Y.*
Martha R. Campbell,	...M.L....*Lawrence.*
Frank P. Mac Lennan,	..E.......*Emporia.*
Kate Stephens,	........Cl......	*Wakarusa.*

SOPHOMORES.

Charles F. Bassett,	....Cl......*Galesburg, Ill.*
George F. Ganmer,	....Sc.....	*Wakarusa.*
May E. Richardson,	...Sc.....	*Lawrence.*
W. F. Sergent,	.......Sc.....	*Lawrence.*
C. W. Smith,	.........Sc..	...*East Lynne, Mo.*
Nelson J. Stephens,	....Cl.....	*Wakarusa.*
H. S. Tremper,	........Cl....*Galesburg, Ill.*
Elmer B. Tucker,	......Cl.....*Lawrence.*
Jas. A. Wickersham,	..Sc.....*Dimon.*

---

10   STUDENTS.

Names.	Courses.	Residence.

FRESHMEN.

Andrew Atchison	.......Cl.....*Richmond.*
Jonathan W. Ball,	.....Cl.....*Olathe.*
Fernando S. Barber,	...Cl.....*Lawrence.*
Bion H. Barnett,	.......Sc.....*Hiawatha.*
Frank T. Botsford,	....M.L....*Bridgeport, Conn.*
A. Gertrude Bullene,	..M.L...*Wakarusa.*
Eliza Emmett,	..........Sc.....*Lawrence.*
Alice Goss	..............Sc.....*Wakarusa.*
May Harris,	..........M.L...*Bowling Green, Mo.*
Abbie A. Holt,	........M.L...*Centre Ridge.*
Kate G. Jenkins,	......Cl.....*Lawrence.*
John H. Long,	..........Sc.....*Olathe.*
Lizzie J. Miller,	.........Sc.....*Lawrence.*
Frank H. Morgan,	.....Sc.....*Leavenworth.*
William Osburn,	......Cl.....*Wilmington, Ill.*
Louisa Rankin,	.....Sc. ....*Wakarusa.*
*A. L. Read,	..........Cl.....*Winona, Wis.*
A. A. Rodgers,	... ...M.L...*Topeka.*
A. C. Scott,	............Cl.....*Carlyle.*
Grace E. M. Scoullar,	..Cl....*Chicago, Ill.*
Kate S. Sneed,	.........M.L...*Lawrence.*
Carrie M. Watson,	.....M.L...*Lawrence.*
Clementine M. Wilson,	.Sc ....*Lawrence.*
Selina Wilson,	........Sc.....*Lawrence.*
Lizzie Yengley,	.........M. L...*Lawrence.*

SELECT COURSE.

Anna Baker,	.................*Hiawatha.*
Ida Baker,	....................*Hiawatha.*
Frank D. Black,	.............*Topeka.*

*Deceased.

Elizabeth's Preparatory School record, showing "Lizzie J. Miller" as a freshman. (*Eighth Annual Catalogue of the Officers and Students of the University of Kansas, 1873-74.* Kenneth Spencer Research Library, University of Kansas)

them, even as he himself did not feel his best. It is no wonder she developed a strong sense of duty to help her fellow humans.

Lawrence papers carried several stories that mentioned Dr. Miller in his role as coroner.

Western Home Journal, Lawrence, December 28, 1876

A very sad case of drowning occurred Wednesday between 11 and 12 o'clock about a mile and a half up the river, at the opening where the Kansas Pacific railroad company is getting out ice. Two boys were skating and one had fallen in. Attempts were made to rescue them but the child drowned. Coroner Miller was notified, and summoned a jury, a verdict being returned in accordance with the facts. The jury also made the following recommendations: We, the jurors, do recommend to the proper authorities that some means be devised for the protection of our children upon the river by the placing of a mark of limit, beyond which they must not be allowed to pass.

Republican Journal, Tuesday, May 23, 1876

Yesterday morning, about nine o'clock, word was brought into town that R.H. Fitts, living about three miles south of town had been found dead in his bed. Dr. Miller, the Coroner, and several citizens, immediately repaired to the spot and found the report correct. His body was found lying in a diagonal position across the bed, his feet hanging off the front, while his head was near the back. No evidence of violence was discovered. His feet were bare, and he was dressed in his ordinary working clothes.

Republican Journal, Sunday, August 19, 1877

Yesterday morning, as Dr. Miller was going down a hill leading to a ford on the Wakarusa east of the poor-farm, the buggy from some cause ran on to his horse's heels, causing that animal to make frantic efforts to get away. In this struggle it kicked the dashboard to pieces, and one of its heels coming in contact with the Doctor's leg, bruised it considerably. He finally ran her into a ditch, and with the aid of a colored man who was at work nearby straightened things up.

Dr. Miller's health was not improving, despite the care he was given by Ella and daughter Elizabeth. Sometimes he was unable to work, and, as the newest doctor in town, his practice was probably not large. The family had enough to live on, but they all needed to work together to support themselves. The brothers, older than Elizabeth, did their part. Frank had a good position in Salina, Kansas, with the Kansas Pacific Land Office and helped financially when he could. Edward was working as a printer in Lawrence.

In the early summer of 1879, Dr. Miller made a decision that would affect himself and the family; it also involved Elizabeth in a very personal and instructive way. Because of the debilitating illness he had contracted in the Civil War, he was eligible for a government pension. He had hesitated to apply for it earlier since he felt many others were worse off, but now his circumstances were getting desperate. There had never been much talk at home about his wartime experiences, but to apply for the pension, he had to provide a detailed account of his service. As Elizabeth helped him with the forms and letters, she learned of the sacrifices he had made and the pain he had suffered. It brought the two of them closer, and she gained a new understanding and appreciation of her father's service to his country.

Civil War pensions were America's first national system of public benefits for the elderly and the disabled. There had been some form of relief for soldiers since the American Revolution, although it favored officers and white males. And, in 1836, widows became eligible for pensions. To persuade men to volunteer for the Civil War, a law was passed in 1862 to address the needs of Union soldiers and dependents. Called "the wisest and most magnificent enactment of the kind ever adopted by any nation," the law formed the basis of the Civil War pension system until 1890. Benefits were available to those with disabilities that could be linked directly to injuries received or diseases contracted in service. Pensions received were graded by rank. A lieutenant colonel could get $30 per month, a private $8 per month. Widows and orphans would receive pensions at the same rate.

The Civil War expanded the costs of the pension system. In 1862 there were 10,700 recipients and costs were $1 million per year. By 1866 recipients numbered 126,722 at a cost of $15.5 million, and costs would grow with each year. Many who were eligible had not applied for pensions: they wanted to forget the war, they didn't need the money, or they refused the stigma of taking a government handout. Many, like Elizabeth's father, simply believed that there were others who needed it more than they did.

In 1879 an act of Congress changed the picture. Theda Skocpol's *Protecting Soldiers & Mothers* tells us that the Arrears Act of 1879 allowed those with "newly discovered Civil War related disabilities to sign up and receive in one lump sum all of the pension payments they would have been eligible to receive since 1860." Even old age became a qualifying disability. Advertisements in the local papers gave all the particulars. By 1881 the average lump sum payment was $953. Valentine's would have been around $1,700.

The Republican party was responsible for delivering this hard-earned help, so it asked for and received special loyalty from the recipients. Republicans were also the party that led the forces that saved the Union, the party of President Lincoln. This may explain why Elizabeth's mother was so determinedly faithful to the Republican party throughout her life.

Civil War Pension Application File of Valentine Miller, 1879, Douglas County, Kansas, National Archives; photocopy in author's possession:

Dr. Miller had mustered into the Army August 21, 1862, as an assistant surgeon in the 64th Ohio Volunteer Infantry. On October 8, 1862, after the Kentucky battle of Perryville and Chaplain Hills, he contracted dysentery aggravated by overwork and excessive fatigue in treating the sick and wounded. This resulted in chronic dysentery. The disease was incurable. He went to Louisville, Kentucky, for treatment and was assigned to duty to the Asylum Hospital and then the hospital in Louisville. He mustered out May 16, 1863 and returned to New Paris. In 1864 President Lincoln called for more volunteers. New Paris furnished 100 men including Valentine. He served as the surgeon of the 156th Ohio Volunteers. He was discharged on September 14, 1864, to reside in New Paris, Ohio and then Lawrence, Kansas after 1872. Before he went into the service, he was of sound physical health and a good physician with a decent practice. After the war he was greatly disabled and found it difficult to keep up his practice.

On August 25, 1879, Dr. Miller and two witnesses signed his declaration for a pension. Nearly a year later, on June 18, 1880, Dr. A. G. Abuela signed the physician's affidavit and Dr. A. B. Ferris of New Paris signed the medical affidavit for this application. Dr. Ferris practiced medicine in New Paris and had known Dr. Miller for many years. He knew Miller had been in excellent health until he got back to New Paris in the fall of 1862 and had attended him on a couple of occasions: during a long case of typhoid fever and during his diarrhea and dysentery in August or September 1864. Dr. Ferris and Dr. Miller had practiced together until Miller's move to Kansas in 1872.

Valentine was still seeing patients in May 1879. When his application for a pension was granted, he began to receive a payment of $8.50 a month, and the Miller family was able to live with fewer concerns about money. But as Dr. Miller's health failed, he was able to practice medicine less and less.

Elizabeth spent those first years in Lawrence getting settled, exploring her new town, and going to school. Children grew up quickly in that time and started to work for the family, or were hired out to others, at a much younger age than we can imagine in the twenty-first century. As Elizabeth approached fifteen years of age, money was again an issue for the family and she considered quitting school to help her parents by getting a job.

And why had Jabez Watkins come to Lawrence?

The documents Professor Malin saved from the World War II paper drive provide that information. Malin, a history professor at KU, personally kept some of those boxes of documents for years. Most were stored in a holding area of the university library, waiting to be accessed whenever an agreement could be reached with the university chancellor. Professor Malin knew a student, Allan G. Bogue, who was interested in the mortgage business during the late 1800s in America's heartland. In 1949, Bogue was the first to begin to sort and chronicle the Watkins papers, and his research resulted in his book *Money at Interest: The Farm Mortgage on the Middle Border.* Bogue gives an account of JB's decision to come to Lawrence, the same year as the Miller family:

> J. B. moved his business to Kansas in August of 1873 to obtain "a wider field of operations, more choice of securities and better rates." Lawrence had a population of around 8300 people. There were probably several reasons for choosing Lawrence: proximity to Kansas City banking resources, the federal court was in Topeka and a working force would be available to him. Lawrence was the county seat of Douglas County, and railroad connections were good. This was an advantageous time to be in this business.

Bogue also notes that JB and his employees had quite a task: "to prove that the farm mortgage was a superior type of investment but also that 'Bloody Kansas' and the 'Great American Desert' were myths—that Kansas was actually a rich and productive state, peopled by healthy, honest and peaceful husbandmen." An advertising campaign would be needed.

With his experience as an attorney who specialized in land values, JB quickly saw the opportunities for a mortgage company. Settlers were moving west and needed cash to buy their land and equipment. Civil War veterans took advantage of the land grant from the government that gave them 160 acres for their service. But they also needed tools to work their

160 acres and supplies to build their homes. JB could provide the money they needed with a mortgage on their land.

In JB's early years in Lawrence, he worked to establish his reputation. He confirmed his references with the local bank, set up an office, and got to work, at first with legal matters, and then, more and more, in mortgages. Watkins's biographer, William Connelley, wrote of JB in 1918: "Mr. Watkins became a resident of Lawrence, Kansas, in August 1872. He is one of the active business men of the city and from Lawrence his operations and interests have extended in many directions and in various fields. He early became identified with the business of handling mortgages and as an investment banker."

For a glimpse at what lay ahead for JB, Connelley also compiled a helpful overview of his businesses up to 1918:

> In forty years, it is said that [JB] directed the investments of over $12,000,000 in lands and mortgages. In 1876 a branch of his business was established in New York, one in London in 1878, one at Dallas in 1881, and in 1883 the business was incorporated as the J. B. Watkins Land Mortgage Company, of which Mr. Watkins is still president [in 1918]. At London he organized the North American Land and Timber Company in 1882, and retained his interests until 1911, when he sold out for property and cash considerations to the amount of $800,000. Mr. Watkins is also president of the Watkins National Bank of Lawrence.

JB was the right man in the right place at the right time in 1872, and his business grew at a rapid pace.

Elizabeth and JB were each going through formative years when they came to Lawrence: JB, in the establishment of his business, and Elizabeth, in her personal growth. Independently, during their early years, they each cemented a lifelong belief in the importance of education. For JB, this is evident in the sacrifices he made to get his education and law degree. These were accomplishments that in no small way contributed to his later success. For Elizabeth, this is seen in her desire for a higher education, a yearning she carried all of her life. It was only her sense of duty to her family that led her to quit school and go to work. JB and Elizabeth had each learned to value hard work and they both demanded much of themselves.

They each had great confidence in their God-given abilities. Their early experiences led them later, together, to develop an overarching principle: lend a helping hand, but never a handout. And thousands have benefited from that principle.

Next come the years when JB hired Elizabeth and they began to work together. Business documents from 1876 until their marriage in 1909 also reveal personal information and show Elizabeth's growth from an inexperienced fifteen-year-old into a savvy, competent businesswoman. She learned quickly from JB, showed close attention to detail, and was completely trustworthy. The complexity of JB's character emerges from the documents. He was frugal, single-minded, and consumed by his business interests. He was under extreme financial pressure and traveled extensively at a time when travel was difficult. He could be exacting and expected those around him to listen to his advice and follow it to the letter. These domineering traits, combined with stress and overwork, led to a period when alcohol became a problem for him. The business letters also hint at JB's sense of humor, love of beauty, and generosity.

In addition, those papers that fluttered to the ground during World War II contained words that gave proof of his appreciation for Elizabeth. Love grew from that appreciation.

CHAPTER 3

Working for JB

Jabez hired Elizabeth in 1876, when she was fifteen years old. A question remains unanswered: How did she happen to end up working for JB? Did she apply at several places? Were there ads in the local paper? Had the Miller family become acquainted with JB? The most logical answer, in the authors' eyes, is that Elizabeth's brother Frank, then working as a clerk in a Salina bank, suggested that JB was hiring. Allan Bogue suggests a compelling reason for this: since 1874, JB's business had doubled yearly.

As the mortgage business grew, it required more people to handle the increased workload. Miles Dart was hired as an office manager in 1874 and was later sent to begin operations for JB in Dallas, Texas. In 1876, JB opened his New York office. By 1877, a force of eight worked in the Lawrence office. T. C. Green was treasurer of the Watkins Mortgage Company and a mainstay in the Lawrence office for his entire life. It was the home, or main, office throughout JB's career. All transactions flowed in and out of there.

Elizabeth was the lowest-ranking person in the Lawrence office, probably making less than $40 a month, but she enjoyed what she was doing. No doubt fascinated by the business dealings with faraway places she had never seen, she was bright and a quick learner. JB Watkins was not often in his Lawrence office because, by 1881, he also had offices in New York City, London, and Dallas. He was traveling a great deal in those years, by railroad and on ocean-going steamships across the Atlantic. Because he was absent from the office for weeks at a time, good communication was imperative so he could keep an eye on all transactions. These days, JB would

E. SUMMERFIELD,
Capitalist.

T. C. GREEN,
Treasurer Watkins Mtg. Co.

C. A. HILL,
Merchant.

L. O. McINTIRE,
Capitalist.

P. H. PEIRCE,
Merchant.

J. W. ROBERTSON,
Furniture.

E. M. ROBERTSON,
Furniture.

J. H. COHN,
Merchant.

PROMINENT CITIZENS OF LAWRENCE.

Thomas C. Green, treasurer of Watkins Mortgage Company and lifelong trusted employee. He is shown with other prominent citizens of Lawrence of the time.
(E. F. Caldwell, *A Souvenir History of Lawrence, Kansas, 1898*)

be called a micromanager. He watched every detail. This period, when his businesses were growing to maturity, was an active and formative time in the lives of both JB and Elizabeth.

The world of opportunity open to women was beginning to change. During the Civil War, women had been forced to do work and make decisions formerly handled by the men. Now, after the war, they were finding they could hold responsible jobs, be self-sufficient, and make their own way in a male-dominated society. Elizabeth may have made a conscious decision early in her life to not marry and to be self-sufficient. Or, perhaps as she worked for JB in his extensive businesses, she may have decided on a career in business. Such a career would have been highly unusual for a single woman, but it would have been unthinkable for a married woman. She had seen her mother cope with financial uncertainty and with her father's absence in her early childhood; she may have wanted to take greater control in her own life. She was also possibly influenced by social and political developments in women's rights during this time.

During her late teens and early twenties, as Elizabeth was absorbing information about business practices, she was also reading widely. She and her mother, Ella, later joined a book club, so we know she was an avid reader. Available from the Lawrence library would have been works by popular authors of the time: Wilkie Collins, Robert Browning, Mark Twain, Oscar Wilde, Helen Hunt Jackson, and Louisa May Alcott. The *Lawrence Daily Journal* periodically listed the new books that Rhoda Trask, the librarian, had put into the collection. By 1880, the public library, part of Lawrence since 1854, was housed in the National Bank building at Seventh and Massachusetts, where Elizabeth worked. That was very convenient and the cost was reasonable: $2.00 per year, $1.00 for six months, or one book for one week for $.10. There are no existing records of patrons' checkouts, but the library had about six thousand volumes by 1880, including newspapers and periodicals. Elizabeth may have been realizing that a woman could have a career and did not have to rely on marriage and a family to be successful or fulfilled.

From 1875 to 1900, women were finding their political voice. Suffragettes were speaking out in Britain and in the United States, the temperance community was active, and women were writing about new possibilities for their lives. The *Lawrence Daily Journal* and the *Lawrence Gazette* reported speeches by women and men that called for equal rights for women. The *Lawrence Gazette* reported in 1888 that "quite a large audience of thoughtful people assembled in the Unitarian church last Friday evening and were greatly edified by remarks from Lucy Stone and her husband Henry B. Blackwell. The subject was, 'Equal Suffrage for Women.'" In 1889 the Blackwells had a farm four miles northeast of Lawrence.* Lucy Stone, editor of the Boston-based *Woman's Journal,* predicted in 1887 that "a woman will be President of the United States in the year 2000." The book *We Unitarians* notes that the Unitarian Church was located at 933 Ohio, about two blocks from Elizabeth's house. She could have walked to these meetings.

---

* The *Lawrence Daily Journal* of March 16, 1889, noted the sale of the Blackwell farm to P. Laptad. The Blackwells had purchased the 240 acres twenty-three years earlier when they were "stumping" the state for women's suffrage.

From another popular work of that time, M. L. Rayne's 1884 *What Can a Woman Do: or Her Position in the Business and Literary World*:

> If our grandfathers could revisit the earth, what would astonish them quite as much as the telegraph, railroads, telephone, and the electric lights, is the position that woman has taken and is so nobly sustaining under all these difficulties of non-fitness and lack of business education. . . . A brilliant coterie of woman has led the way into new fields, where a woman working for her daily bread need feel no shame or embarrassment or trammel herself unnecessarily with the set formulas of a dead past. The world is full of women who must work or starve. There are women who prefer a life of single independence to taking up with one lame offer of marriage. . . . She does not require the genius of a Napoleon to succeed in any profession; very ordinary qualities can be grafted and improved on the tree of knowledge; much depends on the ernestness [*sic*] of what a woman can do to be successful in many fields, including marriage.

It is quite possible that Elizabeth read this book and took it to heart.

When the Kansas Supreme Court ruled that the female municipal suffrage law passed by the Kansas legislature in January 1887 was valid, women suddenly became participants as voters. The small town of Syracuse, in far western Kansas, elected women to the municipal government that same year: an all-female town council. The *Lawrence Daily Journal* ran small articles: "The city council of Syracuse, Kan., is reported to be composed of women" and "Five women were elected to serve on the city council of Syracuse." Also in 1887, Susanna Salter, a member of the Prohibition Party, was elected mayor of Argonia, a small town in south central Kansas, becoming the first woman to win political office in the United States. This was reported in many newspapers across the state. *The Women's West*, edited by Susan Armitage and Elizabeth Jameson, discusses these exciting developments.

Anna Dickinson, Kate Fields, Elizabeth Cady Stanton, and Susan B. Anthony also visited and spoke in Lawrence and Topeka. It is likely that Elizabeth heard them speak or at least read the accounts in the local papers. Influenced by their forward-thinking outlook, she would have been encouraged to decide her destiny for herself.

MISS BESSIE MYERS,
With Consolidated Barb Wire Co.

MISS SARAH RADCLIFFE,
With Russell & Metcalf.

MISS GERTRUDE STANDING,
With Poehler & Mason.

MISS EULA C. LYONS,
With W. W. Nevison.

MISS CATHERINE MENETT,
Deputy Clerk of Court.

MISS ALICE LITCHFIELD,
Treasurer School Board.

MISS MYRTLE ELLIOT,
With McHale & Learnard.

MISS LENA WILBER,
With City Clerk.

YOUNG LADIES HOLDING RESPONSIBLE POSITIONS.

Note that all the "Young Ladies Holding Responsible Positions" are unmarried, with the title "Miss." (E. F. Caldwell, *A Souvenir History of Lawrence, Kansas, 1898*)

These were also busy years for JB, as his business dealings give ample proof. A cursory overview of how JB ran his business is appropriate here. The following quote from Allan Bogue's *Money at Interest* clearly shows at what an opportune time JB chose to go into the mortgage business.

Watkins began his labors in Kansas at a favorable time. The depression of 1873 and its aftermath brought disillusion to many eastern investors. Holders of railroad securities suffered severe losses, while the insurance companies underwent a weeding out process which eliminated many of the weaker organizations and aroused distrust among investors. In some eastern states the savings banks which had been rising rapidly in public favor found themselves in financial difficulties. At the same time, the last forty years of the nineteenth century was a period when capital was being accumulated rapidly in the northeastern states. Not only were large fortunes amassed but clerical and professional workers were often able to lay by modest competences. Finally, the long-term interest

FOUR UNIQUE WOMEN.

KATE FIELD, MRS. LIPPINCOTT, MARGUERITE MOORE, MRS. BLAKE.

Edith Sessions Tupper Writes Charmingly of the Life, Aims and Personality of These Leaders in the Movement That Is Making This the Woman's Age.

[Special Correspondence.]

NEW YORK, April 6.—When one speaks of unique women one thinks instinctively

KATE FIELD.

of Kate Field, who is without question one of the most unique and picturesque characters of the day. There is scarcely anything this lady has not turned her hand to—the stage, the shop, the lecture platform, the writing desk and now the editor's chair. She understands politics much better than most men; she proved more of a power against Mormonism than all the laws enacted against this hideous stain upon our government; she was a splendid "drummer" for the California wine companies, and I am sure she could conduct a post-mortem or preach from any text quite as well as the average doctor of medicine or divinity.

Kate Field, a noted suffragette of the era, who lectured in Lawrence. (*Leavenworth Standard* newspaper, April 23, 1891)

rate was declining, stimulating those who possessed capital or savings to look for new avenues of investment. Conditions were favorable in the mid 1870's, therefore for the western, mortgage broker with his promise of high interest and a security as substantial as the soil itself.

JB opened his New York office in 1876. He wanted to tap into the money being made on the more industrialized East Coast. As Bogue points out, investors, large and small, were looking for opportunities to invest. As

America turned its attention to westward expansion after the war ended, New York was the center of that investing zeal. It was the perfect seedbed for JB's banking and lending business.

With manager Henry Dickinson, he opened an office at 243 Broadway in New York City. Over the years, he would move his offices to 319 Broadway, 2 Wall Street, and 2 William Street. When he first opened the New York office, his letterhead read "J. B. Watkins & Co., Counselors at Law and Loan Brokers." He was getting to know the businesspeople in New York and inspiring their trust in his ability to grow their money, with nothing but his education and imagination to recommend him. Once again, charismatic may not be too strong a word for JB.

In August 1883 Watkins was in New York with William Henry (Billy) Vanderbilt, son of Cornelius Vanderbilt, the patriarch of a Dutch family who made their fortune in America in shipping, both by steamboat and oceangoing steamship, and later in railroads. JB sent a letter to the Lawrence office, dated August 25, 1883, from the St. Denis Hotel in New York City. "Vanderbilt and I and 13,000 other visitors are here, spending money, looking at each other and trying to have a good time. Vanderbilt drives a team of four, one horse of which he paid $40,000, that beats me. [Two of the horses were named Maud S and Aldine.] Van drives himself, other swells have a few—one or more coachmen along."

Back at the Lawrence office, Wilbur Presby was working as JB's personal secretary, a position he would hold for many years. At that time, the position of secretary was filled only by men. JB Watkins ran his business with a tight rein; he oversaw every aspect, even to the smallest detail, and directed comments to each employee, as appropriate, in several letters a week sent to the Lawrence office.

Two years later, in 1878, JB opened his London office at Number 14 Bishopgate. Henry George Chalkley Sr., who managed the office for JB, had moved to London from Lawrence with his family. The office was JB's European headquarters for investment money to flow to North America. By 1882, his English investors had bought shares in the North America Land & Timber Co., Ltd. JB had purchased the company so as to have an already functioning investment vehicle ready for the benefit of overseas customers. The company purchased nine hundred thousand acres in southwestern Louisiana, an area where JB envisioned great growth. JB served as the

American manager so he could influence the direction of the company. He himself kept one-third of the stock and sold the remainder to his English investors.

A Watkins Collection letter dated May 24, 1882, tells about his trip from New York to London on the *City of Rome*, then the newest and largest steamship afloat. P. T. Barnum, a fellow passenger, was on his way to London to purchase Jumbo, a large elephant, for his Grand Traveling Museum Menagerie Caravan & Hippodrome. JB noted that the trip took seven days and twenty hours.

If Jabez thought New York would be fertile ground for capital, London was the motherlode. Britain ruled the waves and, during the reign of Queen Victoria, it dominated the world economy. The Industrial Revolution had made Britain the manufacturing powerhouse of the world; as many families in England became wealthy, they began to look overseas for investment opportunities. For example, Thomas Barlow invested in tea production in Indonesia but was wiped out in the Tea Blight of 1873. Then someone convinced him to plant rubber trees on his tea plantation, just in time for the invention of the automobile. Thomas Barlow and Sons is still listed on the London Exchange; as a girl, Queen Elizabeth II first learned to ride a horse on the family's sprawling estate in Thornbury. As another example, Harry Streeter and, later, other members of the Streeter family of England went to Australia to get in the pearl business. At first the oysters were the size of dinner plates, and the pearls were fantastic and very profitable. As time went on, the oysters and pearls got smaller and so they began to use the oyster shells to make buttons for the textile industry in England and America. During this time, the family acquired 717,000 acres in Australia. In the British view, the entire world was open to them for investment and exploitation. JB sensed this was the kind of atmosphere in which he could attract investors and capital, and he did.

JB's Dallas office opened in 1881. His local manager for that office, Miles J. Dart, moved to Texas in the employ of JB but had lived in Lawrence previously. Dart was a favorite among the home office staff; the *Lawrence Journal World* of May 18, 1881, reported that a festive birthday party held for him was attended by many of the Watkins employees, including Elizabeth.

JB had enlisted Dart to help him expand into Texas because he had sensed that there were starting to be fewer opportunities in Kansas. He did feel some hesitation about the move. During the Reconstruction era after the Civil War, Texas had developed a reputation for bad financial management, which could scare off Eastern investors. Although they saw that there was investment potential in Texas, the move to Dallas was cloaked in secrecy for a time. The following letter to his New York office manager, Henry Dickinson, shows JB's confidence in his own evaluation of the risk.

We . . . shall turn a considerable portion of European capital there, and will place some American capital where it will be satisfactory to the parties furnishing it, but we do not want it to become known in this country that we are doing business in Texas. It is therefore important in soliciting that you do not let the matter be known except to parties who keep their business strictly to themselves. We are confident that as soon as it becomes known we are there other companies will be looking in that direction also and we shall have to compete with them as we have been doing here.

All the transactions from each office passed through the main Lawrence office, so Elizabeth saw how a complicated business was run. Her responsibilities were probably clerical in nature—filing, sorting, keeping all the transactions in order—but she was determined to be an important part of the business. Her working life revolved around Watkins's undertakings. Each of his offices kept him apprised of business dealings through letters, whether he was in or out of Lawrence. When JB traveled, letters followed him wherever he went, to ensure he was current on all matters. The amount of interoffice paper communication in the Watkins Collection is staggering.

JB began to recognize that western farm mortgages were a form of investment that could possibly appeal to a new source of clients. Realizing that his clientele did not necessarily need to be rich to invest, he advertised in religious newspapers in order to reach a new group of investors. JB had seen this type of advertising work during the Civil War; it had been used to entice settlers to move to the territory of Kansas and vote it into the Union as a free state. JB placed ads about investment opportunities in twenty-four newspapers, all of them east of Chicago. Ties with the Society of Friends were very beneficial to JB; he was not a member, but, as Bogue suggested, as a "Pennsylvanian he had great sympathy for their religious tenets." Several of the men whom he had hired had close ties to the Quakers: Silas Deane, Miles Dart, Henry Dickinson, and H. G. Chalkley. Later, when JB worked hard to boost the city of Lake Charles, he used religious and ethnic ties to promote his operations in selected newspapers and journals. This approach tapped into a huge reservoir of savings, albeit from smaller investors.

As mentioned, JB had opened offices in New York City, London, and Dallas. Now, impressed by the land available in Louisiana, he developed a huge, regional plan as he laid the groundwork to grow the small town of Lake Charles.

With the help of the funds he raised in these other cities, JB worked to develop his vision for Louisiana and, by 1883, he had purchased a million acres of land in that state. Based on JB's expertise in evaluating land and its use, he saw potential for rice production in southwest Louisiana; the risk in such a venture was written about in detail by the local papers. The Lake Charles *American* called it a "Gigantic Vision." JB's plan for the region included a railroad, which would be needed to transport agricultural products to the Gulf Coast for shipping. The Southern Pacific Railroad had a monopoly on the route and charged high rates to get to the existing port at New Orleans. JB was likely the first to suggest a deep-water port at Calcasieu Pass, at Lake Charles, to bypass New Orleans.

Following his entrepreneurial instincts, JB founded his own railroad, the Kansas City, Watkins & Gulf Railway Company, which eventually ran from Alexandria to Lake Charles, a distance of a hundred miles. He tried to get financing for a deep-water navigation channel that would allow the railroad to continue to a deep-water terminal at the Gulf. Although money ran short and that part of the project was never realized, we can admire JB's futuristic vision in which Lake Charles would rival New Orleans.

The *Jayhawker* of October 1936 (49, no. 1, p. 11) described the massive new undertaking in this way: "Mr. Watkins went East and won the confidence of Eastern investors. He purchased a million and a half acres of Louisiana land from 1885 to 1890 for fifty cents an acre, then mortgaged it for six dollars an acre. With this profit he drained the land and it became rich rice fields. Then he built a hundred miles of railroads on his holdings."

Once his office was established in Lake Charles, JB spent much of his time there, helping his new settlers. Along with shipping farm equipment

A completed section of the Kansas City, Watkins and Gulf Railway Company, within the 100 miles of finished track between Alexandria and Lake Charles, Louisiana. (Kitchen 8 Archives, Watkins Museum of History, Folder 3/18)

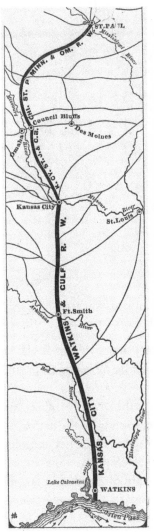

Diagram of Jabez B. Watkins's proposed railway to link St. Paul, Minnesota, with Calcasieu Pass at Lake Charles, Louisiana. (Report of the Water Way Committee for Southern Louisiana, Kitchen 8 Archives, Watkins Museum of History, Folder 3/18)

JB Watkins (*center*) at his Lake Charles office in Louisiana. (Kitchen 8 Archives, Watkins Museum of History, Untitled Folder, Drawer 4)

to Louisiana that his new farmers needed to plant their rice fields, he was also dredging the swampland, creating canals to move the crops, and building his railroad.

In a letter dated December 10, 1883, from JB to the Lawrence office: "We are shipping 85 tons, 10 carloads. We are going to surprise the natives, 16 plows. We'll have them in and any will turn 50 acres a day. They are going to Lake Charles from England."

Leaning on family to work for him, JB brought his brother-in-law Alexander Thomson to Louisiana. Alexander, married to JB's sister Maria, was originally from what became Ontario, Canada. He was a professor of mechanical engineering at Iowa State College of Agriculture in Ames. Iowa State was also well-known as the first veterinary college in America, begun in 1879. JB needed Alexander's engineering skills to help plan the process of draining the swampland in preparation to plant rice. However, even after drainage canals were built, saltwater seeped through the canal walls and back onto the swampy fields.

Undaunted by setbacks, JB brought in Professor Seaman A. Knapp in 1886 to assist Alexander. Knapp, the former president of Iowa State College

JB Watkins established the rice industry in Louisiana; by 1893, the world's largest rice mill was in Lake Charles, Louisiana. (McNeese State University Archives, Lake Charles, Louisiana)

of Agriculture, helped them evaluate the prairie lands that lay around the swamp areas. Making small adaptations to regular farm equipment, Knapp worked with JB and the local landowners to plant rice crops. Both the professor and JB were certain this would work. By 1900, Louisiana was growing 70 percent of all the rice in the United States and Lake Charles boasted the largest rice mill in the world. Although the swampland hadn't worked, the prairie land did.

At this same time, 1883, JB was also buying land in western Kansas with money from Eastern and foreign investors. Western Kansas was in a drought, and JB commented that everything west of Ellinwood was dried up all the way to Pueblo, Colorado. In a letter to the Lawrence office dated July 8, 1883, from the Fifth Avenue Hotel in Pueblo, he wrote: "After Ellinwood is all dried up. Can't say about Stafford County but Edwards is gone up this year."

Watkins worked with investors in America and England, and, Bogue says, he found them to be "deeply impressed by the frailty of human flesh." In other words, they were concerned about what would happen if JB died.

He had already planned for that, remarkably, for such a young man. In the early 1880s, JB had organized a trustee arrangement to carry on the business. The trustees were "Miles J. Dart, his lieutenant since 1874; D. M. Sprankle, Watkins' cousin who was employed at the Lawrence office; and Alexander Thomson, a brother-in-law of Watkins and professor at Iowa State College."

JB frequently hired family members. He also financially supported some relatives, but, with his belief in hard work, he preferred to employ rather than outright support them. And, in return, JB had employees that he felt he could trust.* He bought the St. Charles newspaper, the *American,* and made his nephew J. H. Neal manager. (Neal was married to Della, daughter of JB's sister Ellen.) David M. Sprankle, a cousin on his mother's side, worked for years at the Lawrence office, first in security and later as a secretary. As mentioned above, his brother-in-law Alexander Thomson moved to Lake Charles and helped drain the swamplands that became fertile rice fields.

In time, Elizabeth's family members also became part of this hiring pattern. Her brother Edward would move to Lake Charles to work as the printer for the *American.*

The 1880s and 1890s were years of wealth accumulation in America. The Industrial Revolution led to great wealth for those who could invest or otherwise take advantage of this change in the production of goods. People who were in the right place at the right time, and who also had the vision to seize the moment, generated great wealth in their own lifetimes. JB was one of the first to do so in Kansas. "Pen, Pants and Scissors," an article

---

* JB's family was intertwined with his business life: JB's mother, Barbara Sprankle, lived from 1803 to 1894. She had four children from her first marriage to John Mutersbaugh, who died in 1831: David, Abraham, John, and Mary. David married Ellen; their children were John, Mary, Amanda, Elizabeth, David, Emma, and Rosanna. Abraham married Rachel; their children were Alonzo, Ulysses, and Grant. John married Sarah. Barbara Sprankle's second marriage was to John Watkins, who lived from 1799 until 1853. They had seven children: Hannah, Ellen, Barbara, Ruth, Jabez Bunting, Harriet (or Hattie), and Maria. Barbara married Archibald Neal; their children were Della, Harriet, Ada Ruth, Lillie, James, and Bertha. Ruth married William White; their children were Jennie, Lewis, Grace, and Lloyd. Jabez Bunting married Elizabeth Miller. Harriet married Elery Chandler Walker; their children were Edwin C. Walker, John, George, Harry, and Ida. Maria married Alexander Thomson, a professor at Iowa State; their child was Zena.

in the *Kansas City Gazette* in June 1892, commented, "Jabez B. Watkins of Lawrence is said to be the wealthiest man in Kansas." The January 24, 1907, issue of the Lawrence *Daily Journal* contained an article from the *Financial Red Book of America* with an alphabetical list of Kansas men who, in 1905, were worth $300,000 or more. Included was "Watkins, Jabez B., Massachusetts and Quincy streets. President Watkins National Bank; owner Timber Lands; President St. Louis, Watkins & Gulf Railroad company."

While most of his time was consumed with his business dealings and extensive travels, JB still found time to take care of the women in his family. In the early 1880s, he purchased two insurance policies of $1,000 each for two of his sisters. He loaned money to a niece, Della Neal, for a land purchase in South Dakota. He sent $20 a month to Hattie Walker, his sister who lived in Falls Church, Virginia, and he also supported several nieces with monthly stipends.

JB also supported his mother monthly, as expected of a good, successful son: he paid her bills, paid for someone to care for her in her home, and purchased coal to heat her home in Punxsutawney, Pennsylvania. He also helped pay to fence the cemetery at Perrysville, Pennsylvania, where most of his family was buried.

During this period, 1876 to 1885, Elizabeth and JB each experienced personal and business growth. Elizabeth was developing her talents as she learned about office organization and the mortgage business. She showed extraordinary attention to detail and was acquainted with what went on in each of the offices, the personnel and the transactions. Outside of work, she read and listened to speeches on topics pertaining to women's independence and suffrage.

As JB saw more of the world, he developed his own view of politics. Much has been made of his political leanings. A self-described Democrat in the very Republican city of Lawrence, he championed Grover Cleveland, small government, and self-responsibility. He cast his first vote for Horace Greeley in 1872. JB's politics were no secret; being known as a "Grover Cleveland Democrat" made him somewhat of an outcast in Lawrence society.

The terms "Grover Cleveland Democrat" and "Bourbon Democrat" were used interchangeably and somewhat critically to describe an ideology some considered old-fashioned. Such Democrats were usually Southern (hence the term "Bourbon"); they were conservatives who supported fiscal discipline and were opposed to the high-tariff protectionism that was then in fashion in the Republican party. They believed in business and competition; they opposed subsidies and American imperialism overseas. During a Republican-dominated era from 1861 to 1933, Grover Cleveland was one of only two Democrats elected president.

Elizabeth's political leanings are revealed in her personal scrapbook. A lovely Victorian pastime, scrapbooks could be similar to diaries, revealing their owners' preferences. Elizabeth's scrapbook contains clippings of editorials she agrees with, some with handwritten notes in the margins. In the 1930s, First Lady Eleanor Roosevelt visited Lawrence and paid a call, right next door to Elizabeth's home. Many wondered why Elizabeth ignored this event. The answer may be found in her letters and scrapbook. JB had been a Democrat his entire voting life, which surely had an influence on Elizabeth. But she may also have held on loyally to her Republican upbringing. Remember, her family had been staunch Republicans, in gratitude for the Civil War pension her father received.

~

Evidence of the growing relationship between Elizabeth and JB Watkins, very private people, would be hard to base on the few personal letters in the collection. The business papers give indications of Elizabeth's increased involvement in JB's life and the beginning of their partnership. Small clues show JB's increasing dependence on Elizabeth; it seems clear that he was attracted by her growing abilities, her opinions, her steadfastness, and her ethics.

Given JB's lifelong practice of hiring family members to work in his businesses, it would seem to follow that those relatives would share Elizabeth's loyalty to him. However, in the years to come, some of them would prove loyal, others decidedly not.

CHAPTER 4

The Partnership Begins

The letters from 1885 show the growing partnership between Jabez B. Watkins and Elizabeth Miller, as well as JB's manner of doing business and his life interests. JB began to rely on Elizabeth and eventually became her life partner. Was their marriage born out of love or business necessity? Quite possibly it was a combination of the two.

To understand Elizabeth's life it is crucial to understand her relationship with her employer. In many ways, JB and her work molded her into the woman she became. Day-to-day operations at the various offices were guided by JB's trusted staff, but he visited them all frequently. He tried to oversee every detail, large and small, but with offices in four states (Kansas, Texas, New York, and Louisiana) and one overseas in England, he needed to trust his staff. Still, he was demanding and did not hesitate to point out errors and areas that needed improvement. He valued Elizabeth's intelligence, work ethic, and loyalty; and her responsibilities and her understanding of the business grew steadily.

At twenty-four, Elizabeth had worked at the Watkins Mortgage Company for nearly ten years; her coworkers still called her by the diminutive "Lizzie Jo." By then, however, she had proved herself. Starting in 1885, JB Watkins began to mention Elizabeth by name in his letters of instruction back to his staff in the home office, always located in Lawrence. These letters show her growing role: she had learned the mortgage business and was trusted to take care of details.

From JB's letter to the Lawrence office, dated December 14, 1885:

"Received from L. J. Miller for assignment of tax sale certificates numbers 500 and 901, Pawnee County, Kansas."

She also began to master second mortgages during this time. A second mortgage is money loaned against land or some other security that is subordinate to the initial or first legal mortgage. That is, the original mortgage had to be paid first; the second would be paid if funds were available upon liquidation. Thus, second mortgages were riskier, and a higher rate of interest could be charged for them. In 1894 in the United States, according to an article in the *Journal of Political Economy,* first mortgages accounted for $70 million, second mortgages for $2 million, and debenture bonds for $439,000. Debenture bonds were a relatively new form of loan; JB would soon begin to offer them to his customers, too.

JB's letter dated May 5, 1885, references second mortgages. Written in pencil on this letter is "Miss Miller has them." This is certainly JB's writing. His business letters were typed, but he often wrote additional notes by hand for clarity, in the margins or by his signature.

JB's attention to detail was iconic. Elizabeth learned from him, and it became a habit of hers, also. JB wrote to the Lawrence office several times a week, no matter where he was, giving instructions in detail. In one letter he told the secretary to clean the keys on her typewriter because it gave a bad impression if the type was dirty. A threat to her job was implied.

Letter dated November 10, 1885, from JB to the Lawrence office: "Your typewriter is doing poorer work than in the past. We must have better work if to accomplish it we are forced to get a new machine and operator. The type is not kept clean is one of the difficulties. JBW."

In a separate letter, he criticized Thomas C. (T. C.) Green, his assistant, for not reading a cable (telegram) correctly. He also wanted Green to check the work of a Mrs. Grannis carefully, as shown by the following three letters. Elizabeth Grannis's connection with JB's work is interesting; it shows the type of advertising he was doing at the time to promote his businesses.

Grannis, a New Yorker, had achieved some notoriety for her "denunciation of low-cut gowns" and the evils of "bare flesh exhibited by society women, particularly at the opera." She was the president of the National Christian League for the Promotion of Social Purity and was active in state and national temperance movements. The *Newton* (Kansas) *Daily Republican* called her "a bundle of nerves and energy. Her entire life has been devoted to work." With traits that echoed his own, she would seem to have been a good resource and worker for JB; however, her pace of work seemed to exhaust even him. She oversaw advertisements for JB's businesses that were placed in several publications that were sent to churches.

JB's letter dated September 25, 1885: "Anything that Mrs. Grannis says about talks with me pay no attention. You are to keep careful records and check all of her work. She talks much to me and have no record before me therefore such statements I do not want you to depend upon. JBW."

October 23, 1885: "E. B. Grannis getting $600 expenses. Church music $40, bill enclosed. *Church Press* and *Church Review* $60. Bill to be sent you by Mrs. Grannis."

December 25, 1885: "Send a draft of $500 to Mrs. E. B. Grannis. This is for a special list of advertising. She will send the list with the amount of each and receipted bills to cover the $500."

Advertisements in these publications were meant to entice ethnic and religious groups to settle in Louisiana on land plots that would be purchased from the Watkins Mortgage Company. This type of targeted advertising had been successful before and after the Civil War. Now, JB was using the same tactic to settle his newly purchased land in Louisiana.

Another example of JB's micromanagement involved the mowing of the lawn around the bank building in Lawrence. He wrote about the matter to David M. Sprankle in the Lawrence office. Sprankle was a cousin on JB's mother's side of the family, another example of JB's propensity to hire family members. He worked in security at the Lawrence office and, later, as a secretary.

JB's letter dated April 3, 1889, from Blossom House Hotel, Kansas City, MO: "Sprankle, I wish you to look after the matter and see that Sallis mows the lawn whenever it has grown an inch. The rye will grow that much in good weather every two days. North of the building and around the street needs to be cut now. Especially the border on Massachusetts St. Wherever there is any rye."

Although JB was usually a serious person and a strict boss, one letter he sent the Lawrence office illustrates his sense of humor. He had taken a watch into a New York shop to be repaired.

From a letter dated December 19, 1892: "It had gained 7 minutes in 2 months. The regulator was changed and then it lost 5 minutes each hour.

Not bad—only 2 hours a day, 14 hours a week, 60 hours per month. At least the watch will be right 5 times a month and 60 times a year. Wonderful!"

JB wanted and liked nice things, like roses on his dining table and luxurious vacations. He took repeated trips through the years to Hot Springs, Arkansas, to enjoy its famed amenities. Hot Springs was a unique place in America at the time Jabez visited. What is now known as Hot Springs National Park came under federal control in 1832 to protect the hot spring waters; it was the first area in the country to be set aside to protect its natural features. By the 1880s, the town was thriving. The waters gushed from the hillside at a remarkable 143 degrees Fahrenheit. For many, including Jabez Watkins, the waters seemed to have healing powers. Bathhouses, both simple and luxurious, lined the main street. The Fordyce, restored in 1989, has the stained glass and terrazzo floors of an elegant spa. Extensive water treatment rooms show the types of therapies Jabez could have indulged in at the Ozark Bath House. The Arlington Hotel, established in 1875, was a beautiful and stylish place to stay. Rebuilt after a fire and operating to this day, it is still the largest hotel in Arkansas.

Hot Springs is also known for its baseball history, which had its beginnings during the years JB visited. In 1886, the Chicago White Stockings (now the Cubs) held the first training and fitness camp prior to their season. The president of the ball club sent his team to Hot Springs before the season because it was an ideal setting to "boil out the alcoholic microbes in the hard-living players that were built up during the winter." It may have held the same appeal for JB Watkins. In 1882, Cornelius Jeremiah Vanderbilt, known as "Cornie," brother of Billy, had also visited Hot Springs to "take the cure." JB fared better than Cornie in this regard; Vanderbilt died very young and alcohol was just one of his vices. JB seemed to respond well to the trips to Hot Springs, even if they didn't permanently "cure" his problem.

JB's secret drinking was under control during those years. No successful businessman in Kansas could be exposed as a drinker. Carrie Nation, the most radical member of the Women's Christian Temperance Union, was smashing bars and taverns all across Kansas, which was the center of the campaign to ban sales of liquor, even before the Prohibition Era began in America.

JB's enjoyment of Hot Springs is evident in a letter to the Lawrence office, dated December 17, 1885. We can imagine him strolling along Bath

House Row, then writing from the desk at his hotel: "You would feel much better after you had taken 3 or 4 baths. I feel glorious now. Am being made over new. It clears my brain as well as purified my body and perhaps my soul a little."

Watkins may have been generous with himself, but he also gave generously to others. He supported many Kansas organizations, including Ottawa University, Trinity Episcopal Church, and the Haskell band in Lawrence. JB's ideas of philanthropy had been influenced by Andrew Carnegie, whom he had met when he was buying steel. Their business relationship led to a friendship. When JB became acquainted with Carnegie's theory of giving, he seemed to have adopted it and passed it on to Elizabeth. His philanthropy followed a general rule: he gave to groups or organizations that helped young people get ahead, but he felt that the recipient should also work to get the gift. This fit with JB's personal ethos: one should work to prove oneself, work is mankind's natural state, one must work to have a fulfilling life, and work is essential to personal dignity.

By 1886, Elizabeth's duties had grown, along with her title and responsibilities. JB recognized that she was becoming an astute businesswoman, an integral part of the company. Shown here, a check signed by Elizabeth designates her as "Assistant Secretary," one of the earliest proofs of her role at the company. Wilbur Presby was still JB's personal secretary, but Elizabeth now held a position that was coveted and rare for a woman at the time.

When JB first started his enterprises in Lawrence, he used local banks, particularly the National Bank of Lawrence, where he was the largest individual stockholder. In 1882 JB filed a district court case that charged officers of the National Bank of Lawrence with defrauding one of the stockholders of his stock. This same group of bank officers had used the bank's money to set up the Western Farm Mortgage Company, in direct competition with JB's company. So, in 1887, JB sued the National Bank of Lawrence for $25,000 in damages for alleged mismanagement and for using the bank's funds for their own personal benefit, to his injury. Many Lawrence businesspeople supported JB's competitors in this matter. This is when he got the idea of starting his own bank.

In 1887, JB bought lots 9, 11, 13, and 15 at the southeast corner of Massachusetts and Quincy for $8,400. These lots were across the street diagonally from where he planned to build his new bank. JB gave Douglas

The signature "L. J. Miller, Assistant Secretary" on this check from December 16, 1886, is one of the earliest proofs of the highly unusual position she held within the J. B. Watkins Land and Mortgage Company. (Douglas County Historical Society, Watkins Museum of History, donated by Kitchen 8)

County the deed to these lots for a new courthouse, for the sum of $1.00, as reported by the *Lawrence Daily Journal* on January 1, 1902. Perhaps this was more than a philanthropic gesture. Having the courthouse near his bank building would be good for business. Building goodwill with the leaders of Lawrence could be an asset, too, and may have been needed. It seems there was always some undercurrent of conflict surrounding JB's politics and his business interests. As already stated, he was a Democrat in the Republican town of Lawrence. And, as an active and assertive businessman who was frequently traveling, JB may not have taken the time to develop social relationships with the local businessmen. Jealousy of JB's success may have created friction, and donating this land for a courthouse could be seen as a gesture to placate the town.

There was correspondence at the time about this land that he eventually sold/gave to the county for the courthouse.* Inquiries had been made

---

* Keeping copies of office correspondence before the advent of copy machines was a complicated process. All matter to be copied was handwritten using a special copy ink. The page to be copied was placed under a blank sheet of very thin paper that was later bound in a book. The thin sheet of paper, with a cloth dipped in water placed on top, was run through a roller wringer. All this was put under a press consisting of two metal plates that could be screwed down. When this was undone, a copy had been made. The process, which produced what were called letterpress volumes, was used through 1910 (A. J. Bolinger, *Kansas Boy: The Memoirs of A. J. Bolinger* [Lawrence: University Press of Kansas, 2021]).

about the price of the blacksmith shop and other buildings that were still on those parcels. T. C. Green, JB's assistant, and Elizabeth did not agree on the prices. JB heeded Elizabeth's advice and suggested he was in no hurry to sell. The correspondence also shows that she disagreed with W. J. Patterson, JB's attorney. Hers was obviously a voice JB listened to; he gave her advice equal weight with that of his legal counsel.

From JB's letter dated February 17, 1888, sent from the Lake Charles, Louisiana, office: "I have Patterson's and Miss Miller's of the 13th. You better agree upon something and write Mr. Chalkley. As I understand the position of Green and Miss Miller they are not in harmony. I do not desire to fix any price on the old blacksmiths shop and other buildings on the lot. I am in no hurry to sell."

Elizabeth's responsibilities with the company continued to grow. Her opinions were sought and listened to. In letters to the Lawrence office, JB addressed each of the employees involved with specific aspects of the business, and they would respond immediately in the next mail, with several letters a week back and forth. Elizabeth observed how JB closely monitored his business and learned from him the need to keep an eye on the company's interests.

Deeds dated November 5, 1888, show that JB bought 160 acres in Pawnee County, Kansas, and signed it over to Elizabeth. With this parcel, Lizzie J. Miller now owned almost 82 acres in Calcasieu, Louisiana, and 160 acres in Pawnee County, Kansas, and she paid $9.04 in back taxes. She was beginning to develop an investment portfolio, unusual for a young woman at that time.

Elizabeth and JB had become good friends, and he took an interest in her well-being and that of her mother. With JB's pattern of taking care of family members, it was a sign of his growing affection for Elizabeth when he began to provide for her family also. Elizabeth was asked to locate copies of the *American,* a journal devoted to southwestern Louisiana. Jabez bought the journal in 1897 and moved it to Lake Charles. Elizabeth's brother Edward moved to Lake Charles to work as a printer for the *American.* Later, Edward worked for the Watkins Bank in Lake Charles. In 1896, JB sold 81.61 acres of land in Louisiana to Elizabeth's mother, Ella Miller, for $1,000 because he thought it was a wise investment for her. Elizabeth's family and JB were becoming intertwined.

When Elizabeth's father died, JB promised to look after the family. Elizabeth and her mother continued to live in the family home at 1104 Tennessee. Ella, as Dr. Miller's widow, would receive payments of $17 a month from his Civil War pension until her death in 1909.

Elizabeth's father died in March 1888. According to Dr. E. D. F. Phillips, who examined Dr. Miller hours before his death, he died of heart disease induced by the chronic diarrhea he had contracted while serving in the Civil War. Dr. Miller's detailed obituary in the Lawrence paper showed the esteem in which he was held by the community. It stated that he had shared the office of Dr. Gifford, had held the position of coroner of Douglas County, and, at the time of his death, was a United States pension examiner. The obituary stated that he left his wife, Ella, a daughter, Miss Lizzie, who lived in Lawrence, a son Frank who lived in Salina, Kansas, and a son Edward who lived in Lake Charles, Louisiana. A group of physicians met to honor him and they passed several resolutions that noted his contributions to the community.

In April 1889 JB cabled (telegrammed) Elizabeth the sum of $40,000. He advised her that it was for her use, but also said she should not tie up the money permanently. He suggested she use it in the mortgage business or have it available to use in debenture bonds, as he would probably want to use a portion of it in the future. This clearly shows the exceptional level of trust between them.

Although he was spending more time in Lake Charles, JB was involved in purchasing the old Methodist Episcopal Church at the northeast corner of Massachusetts and Berkley (now Tenth Street) in downtown Lawrence. A new Methodist church had been built at Vermont and Berkley. Because the University of Kansas had outgrown the available buildings at their campus on the hill, the law school had taken over old North College, forcing the music and art departments to move. JB agreed to rent the old church building for "not over $200 a year as the home for the School of Music," according to a note in the First Methodist Episcopal Church history. The university gave $600 for needed repairs and got a four-year lease.

In April 1890, JB wrote to tell Sprankle to be sure that more than one group used the church building for charitable purposes. He believed it should be used to do good for more people. JB questioned in July whether to put a stone or board sidewalk around the church. He chose board since it was not certain how long he would retain ownership of the property. The arrangement with KU held for a number of years, until 1902. The end of the School of Music's residency in this location is related by Phil Leonard in his history of the Lawrence Fire Department. "[March 13, 1902] Firemen saved only the walls of the J. B. Watkins Music Hall, on the corners of Massachusetts and Berkley, this afternoon after a fire almost completely destroyed the building. . . . Loss to buildings and contents $10,000.00. The fire started downstairs in the building by a small boy left there by a mother in a religious meeting upstairs. The boy was trying to learn to smoke."

Documents from 1891 show that JB sent Elizabeth money to cover travel and other expenses, plus her salary. Her salary is not clearly stated, but it was probably $50 a month. Wilbur Presby's salary was raised to $135 a month. Even at $50 a month, much less than a man would earn at the same job, Elizabeth and her mother were living comfortably. That year, she paid $6.40 in taxes in Calcasieu Parish in Louisiana on the land that JB had purchased for her.

The evidence shows JB's and Elizabeth's mutual respect and care for each other. Was theirs a business relationship that became romantic over time? Or had an early mutual attraction led JB to tutor Elizabeth so she would become his partner? They had likely talked of marriage but could see no advantage to it at that time. There were reasons for Elizabeth not to marry JB while her mother was alive. Obviously, JB had been preparing Elizabeth for more responsibilities in the business. She had been taught business procedures, how to deal with investors, shrewd uses of money, honest dealing, investing, and how to evaluate investments. Above all, JB had taught her the importance of using money wisely. She had learned to evaluate causes and donate to good ones. She truly was becoming JB's "right hand," invaluable in helping handle the voluminous business transactions from their four offices, plus England.

By the age of twenty-nine, Elizabeth traveled regularly on business for the company. This was most unusual for a young unmarried woman at that time. Historian Judith Galas calls Elizabeth a "striking, sometimes scandalous exception to traditional womanhood. In the late 1800's, Elizabeth was among the first of her generation to work outside the home in a white-collar job. . . . At a time when respectable, unmarried women traveled only with chaperones, she traveled extensively either alone or with her employer—a man 16 years her senior."

Surely Elizabeth would have been exhilarated by having the freedom to travel and see new places and by her important role in the Watkins businesses. One wonders what her mother or her friends thought about her traveling to a big city like New York in her role as a businesswoman. Did her mother worry about gossip? Were her friends envious or scandalized? Her unusual lifestyle would have made these reactions possible. Surviving gossip and unkind talk about her lifestyle could lead to the rather solitary life she led later. But, for the time being, she enjoyed her business trips to New York; she went by train, her favorite way to travel. She stayed at the Murray Hill Hotel in the city. JB was often there at the same time, as was Presby, his personal secretary.*

In 1899 Elizabeth and her mother became charter members of the Ingleside Club in Lawrence; the women's club was started for the "study of poetry or prose, of any author the club may select." Women at the time were seeking ways to pursue intellectual subjects. Any woman could become a member with the consent of the majority present. Membership was limited to twenty, a number that could comfortably meet in members' houses—respectable women were not encouraged, or in some cases even allowed, to hold meetings in most public places.

The first members included (all Mrs.) M. E. Addison, Marie French, Serena Jamison, Ella Miller (Elizabeth's mother), Louisa J. O'Bryan, Euphemia Riddle, Arabella Barber, Mary Griffin, Lou Moore, Tabitha Street, Maude Harriman Leonard, Sarah Mitzel, Mary Bradley, and three others. Miss Lizzie Miller was the only unmarried member. Why were there no other young single women? It may be that Ella wanted Elizabeth to join along with her because she thought the group would be a proper influence on her daughter. And, given Elizabeth's unorthodox lifestyle, membership would give her respectability and a group of friends who knew her and understood a bit about her unusual life. It might lessen the potential

---

* The Murray Hill Hotel was frequented by the Vanderbilts, P. T. Barnum, and other well-known people. See Anderson Cooper, *Vanderbilt: The Rise and Fall of an American Dynasty* (New York: Harper Collins, 2021).

The Murray Hill Hotel, where JB Watkins and his employees traditionally stayed while in New York. It was built in 1884 and demolished at the end of World War II. Notable celebrities who stayed there included Mark Twain, Jay Gould, Diamond Jim Brady, and Presidents Grover Cleveland and William McKinley.
(Library of Congress)

Interior of the Murray Hill Hotel. Details in the hotel inspired
JB's choices when he designed his bank building in Lawrence.
(Author's collection)

THE INGLESIDE CLUB. ORGANIZED SEPT., 1894.

MEMBERS:—Mrs. Marie French, President; Mrs. Mary E. Addison, Vice-President; Mrs. E. J. White, Secretary; Mesdames Serenia S. Jameson, Julia Spaulding, Ella A. Miller, May Moore, Euphemia Riddle, Tabitha Street, Mary C. Griffin, Louise J. O'Bryon, Sarah H. Grover, Mary Elwell, Cloyd Smith, John Barber, D. M Sprankle, N. J. Hancock, M. G. Field and Miss Lizzie Miller.

The Ingleside Club, organized September 1894. Miller is believed to be
in the top row, second from right. (E. F. Caldwell, *A Souvenir History of
Lawrence, Kansas, 1898*)

gossip, which would make life easier for Elizabeth and, undoubtedly, for her mother.

Both Elizabeth and her mother presented programs, such as "Quotations from Sketch of Aragon," "Life of Washington Irving," and "Description of the Alhambra—Its Towers and Courts." On December 4, 1900, Elizabeth gave a program entitled "What was the attitude of women of leisure to self-supporting women?" As the only single and self-supporting woman in the Ingleside Club, Elizabeth had need of a strong character to give this presentation and mediate the ensuing discussion. After that meeting, according to the newspaper story, goodbyes were given to Miss Miller, who would be absent some weeks in New York.

Elizabeth was setting her own path in life.

The Watkins Bank

In 1887 JB established the Watkins National Bank in Lawrence, motivated by his lawsuit against his former bank. Always considered a bit of an outsider by the Lawrence establishment, JB felt that, to protect and efficiently run his mortgage business, he must set up his own bank. Now in competition with the Western Farm Mortgage Company, organized by his previous bank, he would have his own bank to handle all the land mortgage business that continued to come through his Lawrence office, giving him a competitive edge.

Planning for the new bank building began in earnest. It would stand at the northwest corner of Massachusetts and Quincy (now Eleventh Street). This was a tremendous undertaking, and JB was involved in every aspect with his usual attention to detail, to the extent that he sent back materials that didn't meet his standards, as reported by Jack Newcomb in his book about the construction of the Watkins Bank Building, *Thing of Beauty*. JB hired the architectural firm of Cobb and Frost of Chicago to design and construct the building—with his own constant input, naturally.

As he was planning his new bank building in Lawrence, JB contemplated places he had visited, buildings he had admired. When in New York, he usually stayed at the Murray Hill Hotel, and he duplicated several of its features: he had its terrazzo floor reproduced for the bank portion of his building, but he used mosaic instead because terrazzo was so expensive. A great deal of the lumber used in the building was shipped from his property in Louisiana. JB admired Louisiana's yellow curly pine trees; he had them milled for woodwork and used in his bank building.

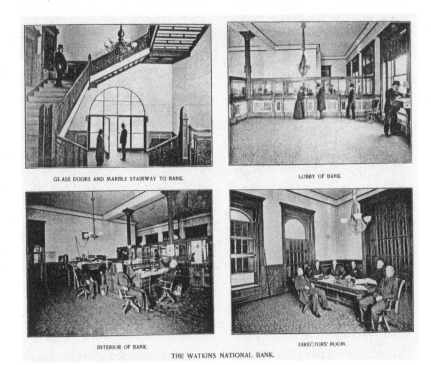

GLASS DOORS AND MARBLE STAIRWAY TO BANK.   LOBBY OF BANK.

INTERIOR OF BANK.   DIRECTORS' ROOM.

THE WATKINS NATIONAL BANK.

Four views of the interior of the Watkins Bank in Lawrence. (E. F. Caldwell, *A Souvenir History of Lawrence, Kansas, 1898*)

There were difficulties with the construction. Shipments of brick did not match and were returned. Terra cotta trim pieces arrived broken, moved from one train car to another with disastrous results. The slate for the roof was not of the quality JB had requested. A marble stairway needed more support than was initially built into the plans. But the final product was a magnificent building; flooded with light from large windows, it was also planned so that natural light would enhance the workplaces of the employees.

JB had a small apartment built into the third floor, up a small stairway. It had a luxuriously deep bathtub for washing off the dust accumulated from driving out to inspect his Kansas farm properties.

The lower level of the building was finished with ash, the second level in light oak, and the third level in Louisiana yellow curly pine. A fireplace in

The deep bathtub built into JB's private quarters on the top floor of his bank and mortgage company building. (Douglas County Historical Society, Watkins Museum of History)

JB's office on the third floor had a lovely mantel made from the pine, with "JBW" carved into it.

From the Massachusetts entrance to the building, the beautiful mosaic floors, majestic white marble stairway, and high ceilings are visible. Such was JB's attention to detail that even the door hinges were heavily ornamented, with "small swinging covers over the keyholes."

Despite JB's constant badgering of the contractors, the building was completed and occupied in October 1888. Moving the business from its old location to the new brought its own issues, as seen in the next letter excerpt.

JB's letter to David Sprankle dated February 5, 1888: "My old desk, if sold, should not be delivered until after I return to Lawrence. When we moved I was not able to unlock the door to the upright case of pigeon holes on the left-hand side of the top of the desk, and I don't want the desk to pass out of my hands until I can get that part unlocked and take out the papers that are filed there."

The new Watkins Bank in Lawrence was so successful that in 1888 they could not loan all the money they had deposited.

JB's office. The fireplace mantel, made from Louisiana yellow curly pine, is carved with his initials "JBW." (Douglas County Historical Society, Watkins Museum of History)

Detail from the marble and metal stairway of the Watkins Bank and Mortgage Company building, again with JB's initials. (Douglas County Historical Society, Watkins Museum of History)

THE WATKINS NATIONAL BANK BUILDING.

The Watkins Bank and Land Mortgage Company, Eleventh and
Massachusetts Street, Lawrence, Kansas. (E. F. Caldwell, *A Souvenir
History of Lawrence, Kansas, 1898*)

During March 1888, JB returned to Hot Springs. He also took camping and fishing trips to Eagle River in Wisconsin and to Maine. The staff
learned that he was now the general manager of the North American Land
and Timber Company, which had initially been incorporated in Maine.
This was the company in which his English clients invested, and his new
role gave him added influence there. Even his vacations turned into business deals, and it seems likely that he took little time to relax and take care
of himself. This intense pace would eventually cause a break in his health.
But for now, with his business interests there, he kept an eye on Maine
politics, which were Democratic at the time, in harmony with his beliefs.

JB wrote to the Lawrence office from the Sea Shore House in Old Or-
chard Beach, Maine, on August 31, 1888: "I found politics all right in Canada, in Clint and Blaine. Who is Harrison anyway? I concluded to come
over into Maine and knock Jim out. I find everything lovely here. The

Dems are scooping them all around. And Blaine, according to the Maine papers 1 have read, is the meanest man in the United States. The Dems have scooped the Republicans on whiskey and fishing and those are two tender spots in Maine politics."*

JB lived at the Eldridge Hotel when he was in Lawrence and stored his clothes there. Frequently he would have Bill, the black porter, send him items of clothing. He read *Pilgrim's Progress,* the *American,* and the *Record,* a Lawrence paper that he eventually also bought.

Elizabeth was now heavily involved in the debenture bond side of the Watkins Land and Mortgage Co. This is a type of bond or debt instrument that is not secured by collateral; the loan is granted based on creditworthiness and reputation and is not backed by a physical asset. Corporations and governments have used debenture bonds to raise funds; they were the unsecured promissory notes, or personal loans, that are in use today.

JB and Elizabeth made the decisions about sales of this type of bond. They advised Henry Dickinson in the New York office to pay a 1.5% commission on the sale of debenture bonds; they could secure a better agent, more likely a local person, if a good commission was offered. It was advantageous to have a local agent who could better assess the reputation of a loan applicant. Elizabeth was advised to furnish Dickinson a list each month of all those ordering reinvestments.

From JB at the Lake Charles office to the Lawrence office, letter dated November 26, 1888: "Miss Miller: 1 have today instructed Dickinson that he may pay a commission of 1½% on the sale of debenture bonds where it is necessary in order to hold or secure a good agent. My reasons for this are that the future efforts by locals will be much more effective than advertising. The day of successful general advertising for investment is past."

Again, from Lake Charles, JB sent this letter on December 12, 1888: "Miss Miller: 1 have just received a letter from Dickinson in which he suggests

---

* Benjamin Harrison, former Republican senator from Indiana, was elected US president in 1888 on the strength of his war record and his support of factory workers and industrialists who wanted high tariffs. Although Grover Cleveland, the Democratic incumbent, won the popular vote, Harrison won with a majority of votes in the Electoral College, an event that would not happen again until 2000. James G. Blaine, the early Republican frontrunner for presidential nominee that year, withdrew when he realized his nomination would require a bitter struggle with Harrison supporters that would not be good for the Republican party.

Sample debenture bond issued by J. B. Watkins Land Mortgage Company, 1914. (Author's collection)

that the Lawrence office refer to him parties who desire reinvestments. He thinks he can get the most of them to accept debenture in bonds. He gives several instances where parties have become dissatisfied with the long delay in reinvesting their money, among them Stephen R. Post and Mr. Curtis, executor of the Wetmore estate. I am telling Dickinson that you will furnish him a list each month of all ordering reinvestments which please see is furnished to him."

Note the use of "please" in the letter to Elizabeth above; it was a word that occurred rarely in JB's correspondence.

While JB was concentrating on his holdings in Louisiana and spending much of his time in Lake Charles, he relied even more heavily on Elizabeth to monitor transactions in the small office in New York. Elizabeth began to travel quite a bit between Lawrence, New York, and Louisiana. The business in Louisiana was expanding. JB was credited, then and now, with making Lake Charles into a prominent Louisiana city.

From the city of Lake Charles website: "The 1880s saw the small sawmill village develop into a boom town, thanks to the innovative advertising methods of a man named J. B. Watkins. With his astounding $200,000 advertising campaign, the town grew 400% in the '80s."

In 1918, Connelley's *Standard History of Kansas and Kansans* gave this overview of JB's enterprises in Louisiana:

In the early '80s Mr. Watkins began an extensive campaign of land buy-ing. He acquired 1,500,000 acres of land from state and federal gov-ernments in Southwestern Louisiana. In 1890 he built and operated 100 miles of railway from Lake Charles to Alexandria, owning all the townsites on the railway. One of his cardinal principles is illustrated in the fact that in all the deeds given for lots in these townsites is a clause forbidding forever the sale of intoxicating liquors on the prem-ises. This decision it should be noted has been sustained by the courts. Lake Charles, one of the most thriving cities of Louisiana, today largely owes its development and growth to Mr. Watkins. [His estate] still owns thousands of acres of land in Kansas, Louisiana and Texas.

A local Lake Charles historian wrote, "The principal operating branch of the Watkins National Bank was located on Broad Street at Hodges, and the principal station for the Watkins Railroad was on Ryan at Clarence. J. B. Watkins, for all practical purposes, was a king in his domain of fi-nance, real estate and transportation."

JB worked hard not only to establish the agricultural business of grow-ing rice around Lake Charles but also to make a good city for those who bought land parcels from him. A local historian said, "Watkins made every effort to fulfill the rural agricultural paradise he promoted and promised." He graded and graveled roads. He brought in the best agricultural experts to help plan the new rice fields. He donated land and money for schools. When the town was struggling to get students out to a newly donated high school building on the edge of town, JB allowed his streetcar line to carry the students out to the site.

In June 1892, JB wrote an ad from his office at 2 Wall Street, New York: "Wanted—good hotel investment near the Gulf Coast and on a beach." Ads were likely put in Louisiana and New York papers. He would donate a liberal quantity of land to anyone who would erect these hotels. Having a good hotel built at Lake Charles would only enhance his business endeav-ors there. By advertising in religious publications, JB was also still trying

The 1910 streetcar crew for the Ryan Street line, Lake Charles, Louisiana. (McNeese State University Archives, Lake Charles, Louisiana)

to entice immigrants of different ethnic and religious groups, including Dunkards, to his Louisiana lands.

As JB's wealth grew, so did requests for money. For example, in February 1889 the Cyclone Club in Washington, DC, asked him for a donation. This was the alumni club of Iowa State College in Ames; perhaps they felt JB should donate out of gratitude. After all, he had hired away two of their professors to assist in the agricultural planning around Lake Charles. He declined because he didn't "see how the expenditure of that money could contribute in any way to the public good." Years later, when she was managing their estate, Elizabeth applied the same standard when she was asked for donations.

JB needed steel rails for his railroad in Louisiana, and Andrew Carnegie was the man with the steel. As mentioned earlier, JB's ideas about charity were based on what he learned from Carnegie: he wanted to help people help themselves. This was a principle he, and also Elizabeth, followed throughout life. They wanted to avoid handouts and, instead, give money in a way to help people help themselves. JB had ordered tons of iron rails from Carnegie for his railroad in Louisiana. Because the Ohio River was too low to ship them by barge, they shipped a thousand tons by rail. Later in the year, Carnegie was able to ship an additional two thousand tons of rails for JB's railroad by way of the Ohio River, a much easier method, passing Evansville, Indiana, and reaching New Orleans in one week.

Often, when they were away from the offices, Elizabeth wrote letters dictated by JB; he signed, with her initials under his signature. She wrote in longhand since she had never learned to type. That fact made her appreciate even more that JB had hired her when she was such an inexperienced young girl. Why had she never learned to type? Remington had produced the first commercial typewriter in 1872, but it hadn't caught on with the public.* This reluctance may have stemmed from the fact that letter writing was seen then as a personal form of communication. Handwritten letters carried the personality of the writer; typewritten letters were viewed as impersonal. When Remington began to advertise to businesses in the 1880s, the typewriter took off and JB bought them for the office stenographers. This timeline explains why Elizabeth would not have known how to type when she was hired and why, by the late 1880s, she did not need that skill. Her responsibilities by then far exceeded those of a stenographer in the Watkins enterprises.

JB and Elizabeth were both in the New York office when they learned of the death of Wilbur Presby's wife, Jenette, in Lawrence in 1891. It was a sad time for them all. Presby was JB's personal secretary and the three of them worked closely together. Presby had been married barely a year, and Jenette was only twenty-one. Both from Lawrence, the couple had moved to New York when Wilbur was promoted. On a trip home to Lawrence to visit her parents, Jenette took ill and died of heart failure.

Simple day-to-day living was challenging in those times. Travel was difficult, slow, and stressful. Health care was not very advanced. JB's letters of 1891 give glimpses of his everyday life. He had some clothes stored in the bank building, probably in his living quarters on the third floor, and needed handkerchiefs sent to him. He wanted copies of pictures taken

* For a good chronology of the typewriter, see Ira Flatow, *They All Laughed . . . From Light Bulbs to Lasers: The Fascinating Stories behind the Great Inventions That Have Changed Our Lives* (New York: Harper Perennial, 1993).

of himself, the most pleasant, to be sent to him. These were most likely for use in newspaper articles being written about him, especially in Lake Charles publications. He didn't want to exchange the Remington typewriter for a Smith-Premier. He asked Miss Bradley to clean her typewriter and not strike it too hard. He did not want the tiger rug sent to New York; however, to keep it from being moth-eaten, he suggested it be powdered with anti-moth preparation for storage. He requested that cousin Sprankle gather his, JB's, clothing in the office, have it laundered, and then pack it away properly. JB was invited to have an exhibit at the 1893 Chicago World's Fair, but he declined the offer. In November 1891 he paid Dr. Thomas in New York $565.88 for medical services he had received, but we do not know what the illness was. These were some of the daily issues in the life of JB Watkins in 1891.

In 1891, JB paid $502.96 in taxes in Lawrence on several properties, including the Methodist Church building, the Robinson land, and the Lawrence Canning Co. Sometimes called the Mount Oread property, the Robinson land lies atop Mount Oread, with a stunning view of the Wakarusa Valley to the south. In 1893 there were inquiries about removing stone from that property. Legend says this stone was used to build the walls around the grounds at the Watkins Bank. JB had purchased the Robinson property in the 1880s for later use. He had ideas of building a house there, although he had not said anything to Elizabeth about it. This property would prove to be important in both JB's and Elizabeth's future.

In 1893, there was a financial crisis in the United States, often called the Panic of 1893; the resultant economic recession lasted until 1897. With many of JB's investors feeling nervous, he sent Elizabeth and Ross Brodhead, another employee, to travel around New York State and reassure them. They visited investors who lived in the area, telling them that the Watkins Mortgage business was still viable. This assignment shows how Elizabeth's position in the business had grown.

During the 1880s, JB had become involved in a number of enterprises in addition to his mortgage company. In Lawrence, these included the Lawrence Canning Company, the Lawrence *Record* newspaper, and his Watkins National Bank. He had also opened a branch bank in Lake Charles. He owned one-third interest in the North American Land and Timber Company, the main investment vehicle for his British investors;

the company had completed the purchase of nine hundred thousand acres in Louisiana. Also in Louisiana, JB owned the Calcasieu Sugar Company, the Lake Charles Sugar Company, and the *American,* a publishing concern. The Orange Land Company, which JB owned outright, owned six hundred thousand acres of land in Louisiana as well. With the exception of his two banks, all these new ventures demanded outlays of money with little immediate return.

When the 1893 depression struck the plains states, JB assumed ownership of all the farms that could not make their payments. In Kansas, these extended from the northwest corner of Phillips County to the southwest corner of Edwards County, then east to Kiowa and Comanche Counties. He had been too optimistic about their land value. This downturn threw more than fifty other loan agencies into receivership. Receivership is a legal remedy when a company cannot pay its bills and must close or reorganize its finances; an individual is appointed by the court to oversee the company, usually with the approval of the creditors. Eastern investors cut their western investments by half, from $6.5 million to $3 million, a reduction that impacted the Watkins enterprises.

The J. B. Watkins Land and Mortgage company held its own through 1893. In September 1892, requests for mortgage loans stood at $400,000, the same as a year earlier; but due to a lack of investor income, JB was unable to fill these loans. This was largely his own doing. He was using $1.5 million from his mortgage company's proceeds to complete the Alexandria to Lake Charles link of his railroad. Failure of the mortgage company seemed imminent in the early fall of 1893.

JB kept his company out of receivership in 1893. He personally guaranteed the payment of securities that reluctant investors agreed to renew. But soon that was not enough. The company was placed in receivership by the US Circuit Court of Topeka on April 5, 1894, with JB appointed as receiver. Within a few months, he had developed a plan of debt reorganization that was approved by the court. The receivership was then terminated.

JB worked to renew confidence in his mortgage company by using advertising to offer safe investments. In late 1893, an ad in newspapers ran as follows: "23 years record. $20,250,000 repaid. Offer safe 6% mortgage investment. Will collect or foreclose defaulted mortgages. JB Watkins Land Mortgage Co., Lawrence, Kansas." This ad was meant to reassure the public and investors, alike, that JB's mortgage company was solvent again.

Elizabeth played an integral part in the survival of the mortgage business during the Panic of 1893; not only did she keep clerical details in order but she also personally visited investors and handled public relations. Both JB and Elizabeth took great pride in surviving this challenge together. JB had been overly optimistic in estimating the value of lands he had mortgaged. He may have led investors astray, but he was not an irresponsible person. For the rest of his life, he tried to the best of his ability to value assets correctly.

In Lawrence in June 1893, the Watkins businesses were still growing, despite the economic downturn; three new stenographers were hired, each paid $45 a month.

An 1893 accounting record from the New York office's petty cash account lists salaries for L. J. Miller at $112.00 and W. F. Presby at $150.00. The company paid for all of Elizabeth's travel and, often, JB would designate extra amounts to her. This notable rise in salary marks her growing importance to the company and to JB.

At about this time, 1893, Elizabeth lived in New York for several years and worked in the office there; support for this idea comes from the fact that her salary was paid by the New York office. She was handling investments for the Orange Land Company in Louisiana, owned exclusively by JB. She was also the resident agent for JB's railroad and handled investors' purchases of shares in the fledgling railroad. Now in her early thirties, Elizabeth was an accomplished businesswoman and a true part of JB's life. With her own portfolio of investments, she was an independent single woman, working and living in New York City on her own. She had truly accomplished her goals.

Another facet of JB Watkins is shown in *The True Money System of the United States*, a book he wrote in 1896. If a copy were available, it would be a fascinating read, given his thoughts about the gold standard and his having just gone through his mortgage company's receivership. For most of the nineteenth century, the United States had a bimetal money system, based on prices of gold and silver. Forty years ahead of his time, JB had a vision of how the monetary system of the United States should work. JB

What a stylish young professional woman like Elizabeth would be wearing in New York City at the turn of the nineteenth century. (*Altman's Spring and Summer Fashions Catalog*, 1915)

may not have been the only one with these ideas, but, always enterprising and confident, he wrote his thoughts into a book.

For most of the 1890s, the United States was in an economic recession. The Panic of 1893 hit JB hard, and, in his book, he blamed the government and its failed monetary policy. JB said the purpose of money was to facilitate trade. The supply of money, he said, was the key to economic growth. In an illustration of his well-known attention to detail, he actually calculated the total amount of physical money in the United States in gold coins, silver coins, government notes, and national bank notes. His estimate was $1.9 billion.

He objected to the use of actual gold and silver coins, as their value was diminished by "wear from much handling." He estimated that if the total US stock of gold at the time was all in circulation as gold coins, the loss from abrasion would be more than $2 million per year.

The value of money was set by the government, based on a percentage of actual gold held by the government in reserve. Generally, the government aimed to keep 20 percent of the nation's $500 million in paper money in gold reserves. At times, this had fallen to only 10 percent.

In the 1890s the value of gold was set incorrectly, according to JB's evaluation. He believed that for the government to fix the value of gold was "against natural laws," that the value should move up and down, following supply and demand. This was a topic of financial conversations in business circles at that time. There was some concern in Europe that America might abandon the gold standard and opt for the silver standard to back its money, which would lessen the value of US dollars held in Europe. JB estimated that, in all, individual and corporate loans from Europe could total $5 billion. Some of these European players no longer wanted to accept US dollars. They demanded repayment of their loans to America in gold, which caused the gold reserve supply to be greatly reduced. The ensuing alarm rippled through the banking institutions of the United States, and the Panic of 1893 was on.

JB's solution was that demand notes, issued by national banks and the federal government, should be replaced. He called for the government to expand the money supply by issuing some type of government securities or savings bonds in which people could invest. This would give the government the people's money to use for a set period of time, in return for interest paid to them. He believed that such investments would be of great value to individuals and would vastly strengthen the government. The nation's debt would be held by the citizens and its currency would be based on that debt. He argued that this would be a strong national bond to unite the people.

In 1929, the US government issued its first treasury bills, the same sort of government-issued security JB had proposed forty years earlier. The end of the gold standard in the United States was effectively 1933, but it was 1971 before the value of gold was no longer set by the government and linked to the dollar, as JB had suggested eighty years earlier.

JB's ideas were ahead of their time. His book is out of print and copies are rare. One is held in the library of the London School of Economics.

In March 1898, Elizabeth's brother Edward died of pneumonia in Lake Charles. He had moved to Louisiana initially to work as a printer at JB's publication, the *American*. Later, he worked for the Lake Charles branch of the Watkins Bank. Edward was mentioned in the local Lake Charles *Commercial* newspaper as one of "our efficient and popular cashiers." He had a wife, Judith, and a young son, Frank Valentine Miller, who would go on to be an important part of the Watkins businesses. Elizabeth and her mother went to Lake Charles to bring Edward's body back to Lawrence. He is buried with his father and mother in the Watkins plot at Oak Hill Cemetery in Lawrence.

In 1900 JB bought a life insurance policy for $3,320 and assigned it to Elizabeth. JB, ever practical, set up the policy so that it would revert back to him if she died first. On the policy itself it reads "the consideration for this assignment is no other than love and affection." This is the earliest known written declaration of their regard for each other.

Elizabeth was again living in Lawrence with her mother at 1104 Tennessee, walking those few blocks to work. In 1903 she contracted with Thomas Sanderson to build a house on lot 11 on Tennessee Street for $3,462.15. It would have double doors on the first story and fancy shingles three feet high around the house. There is no indication that Elizabeth or her mother ever lived there, so it is assumed that this was another of her investments. She was a self-supporting single woman who had her own portfolio of investments in land and houses, a remarkable and unusual achievement.

Life continued in this pattern for several years for both JB and Elizabeth.

TO BE SENT TO THE COMPANY FOR RECORD AS SOON AS EXECUTED.

ASSIGNMENT OF POLICY

No. 254-736 $ 3320

—IN THE—

Mutual Benefit Life Insurance Company
OF NEWARK, N. J.

LIFE OF *Jabez B. Watkins*

FOR VALUE RECEIVED, *I* do hereby assign, transfer and set over unto *Miss Lizzie J. Miller* the above-named Policy of Insurance, and all sum or sums of money, interest, benefit and advantage whatsoever, now due or hereafter to arise, or to be had or made by virtue thereof; to have and to hold unto the said *Miss Lizzie J. Miller during her life time, should she die before the assured this policy shall revert to the assignor the consideration for this assignment is no other than love and affection* the said assignee hereby agreeing that any indebtedness to the Company on the said Policy shall be a valid and prior lien thereon.

IN WITNESS WHEREOF, *I* have hereunto set *my* hand the *14th* day of *Dec*, one thousand nine hundred.——

SIGNED IN THE
PRESENCE OF

Jabez B. Watkins

The Mutual Benefit Life Insurance Company have filed a copy of the above Assignment. If hereafter canceled, the holder should return the original to the Company.

NEWARK, N. J., DEC . 1900

Secretary.

Life insurance policy JB bought for Elizabeth: "the consideration for this assignment is no other than love and affection." Mutual Benefit Life Insurance Company of Newark, New Jersey, dated December 14, 1900. (Kitchen 8 Archives, Watkins Museum of History)

Their partnership and interdependence were settled. Business was good, they were busy working together, and they truly enjoyed their work. Their travels were divided among New York, Louisiana, and Texas. Challenging times lay ahead, but they were now a team. Eventually their partnership would become eternal.

CHAPTER 6

In Sickness and in Health

In 1906, when JB was sixty-one, his behavior became somewhat erratic. The life expectancy for the average man at that time was only fifty-one and a half years. And JB had not led an average life at all. He had traveled extensively, worked at a frenetic pace, lived under tremendous financial pressure, and rested very little. And, in secret, he drank.

Early that year, while in New York, JB seemed somewhat lethargic. Business difficulties plagued him. He was constantly at odds with the board of directors of his Lawrence bank. JB used the bank extensively to finance his own business activities; it was the reason he started his own bank. But the board, largely made up of community leaders in Lawrence, had a fiduciary duty to protect the money of depositors from losses. Their objections to the magnitude of JB's borrowing, the number of notes and overdue paper held by the bank, caused constant friction.

In 1894, following the Panic of 1893, the New York office, managed by Henry Dickinson, closed; this upset investors and led to a decline in business. Until 1910, a small office was still maintained, as a cost-cutting measure, at the Farmer's Loan and Trust Company building in New York City. Elizabeth had been sent to New York to reassure local investors. There is evidence that she stayed and managed this smaller office for several years, working for the Orange Land Company and JB's railroad. When the Watkins Mortgage Business went through reorganization in 1896, it did nothing to calm the nervous investors. Although JB came through receivership with the company and his reputation intact, there would be greater scrutiny and fewer investors in the future.

A mature Jabez Bunting Watkins. (Douglas County
Historical Society, Watkins Museum of History)

Things hadn't been going well in London, either. When the Watkins
Mortgage Company went into receivership in 1896, a committee of En-
glish investors was formed to investigate the losses. H. G. Chalkley Sr., the
London officer manager, was originally from Lawrence and had moved to
England to work for JB. Chalkley Sr. sent his sons, Henry George Chalkley
Jr. and Thomas H. Chalkley, to America to represent those British inves-
tors. Chalkley Sr. was concerned about Watkins's business practices as well
as his mental stability, and he wanted his sons to report back to him from
Lake Charles. It seemed to JB that they were "bent on destroying him."

Dissolution of those joint English–American ventures would be complex because there were ties to and investments in other businesses owned
by JB. Investors' money had gone into the Kansas City, Watkins & Gulf
Railway and the Calcasieu Sugar Company, not just the North American

Land and Timber Company. The cross-Atlantic conflict lasted years, and, by 1905, the London committee sued JB for alleged nonpayment of monthly dividends.

The Dallas office had finally closed. Office manager Miles Dart worked for JB until 1895, when the mortgage business was going through receivership. JB turned his lands in Texas over to local agents to manage when he closed the Dallas office. Perhaps JB was ready to simplify his business life with fewer offices and employees.

Even developing the small city of Lake Charles had its difficulties. In 1903, the state of Louisiana sued JB for not having a "public and visible" office in Lake Charles. This is hard to imagine, following the growth of that city. The Watkins National Bank, where JB had his office, was prominently built at the intersection of Broad and Hodges Streets. The problem seemed to come down to local dislike of a non-Louisiana resident owning 1.5 million acres of land in the state. Although a personal visit by JB to the Louisiana state attorney general seemed to smooth out any difficulties and the lawsuit was dropped, this was just another source of conflict he had to deal with.

Considering all these difficulties, it is highly probable that JB's secret alcohol habit was getting the better of him. In January 1906, he asked the Rev. Samuel L. Bieler of the School of Theology at Boston University to visit him in New York. Although raised in a Methodist family, JB was not a regular churchgoer. He professed that at the age of thirty-three he had "converted, immersed, and joined the Baptist church," and he financially supported many churches. As his dependence on alcohol began to take over his life, he turned to Reverend Bieler to help him gain control of himself through a religious reawakening. Soon afterward, a letter from the Lawrence office to one of JB's relatives mentions that JB's illness had taken a "religious turn." In January 1906, JB seemed to be stable, perhaps with the help of Reverend Bieler. He hired a male nurse to accompany him while he was in New York, perhaps to help him abstain. JB never drank in public but did drink privately in his hotel rooms.

When he returned to Lawrence in February 1906, he seemed to have had a relapse. The *Lawrence Daily Journal* on February 17, 1906, even covered this illness, under the headline "Mr. Watkins Ill."

The Watkins Bank at the corner of Broad and Hodges Streets in Lake Charles, Louisiana. (McNeese State University Archives, Lake Charles, Louisiana)

J. B. Watkins has been ill for several days. He has been over-working for years and at last it has told on him. It is believed that with complete rest, if he can be induced to take it, he will recover completely. Mr. Watkins is an apostle of hard work and big things. He has been dealing in millions for years and the strain has told on him. He is a creditable man to this town; a man who started with nothing and won his millions, and everybody in this town will hope for his speedy recovery.

JB got in touch with Dr. John Punton. The private Punton Sanitarium, built in 1897 by the doctor, was Kansas City's first hospital dedicated to the treatment of mental illnesses and nervous disorders.* He also contacted Dr. C. J. Simmons in Kansas City. Bills paid show that both these doctors conferred with JB about his illness. They recommended a "specially trained nurse," as revealed in a letter from the Lawrence office to JB's relatives on February 20, 1906:

* The Punton Sanitarium is discussed in a report entitled "Preliminary Inventory of Neurological Hospital Association of Kansas City Records, 1935–1972."

It becomes my painful duty to inform you that Mr. Watkins' mind has given way under the great strain under which he has labored for so many years, and that, for the present, he is practically insane. His malady took a religious turn, and for a time amounted to a frenzy. He is quiter [*sic*] now, and just a bit more rational, but we can not by any means call him a sane man. He is in a local hospital, and is attended by a specially trained male nurse from Kansas City. The rest cure is being tried on him, and seems to be effecting a slow, gradual improvement.

The letter continues with a list of relatives who have come to see JB and ends with this line: "Mr. Green, who is Mr. Watkins' cashier here, suggests that you try the effect of what is called among your people the absent treatment." In other words—stay home and leave JB alone to rest.

JB rested, seemed cured, and dove back into his business pursuits. He traveled again to New York. Once again, however, the curious illness recurred. In March 1906, Elizabeth was told by telegram that he was dangerously ill in New York, and, in response, she hurried to join him there.

It is difficult to imagine that Elizabeth was not aware of JB's drinking, especially because they had frequently traveled together. Although he surely would have tried to hide it, she must have suspected, if not known about it outright. A phrase from Shakespeare's *Hamlet* seems to characterize JB's alcohol problem. "The lady doth protest too much, methinks" indicates doubt about the sincerity of someone who expresses over-the-top disapproval of something. JB clearly went out of his way to appear to abstain from alcohol. It is curious that a clause was inserted for every parcel of land he sold in Louisiana, "forbidding forever the sale of intoxicating liquors." Perhaps he was attempting to make Lake Charles a place without temptation for himself? He also required that job applicants provide letters of recommendation to prove they were "total abstainers" from alcohol. The newspaper he owned in Lawrence, the *Record,* had instructions to "support prohibition in all cases." Later, Elizabeth helped him conquer his alcohol problem. At the time, though, when he became very ill, his relatives alone had the legal right to engage doctors or make decisions about his care. Elizabeth could only stand by. But she could, and did, watch over and direct the business transactions carefully while JB was incapacitated.

So, March 1906 found Elizabeth with JB in New York, called there by the emergency telegram. Alexander Thomson, husband of JB's sister Maria, left his work in the rice fields and drainage canals of Lake Charles to come also. It was suggested that JB might benefit from the milder climate of Louisiana, so Thomson, Elizabeth, and a male nurse named John Lyshat traveled with him from New York to Lake Charles. The *Topeka State Journal* on April 6, 1906, had this: "He was brought to Lake Charles about ten days ago, in the hope that the change would be beneficial, but he has not improved."

Then, the shocking headline from the *Shreveport Journal*, April 6, 1906: "INSANITY CASE—J. B. WATKINS IS IN CUSTODY OF FRIENDS AT LAKE CHARLES: Property Placed in the Hands of Administrator Pending His Recovery—Well Known Here."

> Today J. B. Watkins was seized with an attack of mental affection [*sic*] and was taken in hand by friends and is now guarded at his home. . . . Mr. Watkins has been seriously ill for a long time, and recently returned from New York City, where he had been confined by illness. It is not known whether the attack is temporary or otherwise, but that an examination will be had under court supervision to determine his sanity is significant. Alderman Grant Mutersbaugh, as his nearest kin, has been appointed administrator of his property pending Mr. Watkins' recovery.

Mutersbaugh, described above as "nearest kin," was the son of JB's half brother Abraham. He had apparently lived in Lake Charles for some time, and, at the date of this article, was an alderman, which is similar to a city council member in other states. He had grown up in Punxsutawney, Pennsylvania, and had come to work in Lake Charles for one of JB's companies, yet another example of JB's pattern of hiring and helping family.

But the most important headline on April 6, 1906, was from the *Topeka State Journal*:

"Petition for Interdiction of Lawrence Man Filed at Lake Charles."

Interdiction is an unusual legal term used in Louisiana, which is the only one of the United States that operates under the Napoleonic Code of justice. Interdiction is a legal process by which a person may be declared not competent to take care of his or her own affairs. The court appoints a "curator," rather like a guardian, to handle the affairs of the person who is interdicted, and it orders treatment at a specific facility or location. Interdiction lasts until the condition, whether illness or substance abuse, that has caused the person to be incompetent has been resolved. It is similar to a guardianship or a commitment hearing in other states, but interdiction is described as more severe. It is the most far-reaching judgment, short of the death penalty, in Louisiana.

Three people signed this legal document, called a petition for interdiction: Alexander Thomson, Edwin C. Walker, and Miller J. Watkins. Who were these men?

Alexander Thomson, husband of JB's sister Maria, had worked with JB for years at this point and had his trust.

Edwin C. Walker was the son of JB's sister Hattie. JB had given Hattie financial support monthly since the 1870s. This same E. C. Walker would later come to Lawrence, uninvited, upon JB's death in 1921, plague Elizabeth for money, and not leave for weeks. The Walkers and the Mutersbaughs contested JB's will, giving Elizabeth years of difficulty after his death. They argued about the legality of Elizabeth's marriage to JB and repeatedly asserted that they were entitled to more of his estate. Signing this petition was Edwin Walker's first sign of disloyalty to JB.

The third petitioner, Miller J. Watkins, alleged that he was JB's illegitimate son. By all accounts, his arrival in Lake Charles surprised JB as much as anyone. A story was told that he met JB on the sidewalk in Lake Charles and JB "denounced" him. Miller's mother, Maria M. Miller, claimed that she had been married to JB when he lived in Pennsylvania and that he had "deserted" her before her son was born. Her claim, however, surfaced only when JB became known for his great wealth. Perhaps this wealth was too great an enticement for the young man to stay away: he appeared in JB's life now and would return again later. The Brookville, Pennsylvania, *Jefferson-Democrat* reported April 19, 1906: "M. J. Watkins is making a trip to Louisiana to look up the interest and estate of his father. He is accompanied by Mr. Fisher, his attorney, of Punxsutawney." How did they know to come to Lake Charles now, to be a part of this legal interdiction proceeding? Miller had never met JB before this, had never previously attempted to make any contact.

To answer that question, we look to Miller's mother. The Miller family Bible held a Western Union telegram that was sent to Miller J. Watkins in

Punxsutawney on April 6, 1906: "Your father J. B. Watkins insane Court proceedings for possession of estate commences Your immediate presence here positively necessary to preserve the estate and your interest Will you come Wire at once entire office force will back you up. [signed] Ben M. Foster, mgr."

Ben M. Foster was the manager of JB's Lake Charles mortgage office. More questions arise: How did Foster know about Miller J.? Was Grant Mutersbaugh, JB's nephew, the link? Grant had lived in Punxsutawney, as had Miller J. Why did they want to involve Miller J.? Was there a plan to get rid of JB so these younger men could take over the enterprises JB had built? If Miller J. could prove his claim, he would be the nearest relative to JB and would have the greatest claim to run the empire. Had a "deal" been reached between them?

JB was not going to accept this quietly. We don't know whether Elizabeth was still in Lake Charles, or whether she had gone back to Lawrence or New York to watch over business dealings while JB dealt with the interdiction proceedings. Someone—JB, or perhaps Elizabeth, or even the protective T. C. Green—had hired attorney Winston Overton. Overton filed an exception to the interdiction on the grounds that, because JB was not a citizen of Louisiana but of Kansas, he should not be subject to Louisiana law.

Family was important to JB, as he had shown by employing and supporting so many family members. However, he was not going to let anyone take advantage of him, not even family.

The Watkins Papers contain a copy of a curious poster that reads as follows: "At the corner of Broad and Hodges streets at 4 p.m., on Thursday, May 3, 1906, all people of Lake Charles, La., white and black, male and female are requested to hear the statement of the facts which culminated in my imprisonment during the 29 days last past. J. B. Watkins."

JB wanted a public hearing directly in front of the Watkins Bank Building. What would he say to the gathered crowd? "Dried out" by then, he could make an impassioned plea that his nerves had gotten the better of him. He could speak of a religious fervor. He must have been a charismatic and persuasive speaker to be as successful as he was, and he had always been able to talk his way out of things. Still, he could under no circumstances admit to alcohol use. He forbade the sale of alcohol on the

Louisiana townsite properties, and he advertised in religious publications. The temperance movement was quite active in America at that time, and there would be no tolerance for alcoholism in JB. What illness would he claim? Would the people rally around him?

JB's public hearing never took place. A barely legible handwritten note on the poster reads: "Thomas, J. B. had this printed this morning, but the order was stopped before more than 10 or 12 were printed. None got out of the office. B. M. F."*

Ben M. Foster, manager of the mortgage office, sabotaged JB's efforts, denying him his platform to tell his side of the story to the people of Lake Charles. The managers of the mortgage office and Watkins Bank must have thought a public airing of JB's condition could turn out badly and might weaken their business stature. Would people leave their money in a bank owned by a man who ranted on a street corner?

Also, the "Thomas" to whom the note on this poster was addressed was surely Thomas H. Chalkley of the English committee, who was in Lake Charles at that time to protect the interests of the English investors. It may have been the committee, with the help of Grant Mutersbaugh, that enlisted Miller J. Watkins. Although it could be claimed that they were acting in JB's interest by providing a legal heir and continuity to the ownership of the businesses, in the event that JB proved unable to work any longer, it seems they were acting to ensure their own jobs and futures.

On May 4, 1906, the interdiction was granted, and the court called for a family meeting to decide on a curator or guardian for JB's businesses. The *St. Landry Clarion* reported on May 26, 1906, "A stubborn and bitter fight is on in Calcasieu over the succession of J. B. Watkins, the millionaire interdicted." Eventually the curator was named: trusted ally Alexander Thomson.

On May 11, 1906, the *Lawrence Daily Journal* reported: "J. B. Watkins is coming home. He is in a serious condition and the inquiry into his sanity will be made in this city. Mr. Watkins has been getting worse constantly for the past two months and there is now little hope for him. He is getting weaker all the time." The move was actually a positive step, likely

---

* JB ordered the printing of the poster announcing a public hearing; he planned to put it up in prominent places in Lake Charles. A copy can be found at the Watkins Museum of History, Kitchen 8 Archives, Folder 3/18.

orchestrated by JB, Elizabeth, or T. C. Green. Being evaluated for insanity in your hometown, where people and doctors know you, would certainly encourage a friendlier diagnosis.

The fight for control continued in Lake Charles among the family members. Finally, on June 21, a petition was filed with the court to repeal the interdiction, signed by Alexander Thomson, Maria Thomson, and D. Zena Thomson, their daughter. Had they had enough of the family infighting? Were JB's business dealings simply too much for Alexander to manage? In the petition, they attested that JB was completely recovered and fully able to take care of his own person and business.

The *Lawrence Daily Journal* celebrated the repeal of the interdiction order on July 24, 1906, with the headline: "J B WATKINS WON: Restored Yesterday to Full Control of His Estate."

This episode of JB's illness now seemed to be over. Later, Elizabeth's letters reveal that JB's alcoholism had led him to develop delirium tremens, a result of sudden alcohol withdrawal from a person heavily addicted. Symptoms, which can include confusion, hallucinations, and shaking, may begin two to five days after the last drink and may be fatal. It had been severe enough for JB to be declared insane in Louisiana. With the interdiction repealed, the drama with JB's family might have been over for the time being, but his battle with alcohol was not.

In August, JB was in Minneapolis, Minnesota, visiting his sister Ruth (Watkins) White and her daughter Jennie. In typical JB fashion, he had been supporting Jennie with a monthly stipend since February that year. On September 4, 1906, JB also traveled to Pennsylvania for a reunion of the Sprankle family, relatives on his mother's side. In November, when JB was again visiting with niece Jennie and sister Ruth, this time in Iowa, his "illness" returned.

On November 24, 1906, Elizabeth read a letter from Ruth, JB's sister, which was sent to T. C. Green in the Lawrence office.

Dear Friend, I wrote you yesterday in the hospital but do not know if you can read it or not so will write again. My daughter is gaining. Brother [JB] is bad off and I see no other way but have him treated for insanity and that can only be done in the insane asylum. If he had been treated last March he would have been a well man today. I have seen it done on others older than he. As Dr. Abbott says his brain is tired and must have rest. It is worn but can be fixed up if I had money I would take him somewhere. Dr. Abbott thinks now they would not take him to Des Moines, he is so bad off. That is more of a hospital and he wants to be where they treat insanity. Dr. Brooks tells of a good insane asylum in New York state where Dr. are all Christians. I wrote Della [a niece] about coming but she need not come. I was then thinking about Grace [Ruth's younger daughter]. I know I can do more with Brother than she, if I need help Prof. Thomson would be the best. Please let me know what I shall do and send me money.

Yours truly, Ruth A. Watkins

The following day, November 25, 1906, a telegram arrived for T. C. Green in Lawrence: "Come at once take charge." It was signed JBW. This was a call for help!

The staff in the Lawrence office believed JB's problem was overwork. However, Ruth had always wanted to be involved in JB's life and this was her opportunity. His money was very important to her and other family members. Because she was a relative, she had more legal influence over health decisions than his business colleagues did, and obviously more than Elizabeth. Again, Elizabeth had to stand by and help by keeping the businesses running smoothly.

With the advice of doctors, Ruth was instrumental in getting JB admitted to the sanitarium in Battle Creek, Michigan, on December 1, 1906. Run by the Kellogg family, the new institution catered to the wealthy. Gerald Carson, in his book *Cornflake Crusade*, describes it as a sanitarium for the refreshment of body, mind, and spirit. The vast resort offered the combined features of a medical boardinghouse, hospital, religious retreat, country club, tent chautauqua, and spa, all carried out in an atmosphere of moral reform and asceticism. The sanitarium advocated a strict regimen that included special foods and many enemas per day. Ruth moved there, supposedly to supervise JB's care. She was continually writing T. C. Green in Lawrence for money to keep JB (and herself) at Battle Creek.

Ruth was outspoken, and she directed that Elizabeth should not come to see JB. And, if Elizabeth did come, she would not be admitted to his room, per Ruth's orders. In letters to the Lawrence office, she wrote, "No

Letterhead showing the Battle Creek Sanitarium. Note from JB Watkins to
T. C. Green of the main Lawrence office, dated March 4, 1907. (Kenneth
Spencer Research Library, University of Kansas)

one but nurses and I are admitted in the room and if she [Elizabeth] came
it would be instant death." In Ruth's view, Elizabeth meant work and work
would kill JB.

Ruth knew of the close relationship between JB and Elizabeth and was
concerned about protecting her position and her share in JB's money; as a
family member, she had authority to make decisions about JB at this vul-
nerable time. The family was aware that JB and Elizabeth had traveled together for years and had worked closely together. Perhaps they also knew
about the life insurance policy JB had bought for Elizabeth with "love and
affection." The bond between the two was obviously seen as a threat by
Ruth. Ruth wrote that she intended to build a house in Oskaloosa, Iowa,
where she and JB could live after he left the sanitarium. She also asked
about getting a power of attorney over JB, but nothing came of it. Ruth
made it very clear that she did not want him to go back to Lawrence. She

did not want Elizabeth in his life in any way, claiming that she would "bother him to death."

Ruth censored his mail, so he was kept completely away from the businesses he had built over his lifetime. He was not eating well and he spoke very little to Ruth, who complained about his silence in her frequent letters requesting money from T. C. Green. As JB improved, his frustration grew over the lack of knowledge about his empire.

By late December 1906, JB finally made it clear he didn't want Ruth with him. She eventually traveled back to Iowa on January 28, 1907. In another letter to Green, she wrote about her travel plans and once again asked for money. Another niece, Della Neal, daughter of JB's sister Ellen, came to accompany JB as he recovered. Della and her husband, Harry, knew JB well; they had run the *American* newspaper in Lake Charles for him. Della reported steady progress in JB's health: he made conversation and was eating well. However, she added that JB was suspicious that everyone was spending his money, and she alerted the Lawrence office that he was planning to leave Battle Creek.

Ruth wasn't finished meddling yet. On February 7, she wrote to Green in Lawrence from Oskaloosa. She was going through JB's luggage, looking for "a list" in his suitcases and accused Elizabeth of stealing it. "When he went to the Hotel when Miss Miller was here he took both grips (suitcases) with him." She also insisted that JB should stay at Battle Creek at least two more months.

Regardless of Ruth's opinion, JB came back to Lawrence in March 1907. He was much better and was able to look after his businesses with help from Elizabeth and T. C. Green. Things returned to a routine, and he even left for a camping and fishing vacation in Sault St. Marie, Canada, in June.

These episodes of ill health and the intrusion of Ruth and other family members made JB think seriously about how he wanted his fortune to be used when he was gone. Clearly, his family would be happy to use it for their own betterment, but he wanted his fortune to be used for the good of many people. Elizabeth had seen the lengths to which his family would go to get JB's money, and the two of them discussed the situation fully.

During 1906, JB had become concerned about the future of the company and Elizabeth's welfare if he should die. He had written a will in early

1906, but neither he nor anyone else knew what had happened to it. So, he wrote a new will in 1909, and directed the executors that all legacies were to be paid through Elizabeth. The will contains this incredible clause: "Also in trust to pay over to said Elizabeth J. Miller during her lifetime such sums of money as she may request for her own use or for assisting other persons." It was carte blanche for his exceptional, trusted partner Elizabeth.

JB addressed a personal issue in that 1909 will: "Eighth: I have always been a bachelor. I have never been married to any woman. I assert this solemnly as in the presence of Almighty God." The will also contained the novel idea that his fortune should be utilized by an act of the Kansas legislature. This act would use the proceeds of his estate to form "a permanent body having perpetual succession for general educational and benevolent purposes"; however, the Kansas legislature would receive his money only after Elizabeth's death. An interesting idea, but this will was not used when JB died.

After discussions about how to protect the estate from his family, JB and Elizabeth found a solution that pleased them both: marriage. They had worked together for about thirty-five years and had traveled together frequently since Elizabeth's late twenties, sometimes without Presby. They had developed a good relationship; it was not flaunted in public, but those who were close to them were aware of it.

One handwritten letter from JB to Elizabeth in July 1909 ended with him saying that he would be with her in Lawrence in 299 hours—a hint of romance. Also in that letter, JB went to great lengths to establish a timeline of his whereabouts through the years, all to prove that Miller J. Watkins could not possibly be his son. He provided her with a sworn statement from T. G. Wells, who was from that area in Pennsylvania, saying he "never heard anyone in the neighborhood say that they had ever saw Maria Miller in company of JB Watkins. No one took any stock in the marriage story." Was it necessary to resolve the question about the alleged illegitimate son before Elizabeth would say "yes" to a proposal of marriage from JB?

Several biographers and researchers have read through portions of the papers of the Watkins Collection. Monica Gambrell, who read through the collection in 1994, noted that JB and Elizabeth "were together" for some time before marriage. Gambrell also saw something others had

Elizabeth Josephine Miller, at approximately the age she
married JB Watkins. (Douglas County Historical Society,
Watkins Museum of History)

noted. There were periods of time when Elizabeth was not on the Lawrence payroll. She was living in New York, definitely from 1892 to 1894, as
the procurement agent for the Kansas City, Watkins and Gulf Railway and
handling investments for the Orange Land Company. She loved her work
and lived the life of an independent, self-sufficient woman. It has been
suggested that JB may have asked Elizabeth to marry him earlier but that
she had not been ready to give up her independence. While society might
have been ready to tolerate a self-sufficient single woman, a working wife
was another matter.

Certificate and record of marriage between Jabez B. Watkins and Elizabeth J. Miller, certificate no. 9544, recorded by the State of New York on November 12, 1909. Performing the ceremony was William A. Layton, clergyman, of 385 Ninth Street, Brooklyn, NY. Jabez was sixty-four, Elizabeth, forty-eight; it was a first marriage for both. (Kitchen 8 Archives, Watkins Museum of History)

JB may indeed have asked Elizabeth to marry him before 1909, and there may have been reasons to wait, including his problems with alcohol. But for years, Elizabeth had been the one he could always count on. And, with all the recent turmoil in JB's life, now was the right time to settle the matter. If JB died after they married, the fortune would come to Elizabeth, and she could carry out their shared wishes.

Several letters between Elizabeth and Rev. W. A. Layton in New York make it clear that Elizabeth and JB were serious in their intentions. Elizabeth informed Reverend Layton that they planned to marry and would like him to perform the ceremony in Brooklyn. Reverend Layton was a good friend of both and recognized their mutual affection. The decision was made to marry quietly in New York on November 15, 1909.

That day, as Presby rested at the hotel, JB and Elizabeth went out. Presby later recounted that "J. B. and Lizzie supposedly went out 'shopping,'" adding that when they returned, Elizabeth handed him their marriage certificate and said, "Look what we found." James Yeager, a land examiner who worked in their New York office, said that after "Mr. Watkins remarked 'we have been shopping,'" he had shown him the marriage certificate.

The astounding news appeared in the Lawrence paper: "J. B. Watkins weds in New York, Prominent financier figured in a romance in the East, Bride is Elizabeth Miller. They were married Thursday of last week in Brooklyn. Were going to keep the news a secret but it leaked out—both parties are known here."

People in Lawrence were surprised and, at the same time, wondered why the couple hadn't married earlier. Neither was young. Elizabeth was forty-eight and JB was sixty-four. However, there had been reasons for not marrying earlier. Although Elizabeth's mother appreciated all that JB had done for Elizabeth and their family, she did not approve that he drank hard liquor, that he was so much older than her daughter, and, worst of all—that he was a Democrat! As Ella Gardner Miller had passed away in February 1909, all reasons not to marry were gone.

CHAPTER 7

Mr. and Mrs. Watkins

After their marriage, Elizabeth and JB continued much as before. They were still both very involved in the businesses, their lifelong enjoyment. They did have a bit of a honeymoon, for there are notes of money withdrawals and numerous hotel bills paid in those salvaged Watkins Papers. It appears the change this marriage brought to the Lawrence office was taken well by the staff. JB wrote to T. C. Green in November 1909, shortly after the marriage ceremony, "I am obliged to you for your kind expression in regard to the 'romance in the East.'"

JB and Elizabeth were consolidating and transferring ownership of land parcels and shares in the various companies; he wanted Elizabeth to have enough in her own name so that she could live comfortably and have no financial concerns. She retained a room in Mrs. G. A. Carter's house at 1241 Tennessee for $5.00 per month. She used it for the brief periods when she was in Lawrence, and probably stored extra clothing and things from her deceased mother's home there until she and JB could move into their own home.

JB was renting a house at 1244 Tennessee from Professor Ephraim Miller, the cousin of Elizabeth's father who had encouraged the Miller family to move to Lawrence. No longer the superintendent of schools, Ephraim, by then a KU professor, was out of town and wanted a responsible person to look after his house. Elizabeth and JB agreed to do so, and JB also kept his quarters at the Eldridge Hotel for the time being.

Soon after their marriage, JB began to plan for a summer home in Morton County, in extreme southwestern Kansas, where he owned

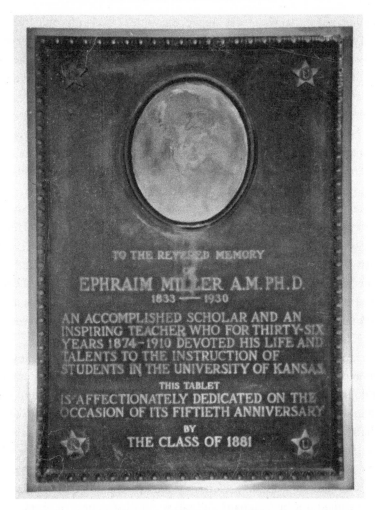

Plaque "to the revered memory" of Ephraim Miller, AM, PhD, given by
the KU Class of 1881. Professor Miller was a cousin of Elizabeth's father;
it was he who suggested the Miller family move to Lawrence. The
plaque is in Strong Hall, University of Kansas. (Author's collection)

fifty-eight sections of land near the city of Elkhart.* He planned to put down
water wells. There was a tremendous "underflow" of water, the Ogallala

* These fifty-eight sections, which make up much of Morton County, are part of
the land that was willed to KU Endowment by Elizabeth Watkins.

Aquifer; when that water was tapped, the value of the land would increase. Sod would be broken, and wheat could be planted. JB could see the potential of this farmland and he enjoyed the open prairie. However, the heat of summer diminished Elizabeth's enthusiasm for a summer house on the prairie, and the project was put on the back burner for a while.

Problems with the English investors of the North American Land and Timber Company continued. Through 1907 and 1908, lawsuits were exchanged on both sides. The London office hired attorney James Moss of Trenton, New Jersey, and accused JB of not paying commissions. JB accused London of insider trading. Then in 1910, oil was discovered on some of the Louisiana land. London gave options to sell the land for $4.11 per acre. JB was outraged at this vastly reduced sale price, claiming it was worth $20 per acre with this possibility of oil. JB charged Chalkley with fraud. On February 8, 1911, the London shareholders of the North American Land and Timber Company held an "Extraordinary General Meeting" in London without JB's knowledge. They voted to buy out JB's 28¼ percent for approximately $800,000, and he eventually agreed. The business continued until 1921, but without JB.

Liquidation of the North American Land and Timber Company was complex. JB estimated in 1911 that the mortgage company had lost millions of dollars through the mismanagement of the Chalkleys, father and sons. Allan Bogue, who wrote about Watkins's businesses, was convinced the Chalkleys had used "their influence with investors to plunder the assets of the mortgage company and Watkins' southern enterprises." Bogue adds, "T. C. Green, who was never one to mince words or to judge Watkins' actions in adulatory fashion, referred in 1909 to 'the fact that certain ones have come into the Company and taken out of the concern or its assets, about $250,000 or $300,000.'" This was less than JB's estimate, but it bears out his assertion of embezzlement.

During this first decade of the 1900s, JB was consolidating the lands he still owned in Kansas, Texas, and Louisiana. He had sold several of his smaller businesses, perhaps to simplify his life. The New York office finally closed, and its furniture was sold. The Lawrence Canning Company was leased to a former employee, Albert Herning, in 1894, then was sold in 1905. Both of his publishing companies, the *Record* in Lawrence and the *American* in Lake Charles, had been sold in the late 1890s. The Kansas

City, Watkins and Gulf Railway had gone through receivership in 1898, but JB had retained partial ownership after the receiver's sale on March 25, 1902, as reported in the *New York Times*. The Calcasieu and Lake Charles Sugar Companies had closed temporarily with the Panic of 1893 and had reopened in 1899. JB was the primary financial backer of both of those concerns, and they operated until his death in 1921. JB still held on to his dream of prosperity for southwestern Louisiana and visited there often. He continued targeted advertising to encourage ethnic groups to move to the Lake Charles area; one surviving advertisement of this sort in the Watkins Museum is written in Hebrew.

After JB and Elizabeth's marriage in 1909, the next nine years were very busy. The couple purchased several lots in Denver for speculation. They often made business trips together to Louisiana, with occasional trips to New York and several to Washington, DC. They truly enjoyed traveling together.

On April 24, 1910, JB received an urgent request for help. There had been a terrible fire in Lake Charles and 109 buildings were gone, along with all the parish records. He agreed to let his bank building be used as a temporary workplace as the town rebuilt.

About this time JB made a luxurious purchase: a car, a Stevens-Duryea Big 6 model 1910 for $4,200. He told how it came about in a letter from New York to E. P. Moriarity in Kansas City. "In front of Marshall Fields, in Chicago, I found a man by a car and said, 'Did you ever see so fine a car?' It was a Studebaker, 4-cylinder, model 1910. The man replied, 'It would look good to me if I had not been touring in a better one.' When questioned further he said, 'In a Stevens Duryea, Big 6 Model 1910 owned by my employer.'" JB right then decided to buy one. Although JB could drive, Elizabeth could not, so he thought it best that they hire chauffeurs, a practice they continued for the rest of their lives.

Their lives were as full as before. However, Elizabeth's day-to-day involvement in the businesses began to lessen as they started another big undertaking. Work had begun on their new home to be built on Mount Oread, the "Robinson Farm" property that JB had purchased in the late 1800s. Up until this time, JB had rented it out to local farmers. It was about five acres, with beautiful views of the Wakarusa Valley and the Kansas River valley to the south and east. At one time, JB had planned to break up the

Stevens-Duryea car similar to the one JB and Elizabeth bought shortly after their marriage. (Photo courtesy of Greg Gjerdingen)

five acres into twenty-four lots; he would keep the middle eight lots and sell the eight lots on the north and the eight lots on the south. But those who expressed interest in the land wanted the whole tract, not portions, and as a result JB retained ownership of the whole five acres. That was a lucky outcome: for them, in 1911, as they planned their home together, and also for many in the future.

Closely involved in its design, JB and Elizabeth poured time, money, and effort into the building of The Outlook, as they decided to call their new home. They were both involved in most of the decisions, and the results show their meticulous attention to detail.

Their careful attention to the quality of the building materials is still evident 110 years later, according to Mark Reiske, the current (as of 2022) university architect and director of Facilities Planning and Development at KU. Noting the craftsmanship of the stucco walls, the terrazzo floors of the porches, and the quality of the hand-selected oak flooring, Reiske added that there is no settling of the home and no cracking of the walls and that the windows are still original to the home.

J. T. Constant was the general contractor for the project. Given JB's stress on quality materials and workmanship, this is a bit surprising, as he was the low bidder. In 1911, a fund of $18,000 was deposited in the Watkins National Bank; this was his money to work from, as he supplied receipts.

The home, in the Neoclassical Revival style, was designed by architect W. J. Mitchell of Lawrence. A bit over six thousand square feet, its distinctive style included pale gray stucco and a green tile roof, with wraparound porches for outdoor living space. The third floor led to a widow's walk, an "eclectic architectural feature more commonly found in the houses of 18th and 19th century New England sea captains," according to KU history professor John H. McCool.

Elizabeth and JB moved into their house during May 1912, with the help of five hired men.

The *Lawrence Daily Journal World* in April 1912 included this detailed description of The Outlook:

Standing on the site of the historic Lawrence fort this residence seems the perfection of the builders art. Three stories in height, with its walls made of gray stucco, a wide veranda extending across the front of the building and half way back to the sides, its broad stone steps leading up to this, the massive cement pillars, its second story porches, the picturesque gables and all surmounted by a green tile roof, it must be declared that from the outside it is one of the prettiest if not the prettiest of Lawrence houses. . . . And to add further to the beauty of the surroundings a two-story garage is to be erected to the southeast. This garage is to be built with the first story on a level with Louisiana street and the second level with the hill. This is to be large enough to accommodate two cars and will contain a repair shop and be fitted out after the fashion of the most modern garage. Inside the house one is beset by even a greater feeling of the grandeur of the surroundings. The wide hall with its large oak doors leading into the various rooms, the broad stairs and the large windows that admit plenty of sunshine all bespeak solid comfort.

All of the wood-work is finished in the natural grain, varnished and polished, the floors are solid oak, the doors are of a pattern known as plank door, in every room there is a fireplace but each is made differently and no two are finished the same. On the first floor there are five rooms, the library, the living room, the kitchen, the dining room and a

Exterior of The Outlook, the home built by JB and Elizabeth Watkins after their marriage. (Douglas County Historical Society, Watkins Museum of History)

Interior of The Outlook, with the front entry and main staircase. (Kenneth Spencer Research Library, University Archives)

Elizabeth Watkins's parlor at The Outlook. (Kenneth Spencer Research Library, University Archives)

den. In addition to this there is the hall, a butler's pantry, the ice pantry, the lavoratory [*sic*], and a closet.

On the second floor there are four bed chambers, an upstairs sitting room, a hall, two bath rooms and nine closets. On the third floor there are three rooms, five closets, one bath room and a hall. The total shows that the home contains including closets, baths and basement thirty-five rooms. Every convenience known to modern times has been installed in the residence, even to the new vacuum cleaning system. This is a novel scheme the pipes being laid in the walls similar to gas pipes and leading to a tank in the basement to catch dust. An electric engine in the basement operates the cleaning plant. The hot water system is used for heating the house while each room is also provided with a fireplace equipped for burning gas. The house is wired throughout for electricity for lighting purpose. Truly it is a modern home and one that Mr. Watkins feels justly proud of.

The article then described Jabez's plans to make a park-like setting. A small lake was to be placed where the fort had been, plus a wide motor gravel road. The "historic Lawrence fort" described in the article was from the Civil War, built for troops there to protect Lawrence from Quantrill's raids. Further artifacts from this fort were discovered when later buildings were built near The Outlook.

On one of their trips together to New York, Elizabeth purchased a baby grand piano from Sohmer & Co. and had it shipped to their new home. Furnishing The Outlook fell mostly to Elizabeth, and she relished the project. She purchased furniture from Kansas City and Lawrence companies. At the age of fifty-one, Elizabeth finally had a house of her own, not her father's or even her mother's, but her own, to set up as she wished.

Once the house was built, they had it landscaped. She ordered trees— three apple, three pear, four peach, and one plum—from Ince Nursery of Lawrence. JB arranged to have sod laid around the home. In typical fashion, he wrote to a Mr. Brooks, who was installing the sod, that "if [T. C.] Green and Billy say it is a fine job, Green will pay you about half. The other half must wait until I approve the work and check quality." That was JB, always watching the details.

Elizabeth had a garden space plowed and harrowed. She had a chicken house built and ordered two hundred incubator eggs, which would furnish chicken for their use. Over the years, they found their cooks by advertising in the Eudora paper or the local German paper. They seemed to prefer German cooks; one, named Bertha, was a special favorite. Although Elizabeth had a large garden set up for The Outlook, for many years she made regular purchases of canned goods from a Mrs. Hughes. They drank Texas Carlsbad Water shipped by rail from Mineral Wells, Texas. Receipts found among the Watkins Papers show us that they consumed lots of ice cream, eggs, and meat.

Still somewhat active in the Ingleside Club, Elizabeth gave programs occasionally, which everyone seemed to enjoy. She also invited the members for luncheons at The Outlook.

Some details of Elizabeth's personal life at the time: she had hats made by Mrs. S. F. Patterson in Lawrence; she purchased ready-made clothes from Emery, Bird, Thayer Dry Goods Company in Kansas City; she also had clothes made for her. She bought the fabric and notions, and a Lawrence dressmaker, Ellen Anderson, sewed for her. Elizabeth was about five foot, six inches, with a waist of twenty-six to twenty-eight inches, and she wore a size 8 narrow shoe. She used White Rose lotion and shopped at Innes Bullene in Lawrence, the precursor to Weavers Department Store.

Living room at The Outlook, with the piano Elizabeth purchased on a trip to New York. (Kenneth Spencer Research Library, University Archives)

Her jewelry was purchased from Sol Marks and Parsons Jewelry in Lawrence. Her very favorite, a long strand of pearls given to her by JB, became her signature piece in all portraits. Perhaps a sentimental favorite, pearls were also the sign of a wealthy woman. Mrs. Alva Vanderbilt wore a "rope of pearls that had belonged to Catherine the Great stretching to her waist" at her famous New York Ball held March 26, 1883. In the 1880s, "before the advent of culturing, a string of perfectly matched pearls was rarer, and more expensive, than diamonds."* At Elizabeth's death in 1939, her pearls were valued at $4,800.00 ($96,000 in 2022 dollars).

Starting in about 1911, Elizabeth and JB began to give loans or outright monetary gifts to students. There are numerous letters from either Elizabeth or JB to then Chancellor Frank Strong, or to heads of various departments at the University of Kansas. They preferred to give assistance to students in partnership with the university. Elizabeth would often send checks to Dr. Ida Hyde, trusting her to find a deserving student to help. They wanted the recipients of their money to do their part, to have

* For a good account of pearls of this quality, see Anderson Cooper, *Vanderbilt: The Rise and Fall of an American Dynasty*.

Letter from Elizabeth to Dr. Ida Hyde,
offering money "to a deserving Kansas girl—
preferably a freshman—whose road is uphill
and a bit rocky." (Kenneth Spencer Research
Library, University of Kansas)

a feeling of having earned the help given. They were generous with their money, but also careful that it went to deserving people. A letter on September 20, 1915, reads: "My dear Miss Hyde, I want to give the enclosed fifty dollars to a deserving Kansas girl—preferably a freshman—whose road is uphill and a bit rocky."

These individual gifts were the beginning of a lifelong philanthropy for Elizabeth, inspired by JB.

On May 14, 1912, Elizabeth's nephew Frank Valentine Miller wrote to "Aunt Lizzie and Uncle JB," asking for a job during the coming summer.

He was the son of Edward, Elizabeth's eldest brother. Frank V. would be a senior in high school in the fall of 1912. This was the beginning of an important relationship for Elizabeth and for the future of the businesses.

In January 1913, Elizabeth and JB took an extended trip to Lake Charles in Louisiana, to Texas, and through St. Louis on the way back to Lawrence, surveying their properties and escaping the cold for a while, at least in Texas and Louisiana. By December 1913, Elizabeth was again concerned about JB's health. She wrote his doctor on December 14:

> My Dear Dr. Bohan, I want to tell you that Mr. Watkins pulse ran up to 120 during his attack some three weeks ago. Under such circumstances, do you advise giving a whole codeine tablet. A number of years ago when he was ill in New York a doctor there prescribed a morphine tablet and it gave him such peculiar head sensations he said he would never take another. Tho [*sic*] the condition may have been due to fever. I am not dictating to you, Dr. Bohan, only want to feel sure I am doing what is right with a full understanding on your part. Yours truly, Elizabeth M. Watkins.

During 1913, JB was focused again on his Morton County farm. He bought equipment in June; he had installed water wells and irrigation had begun. In March 1914, JB and Elizabeth returned to Lake Charles. The city would have been rebuilt by then and JB wanted to check on the crops and farmers. And the old stresses continued to plague him. In a letter to Judge John Wray on August 11, 1914, JB refers to his "15-year fight with Chalkley."

Again, in 1915, Elizabeth was worried about JB's health. With her help, JB had slowly reduced his drinking until he had completely stopped. But other health issues were becoming evident, and she was always aware of the effect that stress had on him. In January 1915, JB traveled to New York to a board of directors meeting; Raymond Rice, an attorney on the KU Law School faculty, traveled with him. This is one of the first mentions of Rice, who became their personal attorney and a trusted ally of both. He would be an even more important ally for Elizabeth in the future.

Attempting to lessen the stress on JB, Elizabeth wrote to Dr. S. L. Beiler on December 3, 1915, asking him to attend a mortgage company meeting in his place. She noted in her letter that he was one of the few they trusted to give an accurate accounting of what would transpire at the meeting.

My dear Dr. Beiler, Mr. Watkins tells me there is a stock holder meeting in Greeley, Colo on January 4, 1916. We have just returned from La after a visit of six weeks. We find conditions very much improved there. The south was slower recovering from the panicky condition than other parts of the country, but rice and lumber interests are more active and people generally are encouraged. Regarding the meetings in the near future, we feel there is a determination on the part of some to make changes that will not be fair to Mr. Watkins' interests. Mr. Chalkley writes you that your presence is not necessary at either meeting. We feel that you might without great inconvenience embrace the two in one trip. Mr. Watkins has not definitely settled in his mind whether he will attend either. Mr. Watkins is in his usual health but I want to reduce the strain for him all I can. I am sure if he is not there and you are not in attendance, we will not get a faithful report of the doings. . . . The struggle has been a long and hard one simply trying to protect what is ours. Now that the end is in sight, there will be a strong effort to keep Mr. Watkins out of his own. I hope you will write to Mr. Watkins that you will attend the two meetings and we should be glad to see you in our home before going to New York.

With kindest regards, Sincerely, Elizabeth M. Watkins.

This encapsulates the role Elizabeth filled, as she looked out for the businesses and tried to protect JB.

The year 1916 brought another new car, a Cadillac Type 53, with room for seven passengers and 60 horsepower. With each ever-larger car, the garage at The Outlook had to be renovated to make space for it. The garage was southeast of The Outlook, with the same stucco and green tile roofing as their home. During garage renovation, the university wrote to JB and Elizabeth, asking whether they planned to keep the road open to the public along the south boundary of The Outlook, continuing east of campus. The address of The Outlook was then on Louisiana Street, which currently runs east of The Outlook. Construction would have hindered traffic around this edge of campus.

About this time, 1916, there is mention of the "White Estate" and there are letters from Louis and Jennie, the children of JB's sister Ruth. Ruth had died, and regardless of their past disagreements, family was family. These are letters of appreciation from her children, thanking JB for helping to settle her estate.

Although Elizabeth had always been in good health, in August or September 1916 she had a hospital stay, under the care of Dr. C. J. Simmons. For several years following this hospitalization, there were monthly bills for "electric treatments" by Dr. Simmons. A bit of history may be called for here. As the country became electrified, beginning in the 1890s, people started to acquire labor-saving devices of all kinds: not only electric lights but also washing machines, saws, and fans. Once people accepted electricity as a friendly and useful force, it started to be used in medical treatments. "Medical battery" treatments were used for every imaginable ailment in the 1910s. The more respectable type of electric treatment was supervised in a doctor's office; a mild current was directed to the affected area and, if nothing else, it increased circulation. These treatments can be likened to early transcutaneous electrical nerve stimulation; in the twenty-first century, TENS, administered by registered physical therapists, is used to treat muscle and joint problems. Whatever her complaint, Elizabeth must have recovered somewhat, for she and JB returned to Lake Charles in November 1916.

Beginning in 1917, the household accounts were in Elizabeth's name rather than JB's. Until that time, he had handled the expenses of their home, and Elizabeth had received an "allowance" of $50 per month. But now her name was on the bills, her signature on the checks. This extended to bills for upkeep and repair of the cars, formerly JB's personal domain. His health was beginning to fail, once again. They traveled to Excelsior Springs, Missouri, just a few hours' drive from Lawrence, to try the therapeutic hot mineral baths there. An early spa experience, the healing waters at Excelsior Springs were discovered in 1880 by a local farmer whose daughter recovered from tuberculosis after drinking and bathing in the water. Years later, the hotel at Excelsior Springs hosted Harry Truman, as he waited for the results of the 1948 presidential election. (He won, contrary to the next morning's headlines.) President Franklin D. Roosevelt also went to Excelsior Springs, seeking treatment for his polio. Excelsior Springs was a closer drive than Hot Springs, Arkansas, where JB had found relief years earlier.

Nurses hired to help JB became a constant feature in their lives. One male nurse, Alvin O. Long, resigned to serve in World War I. On August 1, 1917, JB and Elizabeth drove to Boulder, Colorado, to an "institution," most probably a spa of some type. In a letter to the Lawrence office, Elizabeth compared the cool weather there to the heat in Kansas. JB was ill, she reported, but improving. His signatures were shaky on affidavits for Timber Company lands, on a right of way for the Intercoastal Canal, and on Orange Land Company documents. She noted they didn't travel much during their stay in Boulder. Motoring in the mountains was "not conducive to quiet nerves to make such sharp turns on narrow roads," she wrote. On their way back to Lawrence, she reported that they had a "good dinner at the Brown Palace," a historic hotel that is still in business in Denver.

By 1918 the United States had given up its neutral stance and entered World War I. JB and Elizabeth purchased several Liberty Bonds to help the war effort and they supported Red Cross drives. Several of their nurses and chauffeurs quit to go to war. Elizabeth also donated to the Belgian Relief Fund, which was set up by a young Herbert Hoover. The money was used to feed children starving in Belgium, due to the German blockade of supplies and food into the city. Still revered in Belgium to this day, Herbert Hoover was an expert at shipping and, indeed, he saved many lives. Later, as president, his political career could not survive when he was blamed, erroneously, for the Great Depression.

In 1918 JB bought another car, this one a Cadillac Brougham Type 57 with Imperial body style. He signed for it, but his signature was wobbly. Elizabeth was in good health for a woman in her fifties, but JB was ailing. Since the 1906 episode before they were married, it had been clear that he had problems. Although Elizabeth had helped JB reduce, then eliminate, his alcohol habit, they knew that drinking had damaged his body and that he still needed to be watched. They made several more trips to Excelsior Springs, and the treatments seemed to help them both. They had spent too many years working hard and neither knew how to relax. Still, they had loved their shared life of travel and business dealings.

In September 1918, they bought railroad tickets for themselves and B. A. Sherr, JB's current nurse, to travel to Washington, DC, and then on to New York. JB spent time at a sanitarium or spa in DC, where, after examination of his spinal fluid, a doctor determined that there was nothing to indicate any organic disease of the brain. Several members of JB's family expressed concern over his condition. By late 1918, JB nearly always had a nurse with him. Elfriede Fischer Rowe in *Wonderful Old Lawrence* described him at that time as a "small, stooped man, with piercing eyes."

There were some members of JB's family who tried constantly to access his money. He helped them in small ways but certainly not to the extent that they wanted or felt entitled to, given JB's great wealth. In August 1919, Zena Thomson, daughter of Alexander and JB's sister Maria, wrote to Elizabeth to ask that JB and Elizabeth take over Maria's outstanding loan of $20,000. Elizabeth wrote back that JB would assume $5,000 of the loan but not more. Zena was reassured that JB would "keep" them until they could sell something, likely the land the Thomsons owned in Louisiana. Zena replied with grateful thanks, "I know you have troubles and I am sorry for you. . . . I am getting a taste of it myself, for mother is very like JB and demands my time and attention. . . . I am sorry JB is getting so feeble. It is . . . so hard for you."

Elizabeth foresaw that these demands for money from JB's family would be a problem if she outlived him, which was a real possibility, given that he was sixteen years her senior. The two had talked about the family and JB's wishes, and she had assured him that she would treat them fairly. JB and Elizabeth wanted to use the bulk of the money to benefit as many people as possible. They especially wanted to help young people with their education. They couldn't make every important decision at that time, but JB trusted Elizabeth to carry out his wishes.

In early 1920 many causes requested their help: the Firemen's Ball, the American Legion, the Society for the Friendless, missionary work, the YMCA. They also supported the Presbyterian Church in Lawrence. Elizabeth wrote to the dean of the School of Fine Arts at KU to offer monetary support to a student, if the school would also help the student. Again, this type of support became JB and Elizabeth's signature.

In 1920 they purchased a summer house in Bay View, Michigan, which was rented out when they were not there. This purchase was more for Elizabeth's sake than JB's, because she did not like hot weather. JB made a trip to the Morton County ranch in May; it was one of his favorite places, but not Elizabeth's.

On June 10, 1920, JB Watkins deeded to Elizabeth M. Watkins "for one dollar with love and affection" the homestead known as The Outlook, containing about five acres. Also known as the Robinson Place, the legal description is NE ¼ of Sec 1, Township 13, Range 19 in Douglas County, Kansas.

JB and Elizabeth went to Bay View in July 1920 for an extended stay. At times a nurse traveled with them, sometimes they found someone in the town, but, generally, all the nurses were male. There is mention of one male nurse sent back to Chicago for "work unsatisfactory." A Mr. Olmstead became the favored nurse in the final years of JB's life.

October 1920 brought sadness to Elizabeth, with the death of her brother, Frank C. Miller. Of the three Miller siblings, Elizabeth was the only one still alive. Frank left a student loan or aid fund to the University of Kansas and a bequest to Mercy Hospital for children. He also left a trust for his nephew, Frank V. Miller, with Elizabeth named as the trustee. Frank had had a successful career as a banker, first in Salina, Kansas, and later in Kansas City.

In November 1920, Elizabeth bought five KU football tickets for herself and some friends. A reserved woman, Elizabeth did not have many close friends, but she was known to entertain faculty wives. She may have used the tickets for business friends, employees, or their attorney Raymond Rice. Elizabeth was comfortable in the company of men, having worked among them all her life. JB was not well enough to go to the games, but Elizabeth enjoyed them. She bought a turkey for Thanksgiving dinner and made a trip to Iowa to see family members.

In December 1920, the garage at The Outlook was remodeled again to fit a new car. JB had bought a Cadillac Type 59 Imperial limousine from the Lawrence Buick Company.

In January 1921, JB had $16,000 transferred to Elizabeth for emergency use in case of his death. At this point, he must have been confined to their home. JB's health had not been good for several months. He was seventy-six and Elizabeth was sixty.

On February 4, 1921, JB Watkins, entrepreneur and visionary, died.

"At his death he was principal owner of seven corporations; he also owned personally about 100,000 acres of land in Texas and Louisiana, and more than 200 farms in southwestern Kansas, numbering some 26,000 acres, acquired through foreclosures by the Watkins Land and Mortgage Company," noted John H. McCool, history professor at KU.

Notice of the death of JB Watkins, *Lawrence Journal-World*, February 5, 1921.

Not everyone ascribed the Watkins wealth to "foreclosures," however. An article from the KU Endowment Association, "Whence the Watkins Wealth," gives a different, more humanitarian perspective on the acres owned by foreclosure by the Watkins Land and Mortgage Company. It is a more current perspective, perhaps softened by passing years:

It is easy to see Jabez Bunting Watkins as a ruthless, laissez-faire 19th century capitalist, but as far as the truth can be known now, it's not that simple. He was certainly driven, opportunistic and shrewd; he also had a great deal of initiative and creative imagination. And he was compassionate, as long as compassion coincided with smart business. . . . The company established tenant farmers in 22 counties in Kansas. The management policy was somewhat flexible; farmers in trouble were allowed to pay only their loan interest and stay on the land. J. B. respected the farmers' hard work, and it was in his interest for them to succeed. An inventory of the company's property estimated that only 2 percent of the land came through foreclosure.

Historian Judith Galas wrote in 1998, "Banking, railroads and real estate built J. B.'s empire; and when he died in 1921, his widow inherited an estate valued at $2.4 million. Assets included five Louisiana corporations, 200 Kansas corporations, more than 200 Kansas farms, and about 100,000 acres in Texas and Louisiana. She was, without a doubt, a wealthy woman."

Elizabeth was now left alone with this fortune: a gift and, simultaneously, a burden. However, they had built that fortune together and she knew what was ahead of her. She would be true to JB's wishes and his principles, which had become her own.

CHAPTER

Settling the Estate

In the papers of the Watkins Collection, the first correspondence found after JB's death is a card Elizabeth sent to the Lawrence office staff of the Watkins Land and Mortgage Company. These were Elizabeth's friends and coworkers, the nearest thing to a family she had left. "Dear People of Watkins Mortgage Company, I meant to thank you for the lovely flowers you sent as an expression of sympathy in my sorrow. When I am alone later on, I shall see my friends. Sincerely, Elizabeth M. Watkins."

Elizabeth held JB's funeral on Monday, February 7, 1921, at The Outlook. The pallbearers would "all be members of the bank family," including T. C. Green, JB's longtime head cashier and assistant. The First Presbyterian Church minister, Reverend E. A. Bleck, officiated. Burial was in Oak Hill Cemetery in Lawrence. In the obituary, Elizabeth is mentioned as the "only member of his immediate family." It also mentions his two sisters who survived him, Mrs. Maria Thomson of Lake Charles, Louisiana, and Mrs. Hattie Walker of Falls Church, Virginia.

Hattie wrote to tell Elizabeth that she was unable to attend the funeral but appreciated the telegrams that Elizabeth had sent to each of JB's family members. Hattie's son, Edwin Walker, always a troublemaker, had been one of the petitioners who requested the interdiction of JB. When Edwin wrote Elizabeth now to say, "I think JB would have been better off if he had married you years earlier," how was Elizabeth supposed to interpret this? Edwin had helped in the attempt to declare JB insane, had helped bring JB's alleged illegitimate son to Louisiana as a fellow petitioner, and would soon assert that her marriage to JB was false. The battle lines were forming.

Steadfast supporters of Elizabeth included the children of JB's sister Ruth White, the children of his sister Ellen Barbara Neal, and his sister Maria Thomson and her only child, Zena.

Very quickly the discussion of JB's last will and testament began. Did one exist? Where was it? Various people remembered various wills, one as early as 1880. Elizabeth held that there was no valid will.

When the deceased does not leave a will, the probate court determines the distribution of property to heirs according to state statutes. Usually, this is determined by the probate court in the state where the decedent lived and had legal residence, and sometimes by the probate court in the state where property is located. In larger estates, as with JB's, it can be in both. Kansas and Louisiana would both rule on his estate. This is the normal order of preference to assign assets to heirs: first, the surviving spouse; second, children; third, parents; and fourth, siblings and their lineal descendants.

A surviving spouse almost invariably receives at least half of the decedent's estate and all the property they accumulated together during the marriage, which is called the "communal or community property."

JB's sister Hattie wrote Elizabeth again, asking about wills. Elizabeth wrote a very telling letter back to Hattie on April 21, 1921:

My dear Mrs. Walker, I have your letter of the [April] 13th. . . . In 1909 Mr. Watkins executed a will revoking all previous wills. . . . He destroyed that will some five or six years ago. In that will there was no limit to my use of his property. To his sisters and half-brothers he left $2,000 each and to some of his nieces and nephews a like amount, but to no relative a greater sum. That was his last will—there were two witnesses to it. When I wrote you that he left no will I told you the absolute truth—as all wills he had ever made had been revoked. . . . I had no desire to deceive you but I was willing to pass over to his relatives a much larger amount than he intended. . . . Time and again I tried to persuade my husband to do for his relatives and especially his sisters, something helpful in the way of money. . . . On one or two occasions I succeeded, but I could not always. He believed in everyone carving out his own fortune—he believed that in a much stronger degree than I do. . . . I was willing to do more for his relatives than any one of them would have perhaps done for me under the same circumstances.

Raymond Rice, Elizabeth's attorney, assured her that she had nothing to worry about in Kansas since she was his sole heir. JB had died in Kansas, and, under the laws of intestate succession, the estate would be under Kansas law. Elizabeth would get everything. He checked her status in Louisiana. Legally, there was a difference between property owned by JB before his marriage and "community property," which applied to anything accumulated while he was married to Elizabeth.

A letter, sent to each member of JB's family, clearly stated that Elizabeth intended to divide all the assets in Louisiana between the heirs and to give up her right to keep the community property in that state. The letter noted that she would dispose of the properties as soon as she was able and that she would keep a transparent ledger of what was owned, what was sold, and how much money was sent to each relative. Elizabeth was committed to dividing up the returns from any community property among the relatives, but it would take time to liquidate the property. As she wrote on May 1, 1921, "The community property is a gift by me. That there can be no immediate returns, but we hope for a reasonable speedy conclusion for it." Elizabeth's generosity was not met with the hoped-for pleasant response. Far from it.

Some family members pressed for their share of the estate immediately. In some cases she began paying in increments, keeping track, and deducting the incremental payments from their inheritance. The problem was that she didn't have a lot of ready cash. Her money was tied up in investments and land, and there was indebtedness on some of the properties. JB had often leveraged himself to buy another property. He had given her $16,000 at the beginning of the year, but she had continual expenses, funeral costs, and taxes on all their properties.

Her cash flow problems were hard for many to understand, and some relatives continued to pressure Elizabeth and push to be paid at once. She understood the value of JB's plans for the estate and knew that patience would be required for their assets to come to their full value. She didn't allow herself to be pushed into selling off property to meet their demands, and instead developed a different strategy. She made an inventory and had everything valued. Then, as she could, she bought out the relatives who were most insistent on getting their money now. This way she could maintain control of the assets and sell them when their value was more fully established. A shrewd businesswoman, Elizabeth knew that holding the properties together would increase their worth in the long run.

The court required her to make a full inventory of everything she and JB owned. She hired T. C. Green, along with her nephew Frank V. Miller, and paid them extra to do the inventory. Frank had worked for JB and Elizabeth since high school; he continued to work through his years at KU, where he was a member of the fraternity Phi Alpha Tau. Elizabeth needed Frank especially now; he was a great help and a loyal companion.

One complication in settling the estate was that JB's mother had married twice, and the half relatives wanted their share, also. In the early wills that JB destroyed, he had left $2,000 to his sisters, half brothers, nieces, and nephews. Elizabeth had said she would do better than that. However, she was inclined to be far less generous to those who made trouble for her.

Forthcoming events proved that some of JB's family members were interested in getting as much of his money as possible. JB's half brother, Abraham Mutersbaugh, had told his family that the estate would be worth $15 to $20 million. When the Mutersbaugh wing of the family confronted Elizabeth with this "fact" and she advised them to reduce that amount by $18,500,000, they didn't believe her. Much of JB's estate was land and he had leveraged himself to buy that land. Land can be valued high, if it is developed, or low if it is undeveloped. The normal practice would be to use the lower estimate to reduce estate taxes, but this wing of the family wanted much more than Elizabeth's estimate would give them.

During this spring and summer of heated discussions over wills and the size of JB's estate, Elizabeth discovered that the Mutersbaugh family had started a petition to contest the validity of her marriage to JB, alleging that he was not of sound mind when he married her. Grant Mutersbaugh went to Lake Charles to talk to Dr. Watkins, one of the doctors who had cleared JB of his interdiction. Grant was trying to assert that JB had not been declared sane. The fire in Lake Charles in 1910 had destroyed all the legal records in the courthouse. Edwin Walker, Hattie's son, joined Grant in this line of harassment. Grant went to interview a doctor JB had seen

	Nelson	McCurdy		Dittmer		Crowell	
Challis		MacMurray	Burnett		Hill		Dykes
Miller		Gumbiner	Hutchings		Waldo		Clark

Phi Alpha Tau

Founded 1902, at the Emerson School of Oratory, Boston, Mass.
Installed at the University of Kansas, March 1, 1915.
Publication—"The Phi Alpha Tau Bulletin."
Colors—Green and White.

Active Members

Prof. Arthur MacMurray   Elmer C. Clark   Alton Gumbiner
Prof. Howard T. Hill   Harold B. Crowell   Harlan B. Hutchings
Donald C. Burnett   Otto H. Dittmer   Frank V. Miller
J. V. H. Challis   John H. Dykes   Henry B. McCurdy
Hoyt S. Nelson   Guy L. Waldo

Frank Valentine Miller (*front row, far left*), son of Elizabeth's brother Edward.
Frank was a member of the Phi Alpha Tau fraternity at the University of Kansas.
(*Jayhawker* Yearbooks, Kenneth Spencer Research Library, University of Kansas)

in Washington, DC, for the same purpose. Elizabeth rightly felt she was under attack by the Walkers and Mutersbaughs.

Elizabeth needed an ally in Louisiana, someone to keep an eye on her property and legal dealings there. She hired James Stuart Thomson. Alexander Thomson, JB's brother-in-law (married to JB's sister Maria) was the professor who had come to Lake Charles to assist JB in agricultural matters. J. Stuart Thomson was possibly a relative of Alexander's.* Both were born in Ontario, Canada. J. Stuart's birthplace is known to be Bayfield, Ontario. It seems an unlikely coincidence that the two would arrive independently in the small, newly growing town in Louisiana. However, there is inconsistency in the spelling of their last names, in newspapers and in documents from the Watkins Papers. Given JB and Elizabeth's propensity to hire relatives, a family tie is suspected, although it cannot be proven.

J. Stuart Thomson had become the postmaster for Lake Charles in 1901 and was established there in business and politics. Stuart had worked with Jabez, serving as the secretary and treasurer of the St. Louis, Watkins, and Gulf Railway. He was the Louisiana delegate to the Republican National Convention in 1916. Stuart became Elizabeth's "eyes and ears on the ground" in Louisiana and her business manager there. Although she was clearly independent, Elizabeth began to trust and rely on Stuart as they navigated these difficult years. A great many of the rescued letters in the Watkins Collection are between Elizabeth and Stuart.

A pattern seen in Elizabeth's handwritten letters illuminates her personality. She writes rather formally, and in a careful, dutiful way, she always addresses all the business on her mind first. However, at the end of nearly every letter she adds a little extra that is more personal, especially in her letters to Stuart Thomson in Louisiana. At the end of letters, she speaks about a trip she enjoyed or a drive in her car, her concerns about the scholarship halls she is planning to build, or her loneliness at holidays. These "extras" give glimpses of the private Elizabeth.

Elizabeth kept separate bank accounts, one for her personal use and

---

* There is confusion about the spelling of Thomson versus Thompson. The two families may or may not have been related. Both families had been in Canada at one time, both lived in Lake Charles, Louisiana, and both were important in the lives of Jabez and Elizabeth. Even census records confuse the spelling. We have chosen to use "Thomson" throughout this book.

another for estate business. This process was apparently going to go on for a while, with JB's extended family getting involved as they were. Relatives filed petitions with the Louisiana courts, tying up the properties there. When all this was finally over "there will be no scars on my conscience," she said. "I do not care for JB's property on account of myself beyond keeping up my very comfortable home in its present style as JB wanted me to do but I have work to do for humanity and I feel this property will help me to carry out the plans we have talked over many times. In the past I have never found it difficult to feel the touch of God's hand and I know that He is and will always be near me."

Elizabeth came from a family that valued and practiced religion. Throughout her life, she embodied Christian values of kindness and caring for the less fortunate, taught by her parents. Although her working life often interfered with regular church attendance, she faithfully supported the Presbyterian church in Lawrence. She read religious tracts and was comforted by her faith. During this difficult time in her life, the Christian value of "turning the other cheek" would understandably have proven difficult for Elizabeth.

By April 1921, the inventory of the estate for tax purposes was completed. The value was set at $1,530,000, mostly in land unsold and of uncertain worth. She had a lack of cash with taxes coming due. This inventory, a huge job, had been accomplished with the help of T. C. Green and nephew Frank. She wrote, "I inventoried JBs desk and chair, poor dear. I wonder if he knows of the contention over our property. I say our because I surely helped him make it."

Despite all the estate work and dissension, it was springtime. She had sixty little chicks in the lovely back lawn of her home, which gave her great pleasure, and there was her garden to plant. Elizabeth was closely involved in the daily management of The Outlook, ordering groceries and supplies and planning the garden. Her favorite cook, Bertha, was a mainstay in the household, along with a housekeeper named Lizzie. Elizabeth enjoyed her meals; she lamented that she had lost the touch of cooking, although she still made "good canned peaches and pickles."

That April the Douglas County Probate Court authorized a partial distribution of the estate, giving Elizabeth M. Watkins, as sole heir, ten shares of stock in the Watkins National Bank under the Order of the Court. After those shares were assigned to her, she surrendered them to Watkins National Bank for cancellation and received certificate no. 612 for ten shares in her own name. She then had a new certificate no. 614 for the ten shares made out by the bank to Frank V. Miller, her nephew, son of her brother Edward. Frank, now an officer in the Watkins Bank, had brought her companionship and comfort when she was lonely without JB. He was also beginning to travel for Elizabeth, inspecting the Kansas farmlands and reporting back to her. In May she wrote "had company to dinner. Frank was not here and I could not eat alone."

In May 1921, Edwin Walker turned up in Lawrence, uninvited. He was JB's nephew who, along with the alleged illegitimate son, had tried to take control of JB's estate by declaring him insane. Edwin appeared at The Outlook, wishing to see Elizabeth, late one evening. The next day she spoke with him. He had written one kind letter to her upon JB's death, but she knew he was working against her. She said that "since Ed Walker was here in 1906, I did not mention his name, because JB detested him so very much." Walker stayed for weeks and repeatedly came to The Outlook to harass Elizabeth about the inheritance. Again and again, he went to the Watkins Bank offices and took up T. C. Green's time, as Green attempted to be civil. Walker tried to get an attorney to take the case for his inheritance in Kansas City, but he failed. Finally, in June he relented and left, no richer than when he arrived.

In July, to escape the Kansas summer heat, Elizabeth went to Harbor Springs, Michigan; she wrote to Stuart Thomson, her Louisiana business manager: "Truly Stuart, I miss dear JB more here among strangers or chance acquaintances than I did at home. I would not recall him, for all his sufferings are over, and my loneliness must continue to the end."

Another letter to Stuart, written on July 8, 1921, from Harbor Springs shows a bit of impatience with the family's monetary demands:

Mrs. Olsen [another relative] wrote me on the 5th asking me for $2000, saying I would not miss it from "so many thousands" and that if I were ever poor, I must know how impossible it is to save $2000. . . . I told her that before my marriage I earned every cent I spent, that I often could not see clearly how to meet all demands, that all the time I had a

wealthy brother who did not help me and to whom I did not apply for
assistance.

JB's relatives were trying in every way imaginable to get more of the
estate. They questioned JB's mental condition and, when that didn't work,
they tried to annul the marriage. A letter from the Rev. W. Layton, who
had married the couple, stated, "There is no more chance of annulling
your marriage than there is of proving that I was deceived in performing
the ceremony and married you to another than your beloved husband."
He continued, "It gives me much pleasure to know of your planning for
needy young people." Despite the distractions over the estate, Elizabeth
remembered JB's intention to aid young people, and her ideas of how to
carry this out had begun to take shape.

Elizabeth had a health scare in September 1921. She spent two weeks
at the Mayo Clinic and even executed a will before she left for the clinic.
Thankfully, all was well, for she wrote, "I think I will be spared to do the
things I long to."

In early October 1921, JB's niece Jennie White alerted Elizabeth that the
heirs were organizing. Edwin Walker, trying a new line of attack, had sent
a letter to "thirty-nine or more of the collateral heirs of J. B. Watkins to
meet in Falls Church, Virginia," at the home of JB's sister, Hattie Walker.
The meeting was "to decide what course to pursue for the protection of
their interests in the estate left by J. B. Watkins." Jennie's brother Louis
White wrote that "this [Walker] branch of the family is referred to as 'the
insurgents.'"

Elizabeth wrote to Stuart Thomson in August 1921: "If they expect to
scare me into anything, they will fall short of their guess. I am now in good
fighting mood and when I get back to Bertha's good cooking, I will put on
my war paint and take a bolder stand than ever, for Right will prevail because it is right." Years of business dealings had prepared Elizabeth for this.
She was kind by nature but would not be taken advantage of.

About this time, word reached Elizabeth that James Yeager had come
forward and alleged to have witnessed a valid will of JB's. Yeager had been
employed as a land inspector for the Orange Land Company in New
York while Elizabeth worked there. He had also worked in Louisiana for

the Watkins interests, and now had joined forces with the Walkers and Mutersbaughs.

In December 1921, Stuart Thomson wrote to inform Elizabeth's nephew Frank in the Lawrence office that the Walkers and Mutersbaughs were in the "newspaper stage of their game. They had an article in the American Press last night." In this article, "Collateral Heirs Advancing Claims," Yeager again asserted his claim that there was a valid will from 1909 and that it gave from $10,000 to $50,000 to each of the heirs.

Elizabeth replied in a December 12, 1921, letter to Stuart:

> I have a copy of the original Will of Mr. Watkins which he executed in 1909. . . . I also have a copy of the letter written to the attorney asking if they have in their possession a copy and stating that he did not wish an outstanding copy as he had destroyed the original. His signature was very clear and very firm to this letter. In that Will he leaves to no relative to exceed $2,000.00.The whole proceeding in Louisiana seems to be an effort to frighten me. I am not in the least scared. I cannot say that I am not angry and I have about decided that those people shall not benefit to the extent of one dollar in any of my inheritance through J. B. Watkins. . . . It is "A Grand and Glorious Feelin'" to know that I have not made a single misrepresentation in regard to this Estate matter.

Yeager continued his claims. Refusing to be intimidated, Elizabeth resorted to blackmail. Stuart Thomson was instructed to write a letter to Yeager: "Mrs. Watkins thinks it would be a good plan to let Mr. Yeager know, provided he is considering causing trouble, that Mrs. Watkins has the letters which Mr. Yeager would not care to have come to Mrs. Yeager's attention."

During the time Yeager and Elizabeth had worked together in New York, letters had been sent to him in their office by his mistress. Elizabeth knew of this affair in New York and noted that this unsavory woman "drank punch." This was code for drinking alcohol, seen as a failure of character in a woman of the day. Elizabeth had these letters for proof. After this, nothing came of Yeager's professed "valid will," and his attempts to help the Walkers and Mutersbaughs failed.

JB had been buried in February 1921 in Oak Hill Cemetery in Lawrence, not in a mausoleum as JB and Elizabeth had discussed at one time, but

The Watkins stone marker at Oak Hill Cemetery, Lawrence, Kansas.
The opposite side of the stone reads "Miller." JB and Elizabeth are buried
there, as well as Elizabeth's parents, Valentine and Ella Miller, and
Elizabeth's brother Edward. (Author's collection)

with a stone marker. In December 1921 she decided on a monument of
Light Barre Vermont granite, six feet high on an eight-foot base with urns
and four markers. Interestingly, on the more prominent front, it reads
WATKINS but on the back side it reads MILLER. She intended it to show the
names of both families. It cost $3,122.80. Elizabeth created a $5,000 trust
fund with First National Bank of Kansas City; the income was to be used
for the perpetual care and upkeep of the Watkins lot in Oak Hill Cemetery.
These expenses came from her personal account.

Short of cash, Elizabeth wanted to get rid of some property. But she had
to wait because she refused to sell in a panic and wanted top dollar for the
Louisiana land. There was drilling for oil very close to her land there. And,
she reported to Stuart, "Edwin Walker knows about the oil drilling." The

final estate tax report of JB's gross estate came to $1,903,542.59. Of this there was only $3,631.22 as cash in the bank. Elizabeth was the administrator.

Elizabeth traveled to California in December 1921 to spend her first Christmas without JB with her Miller relatives who lived there. Professor Ephraim Miller, her father's cousin who had first suggested that Elizabeth's parents move to Lawrence, was now retired in California. This was her first trip to the state. She was accustomed to train travel to New York, but this was a longer trip, much of it through parts of America she had never seen. After her visit with the Millers, she stayed at the Hollywood Hotel. She considered living in California, but her lovely home was in Lawrence. She wrote home that Kansas was the "best state in the Union in most respects." But she did enjoy the lovely weather in California and automobile drives along the coast.

Edwin Walker persisted in attempts to establish that JB had not been competent. In March 1922, he met with Dr. Keith and Dr. Bohan in Kansas City to try to prove his point. Dr. Keith simply replied "no," that JB was competent. Dr. Bohan said Elizabeth had been too strict regarding JB's liquor habit. This statement got back to Elizabeth, who knew that her intervention had saved JB and his fortune. She wrote to Stuart on March 23, 1921:

> Dr. Bohan evidently didn't know that I was four years cutting down the daily allowance to nothing and JB stopped finally of his own accord. If dear JB had not drank to the extent of delirium tremens he would never have been declared insane in Louisiana. He was not insane but intoxicated to such an extent that he was incapable of attending to his business. He did not drink at the bar but in his own room and for that reason, his friends did not know the real situation.

In April 1922, Elizabeth finally acquired all the Kansas property of JB's estate under order of the Douglas County Probate Courts—bonds, lands, and stocks. That month she paid $190,000 in federal and state inheritance tax. It took good management to get that money together. Essentially, she had little income, which was hard for people to understand. There were daily requests for monetary assistance, from relatives and charity groups.

The Ingleside Club was invited to The Outlook that April, and Helen Hart, a senior in the fine arts department, entertained the group. Mrs.

Rice, Mrs. McElinny, and Mrs. Reed helped serve two courses and refreshments. It had been over a year since she lost JB, and it was time for Elizabeth to reenter society and entertain.

In May 1922 Elizabeth bought an Imperial Limousine Cadillac, model no. 61 P508. Although she didn't drive, she had acquired a love of cars from JB. She had good help but continued to direct and oversee every aspect of the business personally. Two lots on south Massachusetts Street were purchased; she planned to build a house for her nephew Frank, who worked with her daily. Frank was marrying Louise Monday of Lake Charles, Louisiana. Frank had lived with Elizabeth at The Outlook, but she felt he should have his own home after his marriage. She paid for Frank and Louise's new house over a period of months when her cash became available.

After Frank and Louise moved into their home, Elizabeth often ate at the Colonial Tea Room at 936 Kentucky Street in Lawrence. She did not like to eat alone. She asked Nellie Barnes, who taught rhetoric at KU, to live with her in October 1922. Barnes's varied interests would have made her a good companion for Elizabeth. She brought some of her books with her to The Outlook, including her favorite poetry. Perhaps this influence is seen in the many poems copied into Elizabeth's personal scrapbook. The two attended numerous plays and concerts together.

Once, Frank, Louise, and Elizabeth drove to Manhattan, Kansas, for a football game, ninety miles away. They took their lunch and supper with them and drove home by moonlight. It appeared that Frank was being groomed to follow Elizabeth in the business, and many thought he would be her heir. She had decided that if there was any money left when she died, it would probably go to an institution. She was also thinking of forming a foundation.

There were many travels in 1922, for business, to visit friends, or to escape the heat. Her destinations included Louisville, Kentucky; California; Bay View, Michigan; Cincinnati; and Washington, DC. She needed to go to Louisiana but was afraid that business problems awaited her if she went. She had Stuart Thomson to look after her interests there, as she waited for the court decision about the estate property in Louisiana.

At Christmas 1922, she gave her usual gifts of money, which she always enjoyed. Although she was still trying to sell land, prices were not good, and she refused to sell in a panic.

Nellie Barnes, on the right, with a woman identified only as "Marian." Nellie Barnes was a live-in and traveling companion for Elizabeth after JB's death. (Kenneth Spencer Research Library, University of Kansas)

Early in 1923 she took a trip to Washington, DC, and visited with President Harding and his sister, Carolyn Harding Votaw. She said that no one she spoke with thought President Harding was doing a very good job but admitted that, because she didn't chat with any Republicans, the comments were probably biased. While on the East Coast, she lunched in New York with Reverend Layton and his wife. Layton had performed Elizabeth and JB's wedding ceremony. In a letter to Stuart in Louisiana about her trip, she added, "Frank has written you as I directed," and noted that on that day, February 12, 1923, Frank had turned twenty-seven.

In July 1923, tragedy struck Elizabeth again. Her adored nephew Frank died in a car accident.* He was the only child of her brother Edward, and he had worked for JB and Elizabeth ever since, as a junior in high school in Lake Charles, he had written "Uncle Jabez and Aunt Lizzie" and asked for a job. He was described as "quiet and unassuming in his manner and a pleasant companion. In recent years he has assumed increasing business responsibilities in a creditable manner." At the time of his death, he was a director in the Watkins Bank, and it appeared that he was being groomed to be Elizabeth's second in command. Elizabeth was in Bay View, Michigan, for the summer when she received the tragic news.

Dick Williams had been working for Elizabeth as her helper and personal assistant. Once it became obvious that Frank would be her choice as her successor, Dick took a job in Kansas City, where he was going to work for D. W. Newcomer Sons. It was on the night a going away party was held for Dick that Frank's accident occurred. After the party, a group decided to drive to Topeka for breakfast. Frank was a passenger in a Stutz Bearcat convertible, the last car of four in a caravan. On their way to Topeka, an accident caused the car to roll over and off the highway, killing Frank instantly.

After this sad event, Russell Dick Williams, who had been born in Concordia, Kansas, gave up his new job in Kansas City to stay with Elizabeth and the Watkins enterprises, where his responsibilities soon increased. The tragic accident had far-reaching consequences for Williams, which carried into his long and prosperous future. He stayed in Lawrence and

* An article on page 1 of the *Lawrence Daily Journal World*, July 30, 1923, gives all the details of the car accident that killed Frank V. Miller, Elizabeth's nephew.

had an extended career as Elizabeth's business manager. Then, after Elizabeth's death, his career continued in connection with the University of Kansas.

In the space of two years, Elizabeth had lost her beloved JB and now her nephew Frank. She wrote to Stuart: "Dear Frank, I miss him so—his letters—his love—and close relationship. I feel sometimes as tho [sic] I could not live without him, still I must and there is work I hope that I may do and not leave for others to undertake, without my understanding." She also writes, "I will go thro [sic] deep water every day and every night." Elizabeth's sorrow is evident in her heartbreaking letters. She writes she must keep busy "head and hands, to keep my heartache down."

Elizabeth had not been pleased with Frank's wife, Louise, and soon after Frank's death, their relationship became strained. Before the couple's marriage in 1922 in Lake Charles, Frank had lived at The Outlook. Frank and Louise lived there together for a short time after their marriage and then moved to the home that Elizabeth had built them on south Massachusetts Street. From letters it was apparent that Elizabeth didn't think Louise was "good enough" for Frank. Elizabeth wrote confidentially to Stuart that "it took a right smart sum to pay for her extravagances and they were hers." After Frank's death Louise wanted to be "my little girl," Elizabeth said. But after the two women met again in Lawrence, Elizabeth wrote that "she is out of my life." Louise moved back to Lake Charles and quickly remarried.

About this time Elizabeth began to buy municipal bonds as a steady investment. But as always, she needed cash and lamented the slow real estate sales. She wrote, "Dick Williams is showing ability in my affairs and is working with good results down stairs." Later she wrote, "Dick is working splendid changes." Dick was indeed an intelligent young man; he was learning investment strategies and business tactics from Elizabeth that would help him all his life.

In September she went to Washington, DC, to enroll Lillian Gardner and Margaret Graye, her wards, in school at the National Park Seminary. These young women were related to Elizabeth on her mother's side, the Gardner side. From her letters, it was obvious she had a near-maternal relationship with these young women and found personal satisfaction in helping them begin their education and adult lives.

Elizabeth was now sixty-two years old and had decided not to enter into any new ventures. She was beginning to pay off the relatives, $1,000 at a time. She was also selling her interests in the bank, all except ten shares. By October, she wrote to Stuart, "I am going to begin to build a foundation with which to begin a work that is worthwhile." Philanthropy began to occupy more of her thoughts.

Again, she gave many Christmas gifts in 1923. She traveled to California to escape her loneliness at the holidays, but that year she found it too warm. And she missed Frank. Elizabeth was still waiting for the probate case to be decided in Louisiana. Land sales were stagnant, both in Kansas and Louisiana. She still received many pleas for monetary help. In a letter to Stuart from Hotel Hollywood in California she wrote, "These last years have been a strain. . . . There are certain things I want to do. My future is largely behind me and I'm going to work with all speed I can command." Planning her philanthropy satisfied her need to work and became a fulfilling part of her life.

In January 1924, she took a business trip to New York. While there, she was wined and dined by "a very nice gentleman," a Mr. Patterson, who she thought entertained wedding plans. He was nice but she wanted no "orange blossoms" in her future.

Consider for a moment Elizabeth's journeys. She had been traveling for business since her late twenties. We know she enjoyed travel, especially by train. In December 1923 she was in California and, by January, she was in New York, travel that would involve weeks by train. A glimpse of the kind of train car she would have access to helps us imagine her as she watched the beautiful variety of American landscape glide by the window.

Throughout all these years she was still running her house, ordering groceries, overseeing the garden, and watching her health. Her health was good, but with age came problems. She was getting business matters in order. In time she thought she would take over the Mortgage Company. She was banking in Kansas City now, since she had sold most of her interest in the Watkins National Bank.

The Supreme Court of Louisiana still had not made its decision regarding the community property portion of JB's estate. She had to constantly remind Stuart Thomson, who managed her property in Louisiana, that she was the one who made the decisions on when and if to sell anything. At times her anger showed. From a letter dated June 8, 1924:

First-class railway dining car from the 1920s, the sort Elizabeth would have eaten in during her travels. (Train World Museum, Schaerbeek, Belgium. Photo by author)

Early-twentieth-century first-class touring railcar, similar to ones on which Elizabeth and JB would travel. (Train World Museum, Schaerbeek, Belgium. Photo by author)

Dear Stuart, . . . I am at the head of my affairs and I will not stand by without protest and have my instructions disregarded. I told you in a recent letter that I intended to do as nearly right as I knew, in every way, but will not be ignored in affairs that are mine. I want my business managed while I am on earth, according to my ideas, and when I am gone, I hope to leave what is left with people who do not "take the bull by the horns" and carry their point in spite of heaven and earth. Yours truly, Elizabeth M. Watkins

Dick Williams was her business manager now in Kansas, but his work was still under her close supervision. Elizabeth was still most definitely in charge.

In August 1924, the Supreme Court of Louisiana finally reached a decision on JB's estate. By disputing the estate, the heirs had extended the settlement by years, and Elizabeth had attorney fees to pay because of their lawsuits. Now free to sell those properties and divide the proceeds, Elizabeth sent partial settlement checks to the appropriate relatives. She had kept "ledgers" that showed which relatives had already received advance payments.

December found Elizabeth again in Washington, DC, at the Shoreham Hotel. Her wards, Lillian Gardner and Margaret Graye, visited her there; she wrote Stuart that "the girls have visited and we had lots of fun. There is nothing quite like youth—and old age."

For Christmas 1924, she had a radio installed at The Outlook and once again enjoyed giving many gifts: money to friends, relatives, and employees. She requested that no gifts be given to her. Again, she closed out the year in California.

The year 1925 began with Elizabeth falling quite ill in Salina, Kansas. She went to a sanitarium and then came to rest at home under doctors' care. Dr. Hertzen, a famous surgeon and physician who treated her in Salina, believed she would return to good health quickly.

On March 4, 1925, Elizabeth recorded the final settlement papers for JB's estate in Kansas. It encompassed Hamilton, Wilson, Stevens, Greeley, Meade, Gray, Logan, Haskell, Stanton, Ness, Clark, Grant, Lane, Wichita, Cheyenne, and Comanche Counties.

She was still trying to sell land in Louisiana, but oil had been discovered

Chapter Eight

Portrait of Jabez Bunting Watkins, by A. H. Clark,
commissioned by Elizabeth for Watkins Scholarship Hall.
(Courtesy of Watkins Scholarship Hall, University of Kansas)

and she wanted to maximize her situation. There was talk of selling four thousand acres, but in a "checkerboard" fashion so that she would still own some property if oil was found under it. She humorously commented, "I might have a bilious attack if oil is found on Burton's field, but I will try to be a good sport." This did complicate the liquidation of her landholdings in Louisiana.

In June, she had a sleeping porch built "over the east porch," as she planned to stay in Lawrence that summer. In July she received the oil painting of JB she had commissioned from A. H. Clark. Pleased with the result, she wrote: "I have a wonderful new oil painting of JB. It all but speaks. I will place it in Watkins Hall for girls which I intend to build." This was the first time Elizabeth had related her intention to implement the plans that she and JB had made. By August, she had selected the architect for the scholarship hall.

Also in August 1925, Elizabeth learned of the death of JB's sister Maria Thomson in Lake Charles. As noted earlier, Maria's husband, Alexander, was possibly related to Stuart Thomson, in the web of relatives employed in the Watkins enterprises. In one letter that hinted at that family tie, Elizabeth thanked Stuart for "remaining with Zena (Maria's only child) to the end" and commented "I wish I could be more comfort to her."

The Thomson family had been steadfast in their support of Elizabeth throughout the fight over JB's estate. Now Zena had to adjust to her new life without the burden of caring for her mother. In a letter to Elizabeth, she said she thought she would try a career in real estate, rather than teaching, and asked if she could have her father's (Alexander's) desk, which was in the back room of Stuart's office. Elizabeth gave her blessing—if it was all right with Stuart.

As 1926 began, Elizabeth must have reflected on the previous five years spent in litigation and strife. It is no wonder that she determined that "my greatest object is to realize the most I can from lands and invest it to the glory of God in my lifetime and leave just as little as possible to be fought over when I am no more."

Elizabeth's Dream Come True

It had taken Elizabeth five years to settle JB's estate. Five long years as she fought the family and stood by her belief that she was doing exactly as she and JB had planned with the money she had helped him make. Those years solidified her confidence in herself. Her business experience gave her the determination to find a way to accomplish her goals. She was a formidable woman who was, at the same time, caring and empathetic. During those years, she had thought about how she would spend her time and talent once the estate was settled. Now was her opportunity.

Elizabeth began a great experiment. The desire to help young people "to get an education" was a common thread in JB and Elizabeth's lives. Now, working with "all speed I can command," she took their plans a step further with her idea for designing and building a women's scholarship hall at the University of Kansas. Despite her success in life, Elizabeth always regretted not getting a college degree. She gave serious thought to her "theory" of a hall for girls who, like her, would need financial help to go to college. Her plan was based on her keen insight into the needs of young women and her desire to keep the costs low for the residents.

Elizabeth envisioned a cooperative scholarship hall for women, the first of its kind in America. Watkins Hall opened in 1926 as a residence for deserving but financially challenged young women. In the *University Daily Kansan* of June 1, 1939, Elizabeth is quoted: "I have never done anything into which I have put more of myself. The color scheme of every room, the furniture, draperies and furnishings are results of many months of planning. It is my dream come true."

So much work went into this dream of Elizabeth's; we must look at it more closely.

Perhaps Elizabeth had read the November 1908 KU *Graduate Magazine.*[*] It contained a ten-page summary of housing complaints by Laura Lockwood, an 1894 KU graduate who later taught at Wellesley College. Lockwood's essay compared the advantages of organized living units for women with the existing rooming house system, which she considered "a danger to their health and well-being, and a detriment to their development as examples of wise and noble womanhood."

Shirley Ward Keeler, in the January 1959 KU *Alumni Magazine*, wrote that "Chancellor Frank Strong shared Miss Lockwood's opinion and included a $75,000 request for a women's dormitory in the 1908 University budget, explaining: 'a great many mothers will not allow their daughters to come to the University of Kansas because of the great inadequacy of accommodation. It is absurd to expect that the daughters of the family will go to the University and put up with uncomfortable and unsanitary conditions.' The state legislature thought the [women's housing] situation not quite so pressing, however, and turned down the Chancellor's request—marking the first of a long series of failures in the almost two-decade long battle for a women's residence hall." The "battle" was to obtain public, or state, money to build a women's residence.

Three cooperative houses had been established to provide a good home at a reasonable cost to girls who had to live economically while in school. The first house, at 1127 Ohio Street, was donated by Professor John Ise and opened in fall 1919; money to run it had been given by the women of the university. Residents were expected to learn tolerance, teamwork, and leadership, all through hard work. And, in 1923, a women's dormitory, Corbin Hall, was finally built at KU.[†]

Elizabeth dreamed of something different. She had her own ideas but knew the value of expert advice. After conferring with the faculty of KU's School of Architecture, she chose Thomas Williamson, an architect from nearby Topeka, to draw her "dream." Williamson had already proved his

---

* The *Graduate Magazine* was KU's alumni publication from 1920 until September 1950, when the name changed to *Alumni Magazine.*
† Fred McElhenie's *Making Do and Getting Through: KU Co-ops, Halls and Houses 1919–1966* (Lawrence, KS: Historic Mount Oread Fund, 2006) details the university's journey to provide good housing for its students.

worth, having built a number of county courthouses around Kansas. He designed the Jayhawk Hotel, Theater and Walk in Topeka, and his favorite project was the beautiful Topeka High School; both designs are on the National Register of Historic Places.

Elizabeth wanted to provide a supportive environment for young women, and she used architecture to further that psychological goal. She said, "I planned the hall so that the girls would have the advantages of life in a small group along with those enjoyed by a larger unit." The lower level of the hall had a general utility room used for larger meetings and dinners, and, more importantly, it had seven small kitchens. Women living in the hall were divided into seven kitchen groups, six or seven in each. They prepared meals for each other; each one prepared one lunch and one dinner per week. These kitchen groups became support groups, as Elizabeth had planned. Not only did the women save money by cooking for themselves, but what could be nicer than coming back from class to a home-cooked meal every day? Susan Harshaw Kissinger, who lived in Watkins from 1970 to 1974, noted the advantage of "only having to clean up once a week!" Elizabeth knew these small kitchen groups would become like a small family circle for each girl. Many were from small towns in Kansas, from farms and rural areas, and were away from home for the first time. Conversations around these kitchen tables encouraged and empowered the women, as the alumnae have repeatedly reported through the years.* The kitchens are still there, close to a hundred years later, providing safe and cozy places to talk, dream, plan, and listen.

Companionship was not Elizabeth's only goal, however. Her second unique idea for the hall was that the women would do daily chores to care for their beautiful home. In the beginning, all the residents were awakened each morning by a chime and did their duties before class. This instilled responsibility, discipline, and order—and again, saved them money.

Third in Elizabeth's plan was that the hall would be self-directed. As long as she lived, she personally hired and paid for a mature lady, a housemother, who lived in the small apartment on the ground floor of the hall. The first housemother, Jane Morrow, was paid $60 per month. Her job

* Kitchen 8 is the very active alumnae group of Watkins and Miller Halls. Residents' comments are found in the Kitchen 8 Archives, Watkins Museum of History.

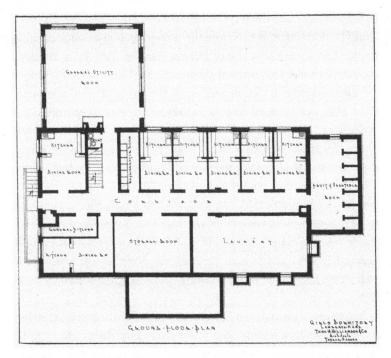

Drawing of the ground floor plan, showing the seven small kitchens unique to Elizabeth's design for her dormitory. (Kitchen 8 Archives, Watkins Museum of History. Reproduction of pamphlet by University of Kansas, *Watkins Hall, Residence for Women* [Topeka: Kansas State Printing Plant, 1926])

was to oversee the young women and be present for advice and in case of emergencies. But the hall residents developed their own constitution and disciplinary rules. A pamphlet to advertise Watkins Hall, printed in 1926 by the Kansas State Printing Plant, states that the hall's "self-government is maintained in harmony with the ideals set forth by the Women's Self-Government Association." The *University Daily Kansan*, May 28, 1939, reported "The purpose of the Women's Self-Governing Association is to foster among women students a feeling of mutual responsibility. . . . Eight years before the National Women's Suffrage amendment, the right to vote was given to women students of the University [of Kansas]. On May 14, 1912, the feminine voters went to the polls to elect officers for their own student government."

To fully understand the importance of these votes in women's history, it should be noted that at this time the university had a policy of "in loco parentis." This means that the university was the parental authority for young women while they were at the university (but interestingly, not for young men). This policy continued until the 1970s. That the women of Watkins Hall were trusted to govern themselves was an example of forward thinking. The Women's Self-Government Association also served as a resource for the university. On October 13, 1986, Emily Taylor, a former dean of women at KU, was interviewed by the *University Daily Kansan.* Back in Lawrence to discuss the changing roles of women at the sixtieth anniversary of Watkins Hall, she said, "When I came here, things were pretty status quo—you remember the '50's .... Some women were still willing to be Victorian. They would go from being dependent on father, to husband, to son. . . . So much needed to be done." It was a historic first step for women students when Watkins Hall was self-directed by its own residents.

As noted, one focal point of Elizabeth's design for the hall was the lower level with its seven kitchens. In a letter dated September 28, 1925, Dick Williams, Mrs. Watkins's personal business manager, wrote to the architectural firm of Williamson & Co.: "We have received the first floor plan of the Girl's dormitory which is to be built by Mrs. Watkins, but we are more anxious to receive the basement plan and get the elevation at the earliest possible moment so that the excavation may be started."

The location Elizabeth selected for Watkins Hall was near her home, The Outlook, just to the north. She could easily watch the construction. The stone removed from the building site was saved for a stone wall that would be built along Lilac Lane in front of Watkins Hall.

As excavation began for the hall, workmen uncovered an old skillet and an army stirrup. Such items had been found earlier when The Outlook, next door, was built; these also were thought to have come from barracks that were set up on Mount Oread to protect Lawrence during Quantrill's raids. The story was covered later by the *Kansas City Star* on February 21, 1938, when there was further construction at the site.

Always financially savvy, Elizabeth watched her money and never paid until the desired outcome was achieved. In a letter of November 20, 1925, she directed Dick Williams to write that Mrs. Watkins had been advised to pay only $800.00, a part of the architect's fee. Dick wrote to ask if this would be acceptable to Williamson & Co. We don't see the reply in the file, but it was obviously "no." In a letter one week later Dick Williams wrote, "I am enclosing, herewith, Mrs. Watkins' check for $1200.00 in payment of the 3% fee on the estimated cost of $40,000.00 for the plans for the girls' dormitory." Paid in full.

Public interest in the construction site grew, as seen in the letter of November 27, 1925, from Dick Williams to Williamson & Co.: "There has been a reporter here several times to see me concerning a cut [drawing] for the Graduate Magazine and I have repeatedly told him that we did not have a cut of the building and he asked me who the architects were and I suppose will write to you. I want to tell you that it will be no favor to us if you put yourself to any trouble for him."

This reporter for the *Graduate Magazine* was a young Fred Ellsworth, who went on to become an important figure at the University of Kansas. He was editor of the alumni magazine from 1924 to 1963, and was later the secretary of the KU Alumni Association for many years. Young Fred did indeed write to Williamson & Co.:

> Dear Mr. Williamson: I am eager to get a story about the Women's Dormitory being built by Mrs. Watkins on the campus of the University for The Graduate Magazine. . . . You are doubtless the only one who could tell us about the building . . . what it will look like, how it is to be arranged, the size etc. etc. I am writing to ask if you will write a short article for the magazine concerning the building, how the work is progressing and whatever other facts you wish to bring out. If it is impossible for you to run out the finished article I would be glad to get enough facts from which I might write the article myself. It would be much better however to get the complete article from you. The magazine goes to press December 2.

Fred Ellsworth got his article and a lovely etching of Watkins Hall for the *Graduate Magazine.**

Elizabeth was not feeling well at this time, not even well enough to climb the stairs to her second-story office at the Watkins National Bank.

---

* An article in the 1925 *Graduate Magazine* by Fred Ellsworth is essentially his speech about Elizabeth's philanthropy.

Etching of Watkins Scholarship Hall. (Kitchen 8 Archives, Watkins Museum
of History. Reproduction of pamphlet by University of Kansas, *Watkins Hall,
Residence for Women* [Topeka: Kansas State Printing Plant, 1926])

She had a desk and a typewriter table moved from the bank to the new dormitory. This way she could oversee the building's construction progress more easily. As always, she was meticulous in supervising her projects. She had learned from JB, and it was second nature to her now.

Of course, there were other events in her daily life to occupy her during the construction of Watkins Hall. Elizabeth's cooks were gone for a bit on vacation, so she tried to cook for herself. She reports not being too pleased with the results. She went to Kansas City to a dentist to see if he could get her false teeth to fit better. "When I get through I might send these to the Near East," she joked. Trying to improve her health, she decided not to eat red meats and acidic fruits.

In November 1925, she bought yet another car, a Lincoln Limousine Car, model 139S for $5,890. On a trip to New York, she again spent the evening with Mr. Patterson, whom she enjoyed but had no interest in marrying. And for Christmas 1925, she had the pleasure of sending many checks to family and friends.

Good progress was being made on the construction of Watkins Hall in early 1926, and she felt she could leave Lawrence and the project for a while. She traveled to Beaumont, Texas, throughout western Kansas, and to Denver. In western Kansas, she and Dick Williams checked on the lands she owned. Mary Gossard Williams, Dick's wife, joined them in their travels. At a number of her farms, wells had been dug for irrigation, and they began to hire people to break sod in preparation for planting wheat. With irrigation, the returns from the wheat fields would be very good.

Elizabeth continued to communicate with Stuart Thomson, her business manager in Louisiana. They were still trying to sell her Louisiana land but wouldn't take a poor price. There was continual speculation about oil and drilling around some of her land. Dick Williams's influence is seen in Elizabeth's letter to Stuart in late 1926: "Dick thinks it's an opportune time as any to accept the Yount-Lee proposition." The letter mentions her hopes that oil would be struck close to her holdings, also that the girls' dormitory was coming along but that it "licks up ready cash." She returned to Lawrence to oversee the hall and as always, relied on Stuart for matters in Louisiana.

As the scholarship hall neared completion, she began to buy furnishings for it. She purchased a clock for the hall from Parsons Jewelry in Lawrence. The furniture was purchased through Rumsey Brothers of Tonganoxie, Kansas. She bought another piano for the hall from Sohmer & Son in New York and ordered dishes from T. M. James & Sons China Company in Kansas City, Missouri. The order was for a service for sixty, plus serving pieces, marked "Syracuse" and also a Bavarian China set, "Irene" pattern, for formal dinners. Silverware was also ordered, to be engraved "Watkins Hall." Linens, ordered from Innes, Hackman in Lawrence, included curtain rods, sheets, pillows, lamps, etc.

A bronze plaque was made for the hall; it reads "Watkins Hall The gift of Elizabeth M. Watkins to the University of Kansas in memory of Jabez B. Watkins 1926." The first plaque delivered had the name error "Jabez B. Hopkins" but that was quickly remedied. Imagine Elizabeth's reaction! And, as planned, she placed the painting of JB by A. H. Clark in Watkins Hall upon completion of construction; it remains there, nearly a hundred years later.

On October 14, 1926, Elizabeth wrote to Stuart Thomson: "The

Bronze plaque dedicating Watkins Hall in memory of JB, Elizabeth's husband, in 1926. (Courtesy of First City Photo, Debra Bates Lamborn, Leavenworth, KS)

dormitory cost considerably more than expected but I do not regret the venture. I think it is a good investment and will prove my theory to be a success and will help many students in the years to come to get an education."

A good investment at $75,000, yes. Nearly one hundred years later, it is still functioning as Elizabeth envisioned. Thousands of young women have been aided by Elizabeth's "theory."

A stone name plate to be placed above the front door had been ordered, but Elizabeth was not pleased with the drawing. Dick Williams again communicated her suggestion to Williamson & Co. A new drawing was submitted, and the name plate above the front door and casements was approved and installed.

The beautiful columned entry into Watkins Hall showed Elizabeth's respect for these young women and their hard work to get an education. Most of the residents had never before lived in such a large, gracious home with a chandelier in the foyer, curving stairway, and fireplace with mantel. Elizabeth wanted "her girls" to experience the better things in life that an education and confidence could bring.

The formal opening of Watkins Hall finally arrived. Elizabeth wrote on October 21, 1926, again to Stuart:

Early photograph of the living room of Watkins Scholarship Hall.
(Douglas County Historical Society, Watkins Museum of History)

View of the front entry with chandelier and formal stairway in Watkins
Scholarship Hall. (Kenneth Spencer Research Library, University of Kansas)

Football game Saturday. I am to be a guest of the Chancellor and wife along with the Governor of the State and members of the Board of Regents. We open Watkins Hall tomorrow to the public. The Chancellor and wife, the House President, the Chaperone, Dean of Women and your humble servant, receive. The house is beautiful and as it was "Homecoming" day for the Alumni the Chancellor thought it would be an appropriate time to give our friends the chance to inspect as so many are anxious to see it. It seems to be a success in every way and it is doing good beyond my expectations.

It was, indeed, a success in every way. Applications came in and the hall was full upon opening. The process of being approved for residency, however, was not an easy one. Elizabeth insisted on giving a hand up, not a handout. Again, from the 1926 pamphlet advertising Watkins Hall:

Candidates must give evidence of high character, integrity, steadfastness of purpose, initiative and capacity for cooperation. All candidates must be in good health and must pass satisfactorily the examination of the University Department of Physical Education. Applicants who are freshmen or new students are to furnish:

1. An official record of their school work.

2. Testimonials from: a. The superintendent or principal of the school or the president or dean of the college which they have attended. b. Their dean of women. c. Another well-known citizen. d. A banker of their community with regard to the applicant's financial need. . . .

Tenure of scholarship is conditioned on the student's continuing to maintain a high standard in conduct and scholarship and on her showing ability to cooperate with her house-mates. The scholarships are awarded for one year, but they may be renewed under certain conditions for another year.

Other house responsibilities are detailed in this publication, such as the requirement that one to two hours a day be spent in hall duties. The hall furnished table linens, sheets, and pillow slips, but each girl was to furnish "her own bed covers, bed spreads, towels and such table and dresser scarfs as she wishes to use."

Although there is little in the written record, Watkins Hall legend reports that Elizabeth would drop by unexpectedly to see if the chores were being done. A place was set for her every Sunday at dinner, just in case she would come. At times, she did! Sunday dinner was a dress occasion calling for the young women to wear dresses, heels and hose. We know from the hall secretary's notes that Elizabeth was especially invited for Thanksgiving dinners. On her birthday, the girls sent her flowers or chocolates, her favorites.

A rare surviving record from those early days of Watkins Hall comes from Harriet Cowles Dyer, one of the first KU students to be selected as a hall resident in 1926. She described Mrs. Watkins as "a queen of kindness, but really down-to-earth." Doris Kent Fox, who lived in Watkins from 1935 to 1937, gives a good mental picture of the sort of young woman Elizabeth's "dream" had helped. In a letter dated March 13, 2000, to Judge Jack A. Murphy in Lawrence, she wrote:

> Your Honor: Winning a residency in K.U.'s Watkins Hall in 1935 meant everything to me, and Mrs. Elizabeth Watkins lived next door. I had no funds for college, my mother received $40 a month to support four children, and the $40 a month I earned writing a column a day in Humboldt for the Iola Daily Register (while commuting to Iola Junior College) barely got us thru. Assured of a K.U. residency (at Watkins Hall), I applied for and was hired as secretary to Professor L. N. Flint, head of Journalism, in between my full schedule of classes. That blessed monthly $40, and such a magnificent residence On Top Of The Hill, how lucky could a girl be? That supported me to my degree in Journalism. Only because of Mrs. Watkins' genius of planning seven kitchens on the bottom floor of Watkins Hall (six women to a kitchen, three meals a day) we took turns cooking, bought supplies wholesale, and each got thru the month on $7. I believe we paid $13 each per semester for Watkins Hall, and $18 for activities fee to K.U.

Doris Kent Fox was the very sort of student Elizabeth wished to reach and soon the hall was full of bright, motivated young women just like her. Mary Ellen Roach Higgins, who lived in Watkins from 1938 to 1942, recalled "meeting Mrs. Watkins twice—Once in the entryway at Watkins Hall and being shown around her elegant home—now the Chancellor's home, I believe. At Watkins she wore a dress of 1890's style—with standing collar."

Elizabeth's kindness and generosity were remembered by Katherine Monroe Cook, a resident of the hall from 1929 to 1933. She related that once Mrs. Watkins took all the women in the hall to a chicken dinner, and then gave them each $10. Cook, who described herself as nearly broke at the time, found the gift very meaningful. Frances Strait Brown, a resident of Watkins from 1936 to 1938, remembered that "Elizabeth Watkins often visited Watkins Hall & I had the privilege of meeting her several times. She was a most gracious and caring person and always interested in the welfare of the students."

In May 1926, Elizabeth even gave monetary gifts to the first Watkins Hall graduates: Mary Jane Crum, Ruth Quinlan, Elberta Weig, Lyndall Nutter, Olive Figge, Esther Settle, Esther Jane Jones, and Mayme Howell.

Housemothers of the hall became the role models Elizabeth had envisioned. Many alumni recall their housemother inviting a few of the girls into her small apartment for tea. These teas provided an opportunity to teach manners to girls whose families didn't have those refinements. This gave these young women the confidence to go into any social setting. Elizabeth understood that such confidence was important as part of a complete education. In the 1950s, Mother Julia Willard was a special favorite of the women. There was an unfortunate situation where a girl had to leave the hall before the end of the semester. At the house meeting, Mother Willard explained the circumstance to all the women in the hall and ended her short speech with "He who is without sin cast the first stone." This loving example of nonjudgmental behavior stayed with a house full of impressionable young women all of their lives.

Now that Watkins Hall was working as Elizabeth had dreamed it would, she prepared to build another—between Watkins Hall and The Outlook. She also hoped to build a similar hall for boys but that dream never materialized.

Elizabeth's thoroughness and attention to detail are evident in the official deed to Watkins Hall, Deed Record No. 118, State of Kansas, Douglas County, which was transferred to the Kansas State Board of Regents on November 23, 1926. The deed contains written stipulations: the university was to purchase adequate insurance, Elizabeth was to choose an

The first class of women to live in Watkins Scholarship Hall in 1926.
(Kenneth Spencer Research Library, University of Kansas)

Watkins Scholarship Hall class of 1945 to 1946, with their beloved housemother
Julia Willard, *center*. (Kitchen 8 Archives, Watkins Museum of History)

appropriate housemother, and a committee was to oversee the rental charges the residents were subjected to. It goes so far as to specify that "fees charged the occupants of said dormitory shall not exceed the sum of Three Dollars ($3.00) per month without unanimous written consent of a committee"—said committee to be composed of trusted town businesspeople and Dick Williams. This restriction on rent was followed for a number of years, but it didn't last long after Elizabeth's death, unfortunately for the residents.

In December 1926 Elizabeth's friends took her to New Paris, Ohio, to visit her birthplace home. The house was there, but the school, church, and remembered people were gone. "No room left for heartaches," she remarked about the trip. On returning to Lawrence, she was ill with complications of flu and intestinal troubles. Her doctor from Kansas City treated her. She received a phone call from Mr. Patterson in New York and relished sending out her usual Christmas gifts.

Each time she was ill, quiet, and resting, it seems she reflected on her relationship with JB and how much they had benefited from each other. "I never for a moment thought I was the only woman in his life but was sure that he cared for me as no one else."

Still concerned about oil exploration and timber on her Louisiana land, she began to think about the future. If a good profit couldn't be made at that time, then she had a plan. She would keep it and give it to KU, telling them to hold it for twenty years after her death. Elizabeth's remarkable foresight established a legacy that would long outlive both her and JB. Watkins Scholarship Hall was just the beginning of her contributions to the public good and to KU.

Watkins Hall helped the young women who lived there, financially and socially, and also contributed to the overall atmosphere and diversity of the university. Many foreign students who came to KU also benefited from Elizabeth's scholarship house. In 1971, two Watkins women became naturalized citizens of the United States. Residents included young women who had fled from their homes: in the 1940s, from Nazi Germany, and, in the 1970s, from communist Eastern Germany during the Cold War. These young women chose to live in Watkins Hall or, later, Miller Hall, the second women's scholarship hall, which Elizabeth built soon after the first. Donna Holm Fisher, resident from 1946 to 1949, called living in Watkins "a truly remarkable living experience, one I think that uniquely prepared me for the diverse world I would live in. The colors, language, customs and cultures brought to the table, moving through the rooms . . . a whole education in itself, fleshing out the one I was receiving in the classroom."

Had Elizabeth thought ahead to this wonderful result? Had she envisioned the dynamic of all these young women, from so many different walks of life, living together in her halls? Had she realized they would learn tolerance and acceptance, along with studying, cooking, and housekeeping? From Elizabeth's own example of appreciating and enjoying all people, it is easy to conclude she had.

CHAPTER

Building the City of Lawrence

Early 1927 found Elizabeth ill again with a sore throat and the flu, but she soon felt well enough to travel to California for her annual escape from the cold. However, while she was there, she developed a temperature and was in bed for four days. She consulted a throat specialist and had "very good care," as she wrote home. It rained a lot but the "hotel didn't leak and the food is good." There was even a slight earthquake for excitement.

Back home in Lawrence, in April and May 1927, she was feeling much better. On April 28 she wrote playfully to Stuart Thomson, her business manager in Louisiana, that she was "entertaining club of 30 tomorrow, invited to three parties this week—gardening and setting 5 hens—So there!"

Elizabeth was greatly attached to her favorite cook, Bertha, and always felt better when at home with "Bertha's good cooking." But now, misfortune struck. Bertha was getting married! In that era, married women did not work outside the home. Although Elizabeth gave Bertha a "substantial wedding present," she was not happy about having to search for, locate, hire, and break in a new cook. She wrote to Stuart rather melodramatically that she "felt abandoned" but that her faith would help her. She was "depending upon the Lord to help me find help. He has a lot of times, in the meantime, I'm keeping my eye out, in conjunction with His assistance." Heavenly intervention must have helped, for soon she found a new cook who made "waffles as good as Bertha's." Elizabeth did enjoy her food!

She had to borrow money to pay her taxes that year; as usual, she was short of ready cash. The oil question in Louisiana was heating up as discoveries were made near her land. Meanwhile, she was in bed once again, with a sore throat and intestinal flu. She sold some bonds to pay off the final $95,000 debt of the Watkins Land and Mortgage Co., proud to remain true to her instincts and true to JB's legacy.

Then in November 1927, oil was found on the Hackney land, near her property. The Calcasieu Oil Company sent a telegram to Elizabeth: "Calcasieu Oil Co. advised that you have granted surface lease to Yount Lee Oil Co. Against your interests. Would enable drilling that would drain your lands." Her reliance on Dick Williams is evident in the letter she wrote to Stuart about this lease; she said she simply couldn't make a decision at that time, as "I haven't Dick's counsel." The plan to divest this land would need to be settled soon, however.

Dick Williams, who had been unwell, continued to travel and work until his illness reached a critical state. He was admitted to the hospital, suffering from septicemia caused by infection in his tonsils, which had to be removed. His recovery was very slow, and, when he was finally allowed to leave the hospital, Elizabeth insisted he recover at The Outlook, with a nurse to care for him. Dick was married, and he and his wife had two small boys, Skip and Odd. Although Elizabeth was very fond of the little boys, she felt Dick needed to rest in a quiet place in order to recover his strength. Of course, his recovery would be good for business, but she showed a level of care that was personal and more than a bit maternal.

On December 31, 1927, she wrote again to Stuart, "Tomorrow is a New Year. How the years fly—truly winged!" Reflections on the year past gave way to plans for the new year. Dick Williams was recovering, and she was ready for another project. She was ready to "take up the new hospital."

The city of Lawrence needed a new hospital badly. In the early 1900s a story was told that a doctor had been called to attend an elderly African American man who had fallen in a fit on the sidewalk near the Eldridge Hotel. At the time there were three small, private hospitals owned by local physicians: Lawrence Hospital and Radium Institute at 1201 Ohio, McConnell Hospital at 744 New Hampshire, and Simmons Hospital at 805 Ohio. None of the hospitals had charity beds available and none would admit the elderly man, who died before he could be treated or even identified. As this story spread, so did awareness of the need for a municipal hospital in Lawrence.

In 1919 the Social Service League bought a frame house at 201 Maine

Street from the George Barker estate. Through a trust agreement, they gave the house to the city to use as a hospital. After about $10,000 was raised for repairs and equipment, Lawrence Memorial Hospital opened on January 17, 1921. It could serve a maximum ten to fifteen patients; and the county's population was 12,456 in 1920. By the mid- to late 1920s, as community dependence on the hospital increased, this capacity was becoming inadequate. The citizens of the county were asked to vote on bonds to build a hospital large enough for a city of Lawrence's size. Some doubted the bond could pass.

Mayor R. C. Rankin related the following story:

While sitting in the mayors' office one afternoon the phone rang and a lady asked if she might come in to see me, and was invited to come. I did not have the slightest idea what her business might be. It is not possible for me to describe my feelings when Mrs. Elizabeth Watkins came in a little later, and when she had regained her breath, after climbing those awful stairs in the Old City Hall, she sat down and informed me that she had come to offer to give the money to build a new hospital for the City of Lawrence. I almost fell out of my chair. If ever a dream came true for me—it did that day. I have never experienced a greater thrill of real joy.*

In an effort to secure the best architect, Elizabeth and Dr. M. T. Sudler made a trip to Chicago, where they stayed in the Hotel Sherman. After interviewing several, they hired Coolidge and Hodgson for the sum of $1,000.00. Elizabeth hoped that the contract to build could be let by February 1928. In July the bids were finally received, and she was getting a bit impatient. When the architect reviewed the contract, which was already signed by all parties, he wanted to make some small changes. Elizabeth thought he was "making a fuss about something that should not bother him." On the hospital executives' insistence, they rewrote the contract and gave it to Dick Williams and Elizabeth to sign and mail. Elizabeth didn't even bother to send or have the architect sign the new contract! She did not "suffer fools gladly" and wanted to get the project moving. Mont Green was to be the contractor and F. A. Russell superintendent of the project.

* Mayor Robert Rankin wrote "An Idea That Grew" about the progression of the idea and the need for a city hospital in Lawrence. The *Kansas City Star,* September 22, 1929, details the hospital opening.

Elizabeth knew Professor Russell, who taught civil engineering at KU, from their joint attendance at the Presbyterian Church.

Elizabeth had purchased five lots in West Lawrence, at the corner of Fourth and Maine, for $800 from the Perkins estate. That was where the hospital would be built. Construction began and the foundations were almost completed by September.

In January 1928, Elizabeth sold 11,285 acres in Louisiana including mineral rights for $1,000,000.00. This was the beginning of the dispersal of all her holdings in Louisiana. The check came by registered mail. Since she would put it in the First National Bank in Kansas City, she would need to keep it at home for a few days until she could be driven to the city. She put it under the corner of the rug in her bedroom!

During 1928 the Watkins National Bank had been in serious monetary trouble. There was the prospect of a merger with Lawrence National Bank. When the merger occurred in October 1928, Elizabeth moved most of her money from the First National Bank in Kansas City back to Lawrence, to the Lawrence National Bank.

On a trip to Houston during 1928, she and Mr. Patterson saw the musical *Show Boat.* She remarked that it was the best performance she had ever seen. She felt it "was true to the book" by Edna Ferber, which she had read. Also, in 1928 she purchased some annuities for herself and relatives Josie Gardner and Mrs. E. M. Davis. Faithful to the commitment she and JB had made to take care of family, she bought those annuities to ensure that each relative would get a monthly income.

In a letter to Stuart Thomson on November 9, 1928, she revealed that she had another generous and practical gift to the city of Lawrence in mind: she contemplated giving the Watkins Bank building to the city of Lawrence to use as a city hall. "I would reserve an office where it is during my lifetime and five years following, if needed."

In this same line of correspondence of November 1928, she suggested that she and Stuart use a "code" for the financial discussions in their letters. The hard bargaining on the price for the remainder of her Louisiana land had begun with Miles Franklin Yount, the oilman from Texas.

Her usual Christmas checks were sent and recorded with delight. She did enjoy treating those she loved and those who helped her. The end of 1928 found Elizabeth again thinking about the future. "There is no use scattering my gifts." She didn't spell out what she envisioned, but it became evident with time.

In early 1929, as dealing with the details of JB's estate dragged on, Elizabeth gave public notice of the dissolution of the mortgage company. This was just one of many loose ends to be tied up because JB died without a valid will and his estate included multiple companies, land holdings, and investments.

Shortly before Lawrence Memorial Hospital was ready to open, Elizabeth presented the Watkins Bank building to the city of Lawrence for use as its city hall. It was a most welcome gift. The new city hall had more space than the previous one, and it was in a beautiful building right on Massachusetts Street. Every resident of Lawrence benefited from this present, which was free of charge, no taxes or bonds required. Another gift that had been on her mind was accomplished. She was giving her fellow citizens a hospital and a city hall.

By May 1929, the hospital building was ready to furnish. Elizabeth used many of the same vendors as she had for Watkins Scholarship Hall: Stickley Brothers Furniture of Grand Rapids, Michigan; Rumsey Brothers of Tonganoxie, Kansas; Missouri China Company of Kansas City, Missouri. The city paid for a bronze dedication plaque. She paid directly for equipment and furnishings. Both she and Dick Williams spent a great deal of time on the hospital. Dick had learned from Elizabeth to check all bills and receipts, as the careful pattern set in place by JB continued.

When Elizabeth had another period of bad health and asked that the formal opening of the hospital be delayed, Mayor Rankin was happy to oblige her request. With her stomach issues, rheumatism, and throat problems, health had become a constant concern. This time stomach problems, along with high blood pressure and rheumatism, sent her to spend some time in the hot baths at Excelsior Springs, Missouri. Elizabeth needed to care for her health because she was determined to continue working as long as she could. When she was "laid up," she passed the time between doctor's visits reading books, including *The Age of Reason, Foolish Virgin, The President's Daughters,* and *Disraeli,* and magazines like the *Literary Digest* and the *National Geographic.* She believed that some of her ill health was caused by her nerves; she said she was on edge because people and things tended to make her nervous.

When Elizabeth returned to Lawrence in June, one of the first things she did was buy a new car. The 1928 Cadillac 7 Imperial 4166 in Olympia Brown had natural wood wheels, a trunk rack, and fender wells and was monogrammed. It cost $4,537.50, and she was given a $1,250 allowance, or trade-in, on the Lincoln.

In July 1929 she went to Crawford, New Hampshire, to escape the heat. She was plagued with chronic colitis and had high blood pressure (210); perhaps now that the hospital was nearly completed, she would feel less stress. She was placed on a careful diet, with no sweets, which must have been hard for her, but her health improved. She lost twenty-five pounds—and later gained it back. Once back home, she purchased two KU season football tickets from Dr. Forrest C. (Phog) Allen for $16.26.

The public and formal opening of the Lawrence Memorial Hospital took place on September 26, 1929. The modern, well-equipped facility had fifty-two beds. Elizabeth had built and fully equipped the lovely Georgian Colonial hospital, at a cost of $200,000; at the formal opening, she sold it to the city for $1.00.

Elizabeth described receiving flowers at her home, sent to express the thanks of many of the local business leaders. She noted that at the ceremony there had been a line a hundred feet long of people waiting to shake her hand and thank her. Although she professed to be "embarrassed about the attention," she pasted newspaper clippings about the event into her personal scrapbook. She must have felt great satisfaction at adding to the quality of the lives of her fellow citizens.

Elizabeth often paid hospital bills for people who couldn't afford them. She called these people "guests." They wouldn't know their bill was paid until they left the hospital. A pond was built in front of the hospital and planted with lilies, but dogs kept getting into the pond and spoiling the lilies.

Once the hospital was finished, Elizabeth saw an additional need. Innately sympathetic to young working women, she noticed that the nurses would benefit from having a safe, clean place to live near the hospital. She hired the architect H. G. Pottenger of Manhattan, Kansas, to design a simple but functional structure. Basil Green was again the general contractor, and the project began in July 1930. The new nurses' home for Lawrence Memorial Hospital staff would be at 345 Maine Street.

Chapter Ten

Lawrence Memorial Hospital on the right, with nurses' home on the left.
(pamphlet, Watkins Memorial Hospital, 1931. Kenneth Spencer Research Library,
University of Kansas)

In a letter to Green on August 14, 1930, Elizabeth directed him to wait
until she was back in Lawrence in September to decide on the interior decoration of the nurses' home. As with Watkins Scholarship Hall, Elizabeth
was an integral participant in the project, not just the source of funds. And
when, in 1935, the nurses' home needed repairs and renovations, she was
again ready to help.

A couple of years later, in 1937, she funded an addition to the Lawrence
Memorial Hospital, bringing the total beds to seventy-five. Following the
principles Jabez had taught her, her involvement in construction projects
extended to the details; she provided the funds and intended to be heard.
During the furnishing of the addition, she questioned the low quality of
some of the equipment being ordered and was told that "poorer, probably
black" people would be housed in that area. Elizabeth, who wanted all economic groups to be served equally, found this unacceptable, and the issue
was remedied immediately.

By 1938, it cost $4,200 yearly to operate Lawrence Memorial Hospital;
when the new wing opened in July 1939, daily rates went up: $2.75 for wards,
$5 for private rooms, and $5.50 for mothers and babies. The question was
discussed whether to raise rates or to request more tax money. Hospital
insurance for individuals was becoming more common at that time.

After intense negotiations, in November 1929, Elizabeth entered into a
contract with Miles Franklin Yount of Beaumont, Texas, for the sale of all

her remaining Louisiana properties, land, and companies. Yount headed one of the most successful private oil companies in the United States. Elizabeth wrote to Dick Williams from the Crawford House Hotel in New Hampshire that July, "I am sending you a copy of the letter received from Stuart Thomson yesterday. . . . I have explained to him that I have heard arguments on both sides, and he should know from past experience that I think for myself and make decisions accordingly." Her patience may have run out, but she remained a sharp negotiator. Elizabeth's ability to complete these negotiations, despite the uncertain economic environment of 1929, was remarkable—the Wall Street Crash of 1929 had begun in September.

After the sale was completed, the Watkins Land Co. had a cash balance of $4,425,761.55. Elizabeth would spend the rest of her life carrying out the plans she and JB had made together for the use of the fortune he had amassed with her help. She had sold the rice land to M. F. Yount for $2 million and the railroad to the Gould System for $1 million. As a side note, a clause in the deed of every parcel of JB's land sold in the South still carried a provision that liquor should never be sold on the premises; although this led to litigation, the clause was upheld by the Louisiana courts. With the proceeds from the Louisiana sales, Elizabeth bought bonds. She also got payments from annuities she had purchased the previous year.

After the Louisiana assets were sold, Elizabeth communicated less frequently with J. Stuart Thomson. Still, Stuart had also become her trusted friend, and he and his wife came to visit her several times at The Outlook. Although she had always relied on Stuart heavily, Dick Williams had truly taken his place by that time. A newspaper article from 1930 details a gathering of the Louisiana circle of Watkins business acquaintances at the wedding of Stuart's daughter. Among those in attendance were Zena Thomson, daughter of Alexander Thomson, and Hannah Chalkley, daughter of H. G. Chalkley Jr.

Much information is available about Elizabeth's interest in the city of Lawrence and the University of Kansas and its students. Less is known about her community involvement. She was a charter member of the Ingleside Club, the women's reading group; however, her full-time work in overseeing the Watkins enterprises may have kept her from being very active in the club. And an undercurrent is often sensed that Mr. and Mrs.

Jabez Watkins were not fully accepted in society in Lawrence. Her ongoing interest in education is seen in a letter to Mrs. Fred Bliesner of Lawrence, who had apparently asked Elizabeth to give an endorsement to a candidate for the Lawrence school board. She replied, "If using my influence for Dr. Kennedy's election as a member of the school board will help the public school situation, I shall do what I can, which might not be a great deal."

In keeping with JB's and her love of new cars, she bought another Cadillac, a 1929 Fisher Custom Line Cadillac Sedan, model 341. The price of cars had gone up to $7,113. She liked elegant cars even though she didn't drive. She always hired nice, handsome, young male KU students to drive her. She paid them a salary and bought their clothes for driving. One such driver was John May Wall.

In a 1993 interview, Wall related that he was her chauffeur for several years until 1931. He lived in the Watkins home on the second floor. He observed that she enjoyed children, especially the Williams boys, Odd and Skip. He would drive her to visit her friends in Lawrence, Mr. and Mrs. Weaver. They would go to Kansas City, where she banked and shopped at Emery, Bird, Thayer Dry Goods Company for dresses and furs. She was not extravagant but always well dressed. He would also drive her on out-of-town trips. Some were nearby, for instance, to Kansas City and Ottawa to buy salt-rising bread. There were quite a few longer trips. They would drive to Bay View, Michigan, and Crawford's Notch, New Hampshire, and even to Boston and Quebec. She never wanted to go anywhere before lunch and rarely went out at night, her former chauffeur reported.

Elizabeth assisted many students by helping with tuition and by hiring them as chauffeurs or for other work around The Outlook. One of these students was Art Hodgson, a Lyons, Kansas, attorney, farmer, and former president of the Kansas State Historical Society. His story, told in a letter written to an alumna of Watkins Hall and preserved at the Watkins Museum of History, illuminates Elizabeth's particular style of giving. The story began in 1927 when Art was a student at KU and was living in a rooming house owned by Coila Morrison, a friend of Elizabeth's. The ladies attended the Presbyterian church together. Art wrote: "I have seen Mrs. Watkins at the home of Mrs. Morrison on numerous occasions and I know that it would not be unusual for Mrs. Watkins to pick up Mrs. Morrison to go to some church affair."

The Emery, Bird, Thayer Dry Goods Company building on Eleventh Street between Walnut and Grand in 1901, some eleven years after its construction. This was Elizabeth's favorite shopping establishment. (Missouri Valley Special Collections, Kansas City Public Library, Kansas City, MO)

Although Art had a job waiting in New York after he graduated from KU, the Depression hit and the job didn't work out. Four years later, Art had accumulated enough money "to buy my law books and my first semester of tuition. I stayed (again) at Mrs. Morrison's and worked for her and I didn't have any other income except that of filling in as a waiter for some of the sororities." Art related that he had "a good-looking pair of corduroy trousers and I did have a handsome suede jacket. That was my wardrobe for all occasions. . . . Those were very difficult times and very few people were living 'very high on the hog.' The law school year of 33–34 was a strenuous one and Mrs. Morrison knew that it would be nice if I had a suit of clothes. She talked to me about it several times and I always told her I was getting along just fine."

One day . . . Mrs. Morrison said that Mrs. Watkins wanted me to come over to her home for Sunday dinner. Although I'd seen her many times and I'd talked with her several times I didn't feel that she knew me at all.

(155)

The sum and substance of it was that I had a nice Sunday dinner and a nice visit with Mrs. Watkins. She had a maid to serve the table and when she wanted the maid to appear she apparently pulled a cord back of the curtains which were just back of where she was seated. I don't remember specifically what the conversation was about but one thing I know, it wasn't about my finances or my wardrobe. . . . In the Spring of '34 I got a check from Mrs. Watkins for $75.00. It looked to me like about as big as $5,000 would look today. I bought a beautiful suit, I think it was $35.00 of good quality and about what I would expect to pay four or five hundred dollars today if I was going to wear that quality of suit. Few things ever happened in my life to give me as big a boost as that check gave me and I wrote her a handwritten letter thanking her. . . .

The second time I dined with Mrs. Watkins, and this would have been after she received my letter, she gave me some timely advice about my handwriting and suggested that I should do all that I could to improve it. I don't know whether she could read it or not but at least she could read it well enough to know that I was thankful and, of course, Mrs. Morrison knew how thankful I was and I am sure that she would have been the one who told Mrs. Watkins about my need and that except for Mrs. Morrison it is not likely that I would ever have gotten to know Mrs. Watkins. . . .

Since I was studying law Mrs. Watkins told us of an experience she had had and she brought suit against someone but she left it up to her attorney to handle it for her. She told me that after the matter was concluded the judge remarked to the attorney for Mrs. Watkins that if Mrs. Watkins didn't care enough about her case to come to court, he was going to find in favor of the other party, which he did. . . . I've never forgotten the story and during my entire professional career I have encouraged my client to be with me even when no testimony was going to be given. I just want them to know what is happening and how their attorney is performing.

A great many people have had a profound impact on my life and one of these people was Elizabeth M. Watkins and she was there in a time of great need on my part and her kindness could not earn her anything of a monetary kind and the only reward she had was perhaps knowing that she had helped one or more of hundreds of other students lessen the load they were carrying and make the sun shine a little more brightly.

He signed this letter of remembrance, "With a thankful heart, Arthur C. Hodgson"

Elizabeth had finally decided against scattering gifts among different locations when she died. Lawrence had been her home for nearly sixty years, so she decided to leave the bulk of her fortune to the city and the University of Kansas. She also gave smaller amounts of money to groups rather than individuals; however, she would make loans to individuals when needed as, for instance, when an operation was necessary.

After selling her Louisiana lands, settling with the relatives, and paying commissions, she didn't make much profit that year. Her income was minimal except for her Kansas land. At the end of 1929 she had lost $673,267.55 from reduced dividends. However, many others had lost everything in the 1929 Wall Street Crash. Elizabeth was very glad that most of her investments were in land and bonds, which didn't seem to be as affected by the stock market crash. She gave the usual number of Christmas gifts to mark the end of 1929, around $300 each. She always remembered family, friends, and those who had helped her. With the start of the Great Depression, these checks must have been exceptionally welcome to family and friends.

CHAPTER

11

Building the University of Kansas

Health is a theme that courses through Elizabeth Watkins's life. Her father's illness had a large impact on her family and shaped her early years. She lived through JB's bouts of illness, brought on by intense work and alcoholism. These experiences would have impressed her with the importance of good health and access to health care. She knew that being healthy was a key part of being able to accomplish goals.

When she built her first structure on the KU campus, Watkins Scholarship Hall in 1926, she included a "hospital room" on the second floor so that any girl who was ill would have a quiet place to recover. Then, in 1928, her biggest and possibly most complex project, Lawrence Memorial Hospital, was built to provide good health care services to all her fellow citizens. The nurses' home, completed in 1930 for employees of Lawrence Memorial Hospital, could arguably be said to have provided for the health of those workers.

Now, in 1930, she turned her attention to the well-being of the students who walked by her home daily, to and from campus. Health was often on Elizabeth's mind, especially in the 1930s, as her personal health began to decline.

In March 1930 KU Chancellor Lindley called her to say he was sure she was "sorry not to include the University in her hospital plans." He said that KU's student hospital, which was then in a residential house at 1406 Tennessee, was inadequate. Elizabeth agreed. The university had no money for new buildings at that time. The entire country was affected by the

Great Depression, and the Kansas legislature had curtailed funds to all educational institutions in the state.

The history of KU's student health facilities is documented in a 1932 pamphlet printed by the university itself. It was published to celebrate the opening of the Watkins Memorial Hospital for KU students, a gift of Elizabeth Watkins. On page 10 of this pamphlet, Professor W. J. Baumgartner gives a history of health issues associated with the campus and the needs of the students:

> The most frequent epidemics were those of typhoid fever which occurred usually in the fall of the year immediately after school started. One of these was traced to the use of bad well water and one to infected milk. The Lawrence City Health officer and the local medical fraternity were alert and co-operated actively with the University authorities to stamp out these recurring epidemics. Many of these autumnal typhoid infections were brought in by the wandering, working students who returned from the threshing crews in the Kansas wheat fields, or the engineering camps in the western mountains. On the campus a very serious epidemic occurred that hastened the work for a hospital. In about 1904 or 1905 a student was stricken with smallpox. The health committee had to take him from among the other students in a rooming house. But the local private hospitals would not admit him. There was no detention house. Finally the health Committee placed him in a cabin on an island in the Kaw River. Here a fellow student brought him his food and left it upon a tree stump not far from the cabin. The boy was not very sick and recovered. But there was criticism in the student and local papers about treating a sick student in such a way, and unpleasant reverberating echoes were heard out in the state. Many of the older faculty members recall the main facts of this incident, but the names of patient and committeemen could not be learned.

Urban legend has long held that this incident, in which a student with smallpox was abandoned on a river island, sparked Elizabeth's decision to build a student hospital. Although that event would have occurred much earlier than Elizabeth's decision in 1930, the incident did lead to various houses near campus being rented and designated, in turn, as the "student hospital." Some of these hospital locations included the Spencer House, the home of ex-chancellor Frank Strong in University Heights, just west of campus; 1134 Ohio; 1300 Louisiana; and, finally, 1406 Tennessee. The last address was the hospital's location just prior to the building of the Watkins Memorial Hospital.

There was another result of this smallpox incident. Student fees to pay for health services, 50 cents per year, were first collected in 1906. Fees grew over the years, but in the early days, the collected fees paid for part of the costs. The university often covered the bills in a contractual agreement with a local doctor or nurse, who was either on call or who kept regular hours at the building appointed for student health.

One interesting note is the role of KU's famous Dr. James Naismith in student health.* Originally a physical educator, he is widely known as the inventor of the game of basketball. However, in spring 1912, "Dr. James Naismith became University Physician, having been relieved of part of his work in the gymnasium. In 1914 Dr. Alice Goetz became his associate, looking after the health of women students." Together they gave "free consultations"; they referred some cases to private hospitals and sent any contagious ones to the student infirmary. Dr. Naismith stayed in this position until he left in 1917 to serve in World War I, stationed in France.

Businesslike, as always, in her approach to projects, in 1930, Elizabeth began research prior to planning the student hospital. Dr. H. I. Canuteson, director of the Student Health Department, joined Joseph Radotinsky, state architect, to form a team for this research. Also part of the team was Professor F. A. Russell of the Engineering Department. Russell, who attended the Presbyterian Church with Elizabeth, had worked with her on the Lawrence Memorial Hospital. The group embarked on a round of inspections of student health centers at several universities, including Urbana University, which later became the University of Illinois; the University of Wisconsin at Madison; the University of Minnesota; and Iowa State University at Ames. Together with Elizabeth, these experts formed a modern plan that would offer complete services for the students.

During this summer of planning, Elizabeth was suffering from high blood pressure and had gone once more to Crawford, New Hampshire,

* For more about James Naismith's role in student health, see Bernice Webb, *The Basketball Man: James Naismith* (Lawrence, KS: Kappelman's Historic Collections, 1973).

to escape the Kansas heat. She continued to work on the hospital, with the help of Dick Williams, and she still carefully checked all letters, bills, and plans. Elizabeth wasn't feeling well. Her feet hurt. Her doctor, Dr. Van Noorden, drew a pint of blood to lower her blood pressure. (Another of his patients succeeded in lowering her blood pressure from 200 to 150 each time blood was drawn.) Around this time, she also began a remodeling project at The Outlook. Its main focus was on modernizing the bathrooms, but she also put in new thermostats and a humidifier.

In February 1931, she went to the sanitarium in Battle Creek, Michigan, for several months to address problems with her stomach and bowels. Again, she conducted her business from Battle Creek with the help of Dick Williams. She was paying the last bills for the Lawrence Memorial Hospital and the nurses' home and the renovations at The Outlook. There had been a robbery at Watkins Scholarship Hall, and individual losses ranged from $1.00 to $80.00. Elizabeth reimbursed these losses to "her girls" from her own purse.

During 1930 to 1931, Elizabeth made repeated gifts to her loyal young female relatives on JB's side: Zena Thomson, Della Neal, and Kate Stear. She took on partial responsibility for paying Reverend Aszman's salary at her church in Lawrence. She had four pencil drawings done of the Lawrence Memorial Hospital, the nurses' home, Watkins Bank Building (then the Lawrence City Hall), and The Outlook. These would later be used to produce postcards.

As the summer heat approached, she returned to Crawford, New Hampshire, her annual refuge. While she was there Mr. Patterson came up for a week from New York. Some people again thought they saw orange blossoms in her future, but she would stay true to JB Watkins. Other visitors were Reverend Aszman and his wife, Mrs. Weaver, and Dick and Mary Williams. From New Hampshire she traveled on to New York, with Dick and Mary Williams as companions.

Meanwhile, planning continued for the student hospital. After careful study, a site just west of Blake Hall was chosen at Elizabeth's request. She thought that the easy availability of that location for students on campus made it more useful. To best fit the site and conform to the location of surrounding buildings, a V-shaped building was planned. Elizabeth always enjoyed having a project near her home, and this was just a block west of

The Outlook. She could easily watch and supervise, as she had done for Watkins Scholarship Hall.

Excavations for the hospital began March 14, 1931, and the Watkins Memorial Hospital was ready for occupancy by KU students by December of that same year, a very quick turnaround. Dick Williams noted that Elizabeth had again used her experienced team for construction. The beautifully designed building was made of Indiana limestone, and it had a red tiled roof and a carving of St. George and the Dragon over the doorway. Instead of an inscription on the front of the hospital there would be a plaque. After some discussion it was decided that the plaque would read "This hospital is the gift of Elizabeth Miller Watkins, in memory of her husband Jabez B. Watkins. Our youth will dwell in a land of health and fair sights and sounds." The last line is a quote from Plato, chosen by Elizabeth. The plaque is still there on the building, although student hospital services have been moved to a new location.

After visiting various stone quarries in Bloomington, Indiana, F. A. Russell, the civil engineering professor, selected Alexander King Stone Quarry to supply the limestone. Their finishing mill, nearly in downtown Bloomington, covered the block between Dodds and Allen Streets, on the east side of the railroad tracks. The outer stone had a carborundum finish, giving it a smoother texture than stone used for any other campus building. Marjorie Whitney, professor of design at KU, made a full-size drawing of the St. George stone carving for approval. She also designed and created unique murals to decorate the inside of the hospital.

All floors of the building were made of reinforced concrete and were finished with terrazzo, linoleum, linoleum tile, or rubber tile. Viewed from the campus (front) side, the building appeared to have three floors, but five when viewed from the back.

The sub-basement held all laundry and mechanical services and, on the back side of the building, there was also a garage with a driveway. An ambulance could pull up directly to the building from the streets on the south. There was an elevator to take the patient up to the examination or surgery rooms.

One floor up from the sub-basement, the "basement" held the nurses' dining room, the main kitchen, and two large storage rooms. There was a bedroom for two students who did the janitorial work, a nurses' rest room,

Front view of Watkins Memorial Hospital on the University of Kansas campus, built in 1931. Note the carving of St. George and the Dragon above the doorway. (Pamphlet, Watkins Memorial Hospital, 1931. Kenneth Spencer Research Library, University of Kansas)

Cover of pamphlet advertising the opening of the Watkins Memorial Hospital. Note the center figure of St. George slaying the dragon of disease, and the healthy and unhealthy Jayhawks. (Pamphlet, Watkins Memorial Hospital, 1931. Kenneth Spencer Research Library, University of Kansas)

and a large lecture room. Beds previously used at the student infirmary were stored nearby for use in case the lecture room was needed for an emergency ward.

The first floor, which opened onto the campus level, held the large entrance lobby with the general office on the left and the pharmacy on the right. The operating room, sterilizing room, and doctor's dressing rooms were at the center of the building at the back. The south wing contained one dressing room, five examination rooms, a general office, and a doctor's office. The north wing contained the x-ray and optometry equipment, a laboratory, a heat and light treatment room, and two living rooms for resident doctors. There were no patient rooms on this floor.

Patient rooms were mainly on the second floor, which contained "32 patient beds being two 4-bed wards and twelve 2-bed rooms." Elizabeth decided to order furniture from Stickley Brothers as she had for the Lawrence Memorial Hospital. She ordered forty-six walnut beds with a Jayhawk carved on the headboard from Batesville, Indiana, at $16.50 each. "Nurses stations are located at the center of the building having a supply room at the back. The station is located to give a full view of the entire length of the corridor in each direction." Meals were brought up from the main kitchen in the basement by way of a dumbwaiter, into small "diet kitchens" on the second and third floors.

The third floor was smaller than the lower floors because of the tiled open courtyards on either end of the roof. This floor had fourteen more patient beds, along with a sunroom that could hold four more beds, if needed. "The north wing of this floor is designed for an isolation ward which can be entirely closed off from the corridor in case of contagious disease. Each of the rooms in the isolation ward is a one-bed room and has its individual toilet room."

Several of those walnut beds with the carved Jayhawk on the headboard are still in existence; there is one at the Watkins Museum of History in Lawrence.

Another unique feature of the Watkins Memorial Hospital is described in the university's 1931 booklet:

One quite attractive feature of the building is the decoration of the Sun Room at the south end of the third floor. The walls are canvassed and

For Watkins Memorial Hospital, Elizabeth ordered headboards for the hospital beds with a carved Jayhawk in the center. (Douglas County Historical Society, Watkins Museum of History)

decorated by Miss Marjorie Whitney of the School of Fine Arts. The special feature of this decoration is the use of the Kansas sunflower and the Jayhawk. On one panel all the Jayhawks are feeling badly, indicating that the location must be unhealthy. Then they discover if they fly up over a door and into another panel, they all get well and feel happy. Then there are the different activities of the University shown such as the football player, soldiers drilling, the painter, the singer, and the engineer surveying.

Several of these panels are preserved in the new Watkins Memorial Health Center, the current student hospital.

An article in the *University Daily Kansan* from Monday, January 4, 1932, reported that the student hospital had opened during the Christmas holidays; there had already been one operation at the new hospital and a number of students had used the dispensary. The day before the article

Murals of sick and injured Jayhawks flying over the doorway, now recovered
and happy, in the sunroom of the Watkins Memorial Hospital. The photo is
believed to show Marjorie Whitney, professor of design, painting the murals.
(Kenneth Spencer Research Library, University of Kansas)

appeared, January 3, an open house held at the new facility had drawn a
crowd of about seven hundred, made up of members of the faculty and
their families. The article noted that "the new Watkins Memorial Hospital has two telephones" and that it could be reached by calling KU 180,
through the university switchboard.

As with Lawrence Memorial, Elizabeth had not only paid for the construction of the building but had also equipped it to meet the high standards
she brought to all her projects. The university booklet lists the inventory
of professional equipment for diagnosis and treatment she provided to
ensure that the students would receive good care: x-ray equipment, a fluo-
roscope, an oxygen tent, ultraviolet and heat lamps, an electrocardiograph,
and an ophthalmic chair. It is noted that the "laboratory though small is
completely equipped for the work required."

More details from the university booklet note: "The building is located
over the heat tunnel which comes from the Power Plant and goes to Blake
Hall and to Fraser Hall. A special steam line for heating the building was

run from the power plant. This service, as well as electricity, water, and gas, was furnished by the University at a cost of approximately $6,500, which is not included" in the final cost below. At the beginning of this project, Elizabeth had promised $150,000 for it. Once the site was chosen, it became evident that it would cost more, so she increased her commitment to $175,000. She again worked with her experienced and dedicated crew of builders and contractors, and the project came in nearly at budget.

One overage is described as "repainting and working over the old equipment moved from the old hospital, as it was Mrs. Watkins' desire that this should be put in good shape and stored ready for use in case of emergency." This was one of her lifelong tenets: Do not overspend, but maintain everything properly, as it will pay off in the long run.

The final cost came in at $176,489. The total equipped cost of the 350,000-square-foot hospital came to 50 cents per square foot. Because it was built in 1931, during the Depression, all purchases were made in a time of "falling market, and unusually favorable prices were obtained making it possible to use better materials and also to add facilities not originally contemplated." It is hard to say what was more remarkable, that the cost was so low or that Elizabeth had the resources to pay for such a project at that time. In any event, the students at the University of Kansas were the beneficiaries.

Elizabeth was very proud of this accomplishment. She had consistently shown a keen interest in students and this project was solely for their benefit. Unlike with previous projects, for which she had avoided acclaim, she had her portrait hung in the students' hospital. Her personal scrapbook contains a clipping of an article entitled "Portrait of Donor is Hung in K.U. Hospital." It describes the painting by A. H. Clark, a former faculty member who had also painted her favorite likeness of Jabez. "Mr. Clark has posed Mrs. Watkins so that she faces squarely the eye of the beholder, bringing out the strong character of a woman whose kindly blue eye shows sympathy for the less fortunate."

For forty-three years, from its opening in December 1931 until 1974, this graceful building served the health needs of KU students. As the student body grew, a larger building was needed. Completed in 1974, a new student health center was built toward the south end of the campus. The Watkins Memorial Health Center, still named for JB and Elizabeth, continues to

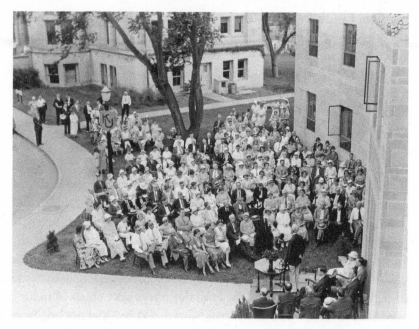

The dedication ceremony for the Watkins Memorial Hospital, June 5, 1932. Chancellor Lindley is at the microphone; Elizabeth is visible seated behind him, dressed in white. (Kenneth Spencer Research Library, University of Kansas)

serve students, functioning as a walk-in clinic and an in-patient hospital. The original Watkins Memorial Hospital building has been renamed Twente Hall and is currently the home of KU's School of Social Welfare.

In December 1930, Elizabeth had her will written at Central Trust in Topeka. Not wanting to dilute her estate, she had decided the bulk of the gift would go to the University of Kansas. She sent a letter to Olin Templin, executive secretary of the University of Kansas Endowment Association (KUEA), outlining what was included in her will and how KU would benefit. Elizabeth had by then been involved in KUEA for several years, serving as vice president (currently called vice chair) of the trustees and as a member of the executive committee from 1934 to 1939. She first became a KU Endowment trustee in 1927, soon after the building of Watkins Scholarship Hall. She had a comfort level with KUEA's current attitude, practices, and board members, and had confidence they would honor her intentions with this great gift.

Elizabeth Josephine Miller Watkins, a portrait by A. H. Clark.
This painting hangs in the current Watkins Student Health
Center. (Author's collection, with thanks to the Watkins
Student Health Center at the University of Kansas)

She did not give her estate directly to the university. To explain why
funds should go to KUEA rather than the university itself, Robert Taft's
book gives this history:

Gift funds to the University are administered by the University Endowment Association, a privately chartered institution which accepts
and administers any trust to be used for the benefit of the University.
The Endowment Association was organized in 1893 as the result of a

peculiar provision in the (Kansas) state Constitution. Through this provision, only the interest on a direct gift to the University may be utilized. To make matters worse, in actual practice any such interest is deducted from the legislative appropriation for the University. In effect, then, the state, and not the University, is the real beneficiary of gifts to the University.*

So, the only practical solution was for the gift to be given directly to KUEA.

Elizabeth did not restrict how KUEA could use most of the money, but she gave them suggestions to consider. She prioritized funds for teaching staff and aid for deserving students, and hoped her gift would be an inspiration to others. She wrote to Templin: "It is my wish to make a gift to the University, not to the state, and so increase its efficiency. By it other individuals might be encouraged to make gifts to the University."

Both she and Dick Williams were having health issues. But at Christmas 1931, she unfailingly gave her usual monetary gifts to friends, workers, and family members. She also planned to build a porte cochere, a covered drive, on the east side of The Outlook.

In 1932 an interesting question involving hiring nurses for the KU hospital arose when a Chinese woman applied, the first member of a minority group ever to apply for a job at the hospital. "As yet we have never been confronted with the race problem in hiring nurses." Race didn't matter to Elizabeth and she saw no reason why the woman shouldn't be hired, as her qualifications were good.

For years Elizabeth had supported the Laurinburg Normal and Industrial Institute of the state of North Carolina for "the training of colored men and women." The school, established in 1904 by Emmanuel McDuffie and his wife, primarily served blacks in Scotland County, North Carolina. By 1932, the school had grown from a single building to a thriving complex. In the early 2000s it was still doing well as a private school and a two-year college, under the direction of McDuffie's grandson.

In the former bank building, now Lawrence's city hall, Elizabeth was renovating the small office space she had retained for her own use. The office, on the north side of the building, had formerly been the stenographic

---

* See Taft's *Across the Years on Mt. Oread: 1866–1941* (Lawrence: University of Kansas, 1941) for a good account of this time of growth at the University of Kansas.

room, and she shared this space with Dick Williams. In May 1932, post-cards were printed from the drawings she had commissioned earlier of Lawrence Memorial Hospital, the nurses' home, Watkins Memorial Hospital, Watkins Hall, and Watkins Bank (now the city hall).

Elizabeth traveled again to Crawford, New Hampshire, to escape the Kansas heat for part of the summer. Most visitors there were elderly, and there were fewer than usual because of the Great Depression. She had not suffered as much financially as many had. Now, at Dick Williams's suggestion she was beginning to buy stocks. She hadn't bought stocks before the Depression, but this was the time to buy: prices were low and few were buying. Some of the early stocks she purchased were US Steel, Bethlehem Steel, and DuPont.

There were still significant landholdings outside of Kansas that she hoped to sell. In April 1932, Raymond Rice and Dick Williams went to Texas and Louisiana, to close on some of the last of these. One West Texas property near the border with Mexico that encompassed sixty thousand acres, or thirty sections, eventually became part of Big Bend National Park. Beyond this, she still owned 11,520 acres in Brewster County, Texas. Closer to home, on her farmland in Western Kansas more sod was being broken in April in preparation for planting wheat.

Elizabeth's health was about the same, but now she often had a nurse staying with her, frequently May Wolsey. In addition to rheumatism, her throat continued to bother her and she had problems with her teeth. She had had all her teeth pulled some years earlier, hoping to experience less infection and pain. Her uncomfortable false teeth felt as if they were "trying to occupy the gallery in my mouth." In December 1932, she enjoyed some time at the Arlington Hotel in Hot Springs, Arkansas. She found the mineral baths to be therapeutic, as had JB, many years earlier.

She made new stock purchases in 1933: General Motors, Standard Oil, and Continental Oil of Delaware. In May, feeling better, she traveled by railroad to Cleveland, Connecticut, and New Hampshire. She began to research having a cooling system installed at The Outlook, perhaps knowing her years of going north to escape the heat would eventually be coming to an end. Travel, although she still loved it, was becoming more difficult for her.

The Watkins papers contain a multitude of receipts for purchases made in 1933. It appeared Elizabeth was refreshing her wardrobe and getting her house in order. At the age of seventy-two, she was not done quite yet.

In January 1934 Elizabeth traveled south to "check on her Gardner relations," her mother's side of the family. She went on to Lake Charles, where she stayed at the Majestic Hotel. In a letter to Lawrence, she wrote about the wonderful roads in Louisiana and how they came to be. She figured Huey Long, the infamous governor of Louisiana, had bought all the gravel pits in the state, compelled the road construction companies to buy from him, and gotten rich! She also described meeting one last time with J. Stuart Thomson, once her trusted business manager there. She asked if he could pay some interest on an outstanding loan he had with her, and he confessed he had lost all his money. Stuart, who had done his banking with the Calcasieu Bank, got nervous during the Great Depression and moved some of his money to the Canal Bank in New Orleans. Both banks had failed. She wrote off the loan to Stuart, a $2,500.00 loss, in 1935. In a letter to Lawrence, Elizabeth wrote that the Watkins relations all had a "tale of woe," and it would be good to get home.

Early in 1934, Dick Williams and Raymond Rice had counseled Elizabeth that her land in Brazoria, Texas, just south of Houston, was "not worth paying taxes on." She had the parcel appraised and then bought it and transferred it to herself personally in June 1934. She then proceeded to pay the back taxes on it, likely because she could not tolerate owing money. In July, she signed an oil and gas lease on that parcel and made a nice profit for herself! No, she was not done quite yet.

The highlight of 1934 was her selection for the Most Distinguished Citizen Award by the Dorsey Liberty American Legion Post in Lawrence. This was a high local honor, and there was a large banquet and many articles in the local papers and those of surrounding cities. The many clippings in her personal scrapbook show how pleased she was to receive this award.

To her great distress, Dr. Charles J. Simmons, her main doctor in Lawrence for many years, died in 1934. Perhaps to buoy her spirits, she made a deposit on a trip to Hawaii for herself, a companion, and Dick and Mary Williams. They set off on this adventure on December 9, 1934.

In 1934 Elizabeth also bought another car, a Cadillac seven-person limousine with many accessories, including a radio. Once again, the garage at The Outlook had to be remodeled so the car would fit. T. D. Funk, a Lawrence mortician, bought her old car, the 1931 Cadillac.

She constantly had business decisions to make. She paid a special assessment to the city for the resurfacing of Seventeenth Street adjoining the Ohio Street lots that she had purchased from Elma Kagi, who lived at 1701 Tennessee Street. The Dust Bowl years had started in 1930, and many of her farms in western Kansas had suffered so badly from drought and high winds that she wondered if wheat could still be planted there. Jackrabbits and dust storms had both done a lot of damage, and there didn't seem to be an answer to either problem. She listed several of the farms for sale.

The housemother at Watkins Hall, Jane Morrow, was leaving for California, for health reasons. To replace her, Elizabeth hired Lena Hayden Esterley, the widow of a Lawrence dentist Elizabeth had gone to. Elizabeth gave a program at the Ingleside Club about the early days of the club. She and her mother, Ella, had been two of the founding members. Elizabeth had retained her membership and attended as she was able. Her 1934 Christmas gift list was no shorter than in earlier years. She always asked that no one send gifts to her as she had all she needed. But she enjoyed remembering family members and friends with her gifts.

As the "Dirty Thirties" continued, 1935 brought no improvements in conditions on Elizabeth's farms in western Kansas. She sold many of her western Kansas bonds at a discount because she feared they might default. She took out annuities for herself and several of JB's nieces and nephews that year, in the amount of $10,000, to provide them with an income for their lifetime.

In spring 1935, Elizabeth still enjoyed growing plants and raising chickens at The Outlook; it may have reminded her of childhood days in Ohio. Maude Landis, the superintendent of the Lawrence Memorial Hospital, became her traveling companion. Elizabeth liked the company of interesting, independent women, and she was still able to enjoy travel.

CHAPTER 12

Her Dream Come True, Part Two

From the *Lawrence Journal World* on June 8, 1936: "Announcement of Another Outstanding Gift is Made Public Today—At Alumni Luncheon—New Hall Will House 40 Women Students and Will Cost $100,000." The article goes on to say, "So pleased has Mrs. Watkins been by the achievement of the women who have held Watkins Hall scholarships, that she now wishes to add a second hall for as many more women."*

Yes, her "dream come true" had shown itself to be a success. So, while she was able, Elizabeth decided to build another. The new Miller Scholarship Hall was named in honor of her brother Frank C. Miller, who had been a banker in Salina, Kansas, and Kansas City, Missouri. Frank was a KU student in 1887–1888 and had bequeathed $50,000 to the university to be used as a student loan fund.

Although the *Journal World* article states that "it is expected that an architect will be on the campus within a few days to select a site and determine the style of architecture," those things had already been decided.

---

* A short history of the *Lawrence Journal-World* newspaper: the title *Journal World* was used first in 1911, but the paper dates to 1858, according to the volume number of the current masthead of the paper. The Simons family moved to Lawrence in 1891 and took over operation of the *Lawrence Record* under a three-month lease. The *Lawrence World* was first issued by the Simons on March 2, 1892. In 1905 the *World* acquired the *Lawrence Journal,* and the two were merged in 1911. The *Lawrence Daily Journal* title, which dates to about 1880, was a continuation of the *Republican Daily Journal*, which dates to at least 1869. The *Republican Daily Journal* appears to have been the successor via sale and/or consolidation of earlier Lawrence newspapers. http://en.wikipedia.org/wiki/Lawrence_Journal-World.

Miller Scholarship Hall under construction, completed in 1937. Its twin, Watkins Scholarship Hall, is on the left. Elizabeth's home, The Outlook, is just to the right of Miller Hall, not visible in this photo. (Kenneth Spencer Research Library, University of Kansas)

A fee of $150 was sent to Williamson & Co. in Topeka for permission to use the same blueprint plans used for Watkins Hall. The plans were borrowed and copied by Lucille Van Swearingen, Dick Williams's secretary, then returned to Williamson & Co., according to the letters typed on Elizabeth's stationery. The new women's scholarship hall was tucked between Watkins Hall and The Outlook; it faced Lilac Lane and was built on an attractive angle between the two existing buildings.

The year 1936 followed a pattern similar to that of previous years. Elizabeth went to Florida in January, but this time she flew on Transcontinental & Western Air. Her trunks were sent by rail. She sent a generous $500 donation to help Republican Alf Landon win the nomination for president. She subscribed to Kiplinger's Washington Agency for their political and financial newsletter. As work started on Miller Hall, she requested a duplicate order of the brick and tile she had ordered for Watkins Hall.

Concerned about the condition of her Kansas farmlands, she hired a Mr. Shetlar to look after the farms that had no tenants. She supported the Wind Erosion Control Committee in Stanton County, and a similar effort in Morton County. She hired a road grader to smooth the fields in Stevens County, so that a crop could be sown. She kept track of her wheat allotments to ensure that the numbers of acres planted complied with the allotment she was given by the US Department of Agriculture. The USDA gave individual farmers allotments to control the amount of certain crops they were allowed to plant, so that there would be sufficient supplies nationwide and prices would be supported.

Christmas 1936 once again brought the pleasant annual tradition of sending approximately thirty gift checks to relatives, friends, and those who had helped Elizabeth.

The year 1937 began busily. Many women applied for the position of housemother for the new Miller Scholarship Hall. Elizabeth chose the widow of Sam Stayton from Wellington, Kansas. There is some evidence that she had met Sam Stayton, a banker and land agent in Wellington, while she was buying or inspecting her lands in western Kansas. When he passed away, his widow was a perfect candidate to be Miller Hall's housemother. Elizabeth's confidence in her new housemother was so great that she directed Dick Williams to have her select dishes and kitchenware. Elizabeth was not feeling well and needed the help. She did manage to order another piano from Sohmer in New York for the new hall, and she commissioned a painting of her brother Frank, with the intention of hanging it in Miller Hall. It still hangs there today, a tribute to Elizabeth's loving relationship with her brother and to the legacy she left with her gift of scholarship halls.

Goods began to be ordered in early 1937 for Miller Hall: kitchen supplies from Smith-St. John Manufacturing, 1518 Walnut, Kansas City, Missouri; china from Jules Grogan of the Missouri China Company, 612 Delaware, Kansas City, Missouri; and R. Wallace silver "stamped in script 'M H.'" Weavers of Lawrence delivered the linens.

Then it was time for a new car again. In June, Tom Reames, her current chauffeur, drove her in the new 1937 Cadillac to Crawford Notch, New Hampshire. She was not feeling well and thought she might not return to Lawrence by September. In the event she didn't get back in time, she left some decisions to be made by Mrs. Stayton, the housemother at Miller Hall. She had given an easement for a diagonal path between Miller and

Watkins Halls that would join the pavement near the Kappa house to the street in front of the halls, which would later be known as Alumni Place Drive. From Harbour Springs, Michigan, Elizabeth wrote to Dick Williams, "I have not felt that I am rapidly improving, but hope in a day or two to be more normal. With love, Elizabeth Miller Watkins."

By August she was in Crawford House in New Hampshire, another favorite place to escape the heat. She had a full-time nurse. Elizabeth wrote to Dick Williams that if he could come to New Hampshire, he could drive her home. While in New Hampshire, she felt well enough to visit Senator Moses, a controversial Republican senator. She related a conversation they had in which she wondered if Roosevelt knew that he was about to "hang himself. I [Elizabeth] would like to attend that hanging." Senator Moses, an ally of conservative eastern manufacturers who opposed protective tariffs, had made a reputation by referring to western progressives as "Sons of the Wild Jackass." This is another indication that Elizabeth's Republican roots had reemerged after years of living with Democrat JB Watkins. Her financial conservatism seemed to align her with the Republican leaders of the time.

Even while in the East, Elizabeth worked. Far from the hot Midwest, she made the same careful choices regarding furnishings, draperies, and color for Miller Scholarship Hall as she had for Watkins, in the joy of building her "dream come true" a second time. Two decades later, when Judy Johnson Niebaum lived in Miller Hall from 1958 to 1961, she remembered, "I was so aware of the beauty of the House . . . its lovely decor, drapes, furniture, dishes, so stylish and elegant to my eyes!" Now in two locations, lucky young women had the opportunity to live in a beautiful, columned home with a chandelier, curving stairway in the foyer, and large living room with fireplace. As Sarah Wohlrabe Shortall, who lived in Watkins Hall from 1972 to 1976, pointed out, not many people can say they lived in a "Neoclassical home with Ionic columns" during college.

Miller Hall had a few differences from its twin, Watkins Hall, even though the same blueprints were used. According to the building scrapbook in KU's University Archives, the internal structure was now made of steel, a mark of the changes in the construction industry in the eleven years since Watkins had been built. Another change was the elimination of the hospital room on the second floor. Now that Elizabeth had built a

Panoramic photo of Watkins and Miller Halls at the University of Kansas. (Photo courtesy of Debra Bates Lamborn, First City Photo, Leavenworth, KS)

hospital for students, just down the street, this space could be used as another study room for the residents. And, true to her thrifty habits, it came in under budget, at approximately $89,000. She had used her usual cadre of builders and contractors.

This lovely twin sister of Watkins Hall, Miller Scholarship Hall, was ready for occupancy in fall 1937. Mrs. Stayton was the first housemother to chaperone the Miller women. Ruth Green Saffel, who lived in Miller Hall from 1942 to 1946, remembered, "During my freshman year 1941–42, my housemother was Mrs. Stayton. She had been a personal friend of Mrs. Watkins and was therefore very aware of Mrs. Watkins' wishes for the halls she gave to the University. Mrs. Stayton often spoke of her friend and how Mrs. Watkins regretted not being able to afford a college education when she was young, and her great satisfaction in being able to make it possible for talented girls of limited means to attend with their scholarship hall awards." They were indeed friends; the *University Daily Kansan* wrote that "She [Mrs. Stayton] was at the bedside when Mrs. Watkins passed away."

Pat Gardner Stein, a resident of Miller Hall from 1953 to 1957, noted a later point of pride in Miller Scholarship Hall: "Miller Hall was the first

scholarship hall to be integrated. We took a vote as to whether we wished to integrate. . . . We received two black students in 1955. [They] were accepted fully in life there [in Miller Hall]. . . . I do remember a few of us and Harriet went downtown to eat one evening and the waitress refused to serve us."

Miller Hall quickly filled up, as Watkins Hall had. Elizabeth had tapped into a great need for young women wishing to get an education. From an article in the *University Daily Kansan* on Sunday, May 28, 1939, we learn: "The women of the halls have drawn up a constitution, and they call themselves the Watkins Hall and Miller Hall Self-governing Association. Officers elected annually were the President, Vice-President, Secretary, Treasurer, Historian, Intramural Manager, and a Social Committee. These officers have charge of running the halls. The President makes out a chart every nine weeks of the house duties that each woman is expected to do daily. Every morning before classes begin, each resident of the hall does a certain house-cleaning job, and in a very short time the house is clean for the day."

Sharing a blueprint with Watkins Hall, Miller Hall had the same seven small kitchens on its lower level. Elizabeth had seen how these small kitchen groups supported and nurtured young women, some away from home for the first time. Creation of this atmosphere was key to the success of her great "theory."

Another unique feature of both Watkins and Miller Halls is the communal sleeping porches, two per hall. Set at the back of the buildings, on the second and third floors, these large airy rooms are lined with windows. They are filled with rows of bunk beds and are strictly kept silent. In each hall, one sleeping porch is designated as warm and one as cold, to allow every woman to find the temperature that suits her sleep. If absolute quiet was needed for study, there was always the refuge of the sleeping porch.

In November 1937, in a codicil to her will, Elizabeth bequeathed 250 shares in Employees Reinsurance to the First Presbyterian Church. The stock was in her name, but the church would get all the yearly dividends, about $10,000. It is worth noting that this gift still provides funds to the Presbyterian Church of Lawrence even today. In 2022, the church is still reaping the benefits of Elizabeth's thoughtful gift.

As every year, there were many and varied contributions to her usual charities in 1937. One of the year's most unusual requests came from KU's business manager Karl Klooz, who asked for help in purchasing a wooden leg for a student.

Although Elizabeth had not felt well during the past year, she stayed true to her word to proceed with "all speed I can command" and began two more building projects. She had the state architect, Joseph Radotinsky, draw up plans and specifications for a home to be built near Watkins Memorial Hospital for the nurses who worked at the hospital. The stone above the doorway was engraved simply "Watkins Home," and it was to be located east and south, down the hill from Watkins Memorial Hospital. Using her usual construction crew, she had it built on a "cost plus basis."

A large pile of native limestone was left when the two scholarship halls were completed. To put it to good use, Elizabeth had a small cottage built behind The Outlook. Although there is no record of exactly how Elizabeth initially used this lovely little cottage, it would later be used as a guest house for academics visiting KU. Student caretakers lived in the lower level. It was a small but comfortable stone home with a leafy view, looking east toward downtown Lawrence.

By train was Elizabeth's favorite way to travel; she always took the Santa Fe to California. But in December 1937 it appears that she flew to Miami

Simply marked "Watkins Home," this dormitory was originally built for the nursing staff of the Watkins Memorial Hospital. (Author's collection)

This lovely stone cottage has welcomed guests to KU for decades. The Outlook is above and just to the left. (Author's collection)

and then later traveled, possibly by train, to Louisville to visit relatives. In January 1938, Elizabeth spent some time in the Flamingo Hotel in Miami Beach, Florida. She was feeling better overall, but the effects of sciatica and shingles lingered.

Beginning in 1938, The Outlook household began to use pasteurized milk from the JayHawk Company, the only plant around using the method. The cost was $.10 per quart for skimmed milk, $.15 per gallon for cream, $.40 per quart for whole milk. Pasteurization was a new process to make milk safer to drink; before that only raw milk had been used. No one seemed to object to the taste of the pasteurized milk. Drinking water was ordered from Dr. Pepper Bottling Company.

Elizabeth ordered fountains to be installed on the grounds of The Outlook. The Lawrence Memorial Hospital needed an addition, and she funded the new wing, which would open in July 1939. She also paid for an addition to the Watkins Memorial Hospital for students. We know that she had also planned to build a scholarship house for young men. So many projects—would she have time to complete everything she dreamed of? Perhaps she sensed she was running out of time. She and Dick Williams attended to the multitude of details and checked the bills.

Elizabeth's first-in-the-nation concept of scholarship halls for women had garnered some publicity by this time. This idea of a communal dormitory for young women who had financial need and were also high academic achievers intrigued First Lady Eleanor Roosevelt and inspired her to visit the halls in 1938. She was scheduled to give a lecture to the university student body and took time to visit Miller Scholarship Hall. She recounted the visit in her column My Day from October 24, 1938: "We stopped for a few minutes at a girl's dormitory run on a cooperative plan where $15 a month covers all living expenses and, at the same time, the girls receive excellent training in housekeeping. To remain in the house they must have better than a 'B' average in their school work. This means that the leaders of the future are probably going through on this basis."

Eleanor Roosevelt had stipulated that no fees were to be charged for her lecture at Hoch Auditorium; however, the university did charge admission and applied the proceeds to the student loan fund, according to Mrs. C. E. Pontius, president of the Lawrence Women's Club. Roosevelt's entertainment during her time in Lawrence was organized through the Lawrence

First Lady Eleanor Roosevelt visited Miller Hall in 1938, accompanied
by an unidentified Kansas highway trooper and Miller Hall president
Sophia Schellenberg. (Kitchen 8 Archives, Watkins Museum of
History, with thanks to the family of Corrine Martin Ervin)

Women's Club and the university. Elizabeth neither received the First Lady
at The Outlook nor met with her. Whether this was due to her declining
health or simply because she was not a fan of the Roosevelts is open to
speculation. There is evidence that Elizabeth did not agree with President
Roosevelt's new social program, the New Deal, a policy she regarded as

too generous. She and JB had always lived by the tenet of "a hand up, not a handout."

In October 1938, the deed for Miller Hall was sent to Chancellor Lindley. With provisions similar to those for Watkins Scholarship Hall, it is Deed Record No. 140, State of Kansas, Douglas County. These gifts were given to the Kansas Board of Regents, not directly to the university. Elizabeth stated her intention of hiring and paying for housemothers as long as she was able, and, with her usual attention to detail, there were instructions concerning insurance coverage. She also gave specific instructions and set up a committee to review and keep the rental rates low for the young women chosen to live in Watkins and Miller Scholarship Halls, a stipulation that was sadly violated some years after her death.

In a later addition to her will, Elizabeth made a separate trust for the benefit of Watkins and Miller Scholarship Halls, designed to make them self-sustaining and, again, to keep the rent very low for the residents. The income from this trust was to be used for "care, maintenance and upkeep" of both halls, "share and share alike." The trust has been used for this purpose, but the university has also used it for other expenditures throughout the years.

The care and attention Elizabeth had put into designing and maintaining these two dormitories for young women is obvious. It is seen in the requirements listed in the deed to each hall, and it is seen in the specific trust set up for them, in perpetuity. These halls were indeed Elizabeth's "children," and the young women living in them, in a fashion, her "daughters."

For the first time, in December 1938, she did not feel up to sending her usual Christmas gifts.

CHAPTER

*The Real Mrs. Watkins:
A Closer Look at Elizabeth*

Remember those pages that fluttered to the ground from the windows of the former Watkins National Bank during the World War II paper drive? Although a great many were saved and are now in the Spencer Research Library at the University of Kansas and in the Watkins Museum of History, Elizabeth's personal letters, for the most part, are not there. But her personal scrapbook was preserved and is in the Watkins Museum of History.

As mentioned before, Elizabeth had a pattern she followed in her business letters, seen especially in letters to those she communicated with frequently, such as J. Stuart Thomson. Duty first—she addressed all business matters first in her letters. Only in the last few lines of each letter did she refer to her personal life: her cares, travels, concerns, feelings. This was also the way Jabez had approached his correspondence. With no diary or personal letters left to read, Elizabeth's scrapbook with its hand-selected poems, magazine articles, and favorite newspaper clippings is the place to seek glimpses of her personality. She was a real woman, smart and headstrong, with struggles and imperfections.*

* Store receipts dated 1929 to 1935 at the Spencer Research Library give glimpses of items used in Elizabeth's everyday life.

From Rankins and Round Corner Drugstores: horehound candy, Bromo Seltzer, vanishing cream, Absorbine, Jr., Anacin, catarrh jelly, Jergens soap, rubbing alcohol, paregoric, Benzedrine, Canada Dry, salty tablets, Epsom salts, Listerine, Campho Phenique, Carters Little Liver Pills.

From Emery, Bird, Thayer in Kansas City, Weaver's in Lawrence, and some New

Scrapbooks were a common occupation for a woman from that Victorian era. The left inside cover of her personal scrapbook has this: "Mrs. Elizabeth M. Watkins, March 8th, 1933." This was a scrapbook of her thoughts and inspirations at a later point in her life, as she looked back on all she had lived through and accomplished.

Written in her own hand, the opposite page has her first entry, the words to a hymn. She titled it:

"My Creed—Also"
I will be true for there are those who trust me,
I will be pure for there are those who care.
I will be strong, for there is much to suffer,
I will be brave, for there is much to dare.
I will be friend to all, to foe, to friendless,
I will be giving and forget the gift.
I will be humble, for I know my weakness.
I will look up and love and laugh and lift.

It is easy to imagine Elizabeth needed this inspiration to keep up her mental strength during her years of assault by factions of JB's family. Her own rather unconventional life, it is also easy to believe, was a challenge for her in several ways. With work consuming so much of her life, she may not have had the usual friends for support that many enjoy. She had learned to rely on herself and was therefore a rather solitary person. JB had also taught her to be cautious about those who would befriend them with designs on their fortune.

York stores: Kleenex, dress patterns, thread, satins, linen, dimity, crinoline, crash (coarse linen), chemise ribbon, underwear, buttons, sheeting, velvet, handkerchiefs, kitchen equipment, ostrich trim, lace, Vogue pattern book, dress weights, gloves, dresses, suits.

Food items included lots of cream, Fritzel's Dairy-milk, whipping cream, buttermilk, coffee cream (one month's order included fifty-one quarts of milk and twenty-one quarts of whipping cream!), lemon soda, three dozen eggs about every other week, pecans, walnuts from Wagstaff Produce, two nineteen-pound turkeys at $.20 per pound, vegetables and fancy meats, cantaloupe, grapefruit, peaches. And *lots* of ice cream.

Garden and chicken supplies: From Barteldes, garden plants and seeds; from Underwoods, hen scratch, straw, mash.

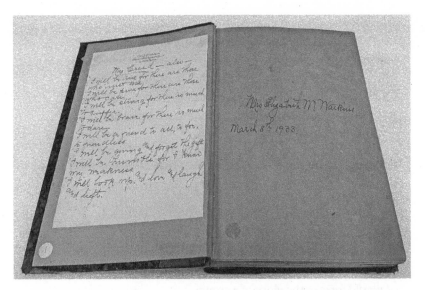

The inside cover of Elizabeth's personal scrapbook displays her signature, the date she began the scrapbook, and "My Creed—also" in her own handwriting. (Douglas County Historical Society, Watkins Museum of History)

Elizabeth's family was all gone by 1933 when she began her scrapbook. She had lost not only JB but both of her brothers. She had also lost her dear nephew whom she hoped would take over the businesses. We know she was a solitary woman, but one who took solace in her innate gifts and her ability to use them for good, especially the public good. Perhaps the admonition to "be humble" in "My Creed—Also" refers to her great confidence and pride in herself and her accomplishments. She recognizes her pride and reminds herself to be humble. She also was devout; prayers are scattered throughout her scrapbook. A poem she chose for the first page of her scrapbook shows these attributes:

"Life's Stewardship"
If I have strength, I owe the service of the strong:
If melody I have, I owe the world a song.
If I can stand when all around my post are falling.
If I can run with speed when needy hearts are calling.
And if my torch can light the dark of any night,
Then, I must pay the debt I owe with living light.

... For any gift God gives to me I cannot pay:
Gifts are most mine when I give them all away.
God's gifts are like his flowers which show their right to stay
By giving all of their look and fragrance away:
Riches are not in gold or land, estates or marts,
The only wealth worth having is found in human hearts.
  Author unknown

Another poem on this first page suggests that Elizabeth was missing her dear JB:

"Could You Come Back?"
Dear love of mine, could you come back tonight
To sit a while within this empty chair
Where you were wont to sit but yesterday
I would forsake the glory of a crown,
The wealth of Midas or a Shakespeare's fame
To feel and know and see you sitting there.
... And then I'd lay my head against your heart.
To go to sleep—forgetting all my pain:
But praying God that I might never wake
To know the aching loss of you again!
  Ruth Bassett

Much has been written about a modest Elizabeth who did not wish to receive accolades for her great gifts to the community, but she was human! Many articles about her accomplishments are pasted into her personal scrapbook. One that obviously had great meaning for her was a local Lawrence award. The Dorsey-Liberty American Legion Post of Lawrence named her the Most Distinguished Citizen in 1934, and she kept articles from the Kansas City *Journal-Post*, the Fort Scott-Iola *Register,* and newspapers from Abilene, Kansas. She also kept the article about the award banquet; it mentions the shortage of tickets (at $.60 each) and reports that many organizations rescheduled their meeting times so members could attend. Quite a tribute to Elizabeth Watkins!

Zula Bennington Green, a regional columnist who wrote under the name "Peggy of the Flint Hills," reported on the American Legion award.

In the column, which Elizabeth saved, Peggy wrote that Elizabeth wore to the banquet a "pretty dress of white sheer, some kind of a fine dimity or batiste with a little figure in it and trimmed with neat little bands of lace," and she called the outfit "a perfect setting for keen blue eyes and fresh skin." Peggy's last paragraph reads: "And no one in Lawrence is more beloved than Mrs. Watkins, who gives not only her money, but herself, to help make the university a finer place for the young people of the state." At the bottom of this clipping, Elizabeth had written "Amen" and her initials. She approved.

This isn't the only handwritten notation to a news item in her scrapbook. In the margin of a clipping from the Kansas City *Journal-Post* entitled "Widow is Giving Away $3,000,000" she wrote "A false report—E. M. Watkins." The article reported that she was "giving away $3 Million" but had "$2,000,000 Still on Hand." Elizabeth was always sensitive about overestimates of her wealth, when, in fact, she was habitually short on cash. This particular article does, however, reveal another instance of her generosity, going on to say, "Only recently it was learned that an entire community of farmers whose crops were wiped out by last season's drought are being provided for by Mrs. Watkins." She truly had a generous heart toward those who worked hard and had troubles not of their own making.

Two pages of clippings with handwritten notes show her love for her brother Frank. "The clippings on this page and one opposite were scraps found in my brother's 'bill folder' the day he was stricken and died. EMW." These entries, including inspiring poems, show that Frank had the same spiritual leanings as Elizabeth. One hand-typed little poem, "The Worry Cow," has her handwritten note: "The above is a bit of my brother's composition F. C. Miller. He had a keen sense of humor, as well as a serious strain—Elizabeth M. Watkins."

These touching pages of tribute to and remembrance of her beloved brother Frank kept his memory alive. She preserved these bits of his writings, to read again and again.

Elizabeth shared Frank's "keen sense of humor"; there are numerous amusing stories and jokes sprinkled throughout her scrapbook. Elizabeth and her brother also shared a sense of civic duty. The scrapbook includes an editorial from the *Kansas City Star* dated July 29, 1920, entitled "His Wealth to the Public." It reads, "The will of Mr. Frank C. Miller is an example of fine public spirit" and adds that, after having provided for his wife, he established two funds. "Both funds are for the aid of young people—one for the children of Mercy Hospital, and the other for loans to deserving students of the University of Kansas. What a satisfaction it must have been to Mr. Miller to look forward to generation after generation of children and young men and women, whose return to health or whose education had been made possible through his bequest."

In the Miller household, the value of public service had been taught and lived out by parents Ella and Valentine and had been passed on to their three children, Frank, Edward, and Elizabeth.

Elizabeth was described by some of the women who knew her best, housemothers at Watkins and Miller Scholarship Halls, as "sweet and simple." This description seems to defy logic, given Elizabeth's outstanding business acumen and her management of the Watkins fortune. However, the following poem in her scrapbook, written in her own hand, shows how she would define "simple."

"The Simple Things"
I would not be too wise, so very wise,
That I must sneer at simple songs and creeds,
And let the glare of wisdom blind my eyes
To humble people and their humble needs.
I would not care to climb so high that I
Could never hear the children at their play,
Could only see the people passing by,
Yet never hear the cheering words they say.
I would not know too much—too much to smile
At trivial errors of the heart and hand,
Not be too proud to play the friend the while,
Nor cease to help and know and understand.
I would not care to sit upon a throne,
Or build my house upon a mountain-top,
Where I must dwell in glory all alone
And never friend come in or poor man stop.
God grant that I may live upon this earth
And face the tasks that every morning brings,

Elizabeth, shown reading in her home. (Kenneth Spencer Research Library, University of Kansas)

And never lose the glory and the worth
Of humble service and the simple things.
  Edgar Guest

Elizabeth's political views were also anything but simple. As noted before, she and JB had shared the burden of being Democrats in the Republican town of Lawrence, but their views were at odds with President Franklin Delano Roosevelt's New Deal policies, which they saw as too much of a handout. Several editorials in her scrapbook are critical of Roosevelt. Remember that even when the First Lady visited Elizabeth's beloved Miller Hall in 1938, Elizabeth did not welcome her personally or even bother to invite her to tea or show up at the luncheon at the Women's Club.

An interesting side story is that most of the numerous political essays in her scrapbook were written by Boake Carter, a well-known journalist of the day. Carter was born to English parents in what is now Baku, Azerbaijan, where his father, who was in the oil business, was the British honorary consul. Carter moved to America in 1921 and later became a naturalized citizen. He was an unknown, fledgling reporter at the *Philadelphia Daily News* when he got a break. A rugby match was to be held, and Carter, who had done part of his growing up in the United Kingdom, was the only one on the reporting staff who understood the game. He later achieved fame when he covered the Lindbergh baby kidnapping in 1932, and he parlayed that into greater fame in radio broadcasting in the 1930s. In 1936, he reportedly had more listeners than any other radio commentator.*

Carter criticized FDR for spending too much and not letting capitalism work; he said that in the five years since the Depression there had been no "long-term fix," no increase in jobs. His stance was not popular, and funding for his radio show slowly dried up. When he wrote an article stating that "responsible statesmen" in Europe were not concerned about Germany's invasion of Austria and the Sudetenland, and that there would be no World War II, his career was over. But in the 1930s his was an accepted voice of political dissent, critical of the massive spending of the New Deal and claiming that capitalism would work if simply let alone by regulators. His political and economic views aligned with those held by JB and Elizabeth. However, Elizabeth, always an independent thinker, judged each political issue by itself, for herself. At times, her family loyalty to the GOP showed itself. She contributed to the Republican Party in support of Kansan Alf Landon's run for president.

Elizabeth often spent an afternoon at the movie theater, the Granada, across from the Watkins Bank building. Emory Frank Scott, in his book *One Hundred Years of Lawrence Theatres,* wrote: "One of the regular Granada matinee patrons, she would arrive out front in her KU student chauffeured sixteen-cylinder Cadillac. With her summer white shoes, white stockings, and white dress, Mrs. J. B. Watkins, who would become Lawrence's outstanding benefactress, would alight gracefully, assisted by the liveried attendant, after he had purchased her ticket, then smiling to all present, made a regal entrance to the theatre. If Lawrence ever laid claim to a queenly individual, this former employee, who married her employer, would, to this writer's judgment, certainly qualify."

---

* Information about Boake Carter comes from Elizabeth's scrapbook at the Watkins Museum of History and is available at www.liquisearch.com/boake_carter.

Nancy Helmstadter of Lawrence remembers that, as a small girl, about five years old, she once sat with Elizabeth Watkins in the theater. Elizabeth told Nancy that she appreciated that she was wearing white gloves, and Nancy confessed that she did so to keep from biting her fingernails. At one "scary" part in a movie Nancy scooted down beside Elizabeth and asked if she could sit beside her. Nancy's grandfather, C. E. Friend, had built the Granada Theater. Here is a selection of movies shown at that time: *Camille* with Greta Garbo and Robert Taylor; *The Devil Is a Sissy* with Freddie Bartholomew, Jackie Cooper, Mickey Rooney, and Ian Hunter; *Born to Dance* with Eleanor Powell, James Stewart, Buddy Ebsen, and Frances Langford; and *Libeled Lady* with William Powell, Jean Harlow, Myrna Loy, and Spencer Tracy.

Elizabeth's religious faith supported and sustained her throughout her life, and, in characteristic fashion, she supported Lawrence churches monetarily. In 1930, she began paying $400 toward the salary of Reverend Aszman, pastor of the Presbyterian Church, and she continued to help pay his salary as long as she was able. Even though she belonged to the Presbyterian Church, she also was sympathetic to the needs of other churches. She gave $400 to Trinity Lutheran for pew cushions.

Elizabeth's home, The Outlook, was at 1500 Louisiana, as the address appears on her personal stationery. At some point the street name was changed to Lilac Lane, by a process that will become clear. Obviously, the street was named for the abundant lilacs that historically grew all along it. The old lilac bushes that grew along the street behind Fraser Hall (both Old and New Fraser Halls), across from The Outlook and the Watkins and Miller Scholarship Halls, lasted until 2016, when the aging bushes were removed and new ones were planted.

The renaming of the street may be explained here. For years, the women of Watkins and Miller Scholarship Halls held a Mother's Day Breakfast in May. Over the years, the event developed into an Alumnae Tea. Whatever the name, from the beginning, the day has been a special occasion for the halls to shine. The residents plan a program of entertainment and prepare lovely refreshments. Poetry readings, singing, and instrumental music have all been parts of the performances. The alumnae association for Watkins and Miller Halls is known as Kitchen 8, a metaphoric reference to graduation from the seven small kitchen groups in each hall to belong to a new group, Kitchen 8. The alumnae group's Kitchen 8 Archives, held at the Watkins Museum of History, contain the following document, which was typed on Elizabeth's personal stationery. She likely read her message in person at the celebration on May 2, 1937.

Miss Nelson and Friends: I know no better way in which to assure you of a royal welcome to Watkins Hall than to tell you the story as it has come to me of the planting of the Lilac Hedge more than sixty years ago by young men just from New England who had settled here and were eager to beautify their new home in The West. The cuttings were furnished by the nurserymen and the work was done by students directed by The Savage Brothers, Joseph and Forrest. Their work still stands as a monument of beauty to that early day desire for trees and shrubbery—how little they guessed it would last so many years! It seems to me fitting that the poem that Dean Arvin S. Olin wrote many years ago should be read today as that hedge seems to have bloomed for the trimming of This Mother's Day Breakfast at Watkins Hall. Certainly nothing could be more suitable ON LILAC LANE as Mr. Lemuel Rothberger, a Taxi Driver, named it and The City Council legalized it, at my request. May the second, 1937.

So, it was Elizabeth who requested the change of street name. Given her gifts to the city and the university, the city council must have been quick to grant her request and make it official. It was another example of that attention to detail, ability to get things done, and confidence in her own judgment that were evident throughout the life of Elizabeth Miller Watkins.

In the middle of Elizabeth's personal scrapbook is a prayer that seems to speak to the emotional injuries she had experienced during her life. By the time she began assembling the scrapbook in the 1930s, she had increasing health problems that were largely the result of years lived under intense pressure. She had been under siege from JB's alleged heirs and greedy relations. She was only human and needed help to not mind "treachery or meanness." This prayer reads:

O God, give me courage to live another day. Let me not turn the coward before its difficulties or prove recreant to its duties. Let me not lose

One of the last formal portraits taken of Elizabeth. It shows
her keen, intelligent eyes, her love of elegant fabrics, and her
favorite long strand of pearls. (Douglas County Historical
Society, Watkins Museum of History)

faith in my fellowmen: keep me sweet and sound at heart, in spite of in-
gratitude, treachery, or meanness. Preserve me, O God, from minding
little stings or giving them. Help me to keep my heart clean and to live
so honestly and fearlessly that no outward failure can dishearten me or
take away the joy of conscious integrity. Open wide the eyes of my soul,
that I may see good in all things. Grant this day some new vision of Thy

Truth. Inspire me with the spirit of joy and gladness, and make me the cup of strength to suffering souls. In the name of the strong Deliverer. Amen.

The last page of Elizabeth's scrapbook is also a prayer, with a focus on the serene natural world and a plea to "know ourselves to be safely held in Thy strong hands."

In the early morning of June 1, 1939, Elizabeth Josephine Miller Watkins died of a kidney infection. She had been ill for seven weeks.

The *University Daily Kansan* wrote on the day of her death: "Death deprived the University of one of its best friends this morning. Mrs. Elizabeth M. Watkins died suddenly at 9:05. She was an influence in the lives of countless University students for years. Her gifts to the University made it possible for many women to continue their education. Through her philanthropies, Mrs. Watkins will be forever remembered by the students who comprise the University of Kansas."

The accolades were many, but she probably would not have wanted that. Mrs. Samuel Stayton, the first housemother Elizabeth Watkins had hired to chaperone the Miller Hall women, was at the bedside when Elizabeth passed away on June 1. A personal friend, she was aware of Elizabeth's attachment to the scholarship halls she had given KU. Mrs. Stayton had often told the hall residents about Elizabeth, her regret at not being able to get a college education when she was young and her great satisfaction in being able to help these young women with the scholarship hall awards.

Lena Hayden Esterly, the Watkins Hall housemother at the time of Elizabeth's death, said "Mrs. Watkins was simple, sweet, modest and retiring. She knew what women need and gave wisely, generously and nobly. There are no other houses on other campuses like Watkins and Miller Halls. Mrs. Watkins hated long illnesses and had been feeling poorly for a long time before she took to her bed. Her place in this community will never be filled. Her name will always live." And Elizabeth's name does live on. Not only in the good health of Lawrence residents and KU students but also in the education of thousands of young women who, with the help of their Watkins or Miller Scholarship Hall award, could afford to attend college.

As Chris Lazzarino wrote in 2011 in the *KU Alumni Magazine*, "The 150th anniversary of Mrs. Watkins' birth was January 21 and the testament

PALL-BEARERS
HONORARY
CHANCELLOR E. H. LINDLEY
DR. M. T. SUDLER
OLIN TEMPLIN
HUGH MEANS   A. D. WEAVER
T. C. GREEN   W. C. SIMONS
I. J. MEAD
ACTIVE
DR. R. I. CANUTESON
E. H. TAYLOR   DICK WILLIAMS
A. B. WEAVER   DOLPH SIMONS
T. J. SWEENEY, JR.
RAYMOND F. RICE
A. B. MITCHELL
C. B. RUSSELL
GENE HARRIS

Crossing The Bar

Sunset and evening star,
   And one clear call for me!
And may there be
   no moaning of the Bar
When I put out to sea.

+   +   +   +   +   +

For tho' from out our bourne
   of Time and Place
The flood may bear me far,
I hope to see my Pilot—
   face to face,
When I have crost the bar.
   —Tennyson

SERVICES

FOR

ELIZABETH M. WATKINS

BORN

JANUARY 21, 1861

NEW PARIS, OHIO

PASSED AWAY

JUNE 1, 1939

LAWRENCE, KANSAS

SERVICES HELD

AT

FIRST PRESBYTERIAN CHURCH

JUNE 3, 1939

CLERGYMEN

REV. THEO. H. ASZMAN

CHANCELLOR E. H. LINDLEY

INTERMENT

PRIVATE

In MEMORIAM

Funeral card for Elizabeth's service, with many well-known names:
Chancellor Lindley, KUEA's Olin Templin, Hugh Means (one of her executors),
A. D. Weaver, T. C. Green (lifelong Watkins employee), W. C. Simons,
Dr. Canuteson, Dick Williams (her business manager and another executor),
A. B. Weaver, Dolph Simons, and Raymond Rice (her attorney), among others.
(Kenneth Spencer Research Library, University of Kansas)

to her sincerity, vision and action is that young women born more than a
half-century after her death consider her a friend and threw her a birthday
party."

Elizabeth had been praised as Lady Bountiful. Earlier, she and JB had
not always been accepted into society in Lawrence, and she didn't have
many close friends in town. However, she didn't let that stop her from

leaving the town of Lawrence and the University of Kansas in much better shape than when she arrived in 1872.

A quote from the eulogy given by the Reverend Theodore Aszman of the Presbyterian Church on June 3, 1939, poetically sums up Elizabeth's life.

The fragrance of the flask of perfume
Of her thoughtful acts lingers on, and
Will linger, down through the years . . .

CHAPTER 14

The Lasting Watkins Legacy

Elizabeth Miller Watkins has been the focus of this work, but it is impossible to overstate the influence JB and Elizabeth had in each other's lives. When JB decided to move his business to Lawrence and Elizabeth's family moved to the city as well, events were set in motion that have had a lasting effect on the city of Lawrence, the University of Kansas, and thousands of young lives. Examination of Elizabeth's and JB's childhoods and adult business lives leads to an understanding of their philosophy of giving and their belief in the importance of education for the young, their most enduring legacy.

Elizabeth gave so much to the city of Lawrence and the University of Kansas; but one truly remarkable statistic stands out. When Elizabeth inherited JB's estate, the total value was estimated at $2.4 million, and when she died, her estate was worth roughly $3 million. She built, equipped, and furnished Watkins Hall, Lawrence Memorial Hospital, Lawrence Memorial's nurses' home, Watkins Memorial Hospital, Miller Hall, Watkins Memorial's nurses' home, and the guest cottage, not to mention additions to several of these projects. There can be no doubt she was a successful businesswoman, ahead of her time. She not only survived the Great Depression of the 1930s, but came through with more money than when she started.

The *Sunday News and Tribune* of Jefferson City, Missouri, commended the Watkins legacy on March 3, 1935:

Out in Lawrence, Kansas, for the past half century Mr. and Mrs. Jabez B. Watkins have been making money. When they had accumulated an estate of $3,000,000 they set about administering on it. Having had a great time together making money, they wanted to have a still greater time spending it where it would do the most good. After giving away about $1,000,000 to benevolent enterprises, Mr. Watkins died, and now his widow is carrying on and expects to give the other $2,000,000 away before she goes to join her late husband. There were no children in the Watkins home, so she is administering on the estate of her husband by giving what they made "for the good of humanity." And another fine thing about her bounty is that the money is to be given in Lawrence where they made the money. This Saturday Night we are singing the praise of this couple. They had a great time making their money and they are having a greater time doing good with it. They could have gone on making money until death called Mr. Watkins, and then Mrs. Watkins could have hugged every nickel to her soul until she died, and then lawyers could have had a picnic settling up the estate, distributing it to distant relatives. But they chose the better way—we wonder why more folk who have made money do not follow the way of the Watkins.

Elizabeth and JB left a bountiful legacy. They left buildings, trust funds, and thousands of acres of Kansas farmland. But the more important and longer lasting legacy is their provision for young people's education combined with their example of thoughtful and careful giving.

Most of the buildings they planned and that Elizabeth built are still standing, testaments to their generosity. The first, built by JB Watkins in 1888, was the Watkins Bank and Watkins Land and Mortgage Company at Eleventh Street and Massachusetts. This striking building, which Elizabeth gave the city of Lawrence, served as the city hall from 1929 until 1970 and now functions as the beautiful home of the Watkins Museum of History. It is still a vibrant part of downtown Lawrence and the culture of the city.

Next was their home, The Outlook, built in 1909. The Outlook still serves as a home to each chancellor of the University of Kansas; nearly every chancellor since Chancellor Malott has lived in the elegant Neoclassic house. It is a tradition to renovate and redecorate prior to a new chancellor moving in. Some features of Elizabeth's time have gone by the wayside: no longer needed is the coal chute and gone are the chicken house and the ahead-of-its-time vacuum system. Some unique architectural features of the home are visible to those who walk by, including the columned entry and the widow's walk along the roofline. Another signature feature is the carpet in the entry. A replica of a carpet in Cedar Crest, official residence for Kansas governors, it has a dark blue background with the Great Seal of the State of Kansas woven into a large circular design.

Traditionally, chancellors are free to choose artwork to decorate The Outlook while they live in the home; these pieces are generally provided by the Spencer Art Museum. Carol Shankel, wife of former Chancellor Del Shankel, enhanced that tradition, decorating The Outlook with pieces that showcased the talents of professors from KU's art department. As a sign of her affection for the lovely home, Gretchen Budig, wife of former Chancellor Gene Budig, gifted an antique pier mirror to The Outlook.

The home's first floor is used for entertaining university guests. Carol Shankel remembers how easily the rooms, and therefore the guests, flowed from one area to another. The dining room, where Elizabeth's portrait still hangs, could host a formal dinner for twelve, but, because the living rooms flowed into each other, small tables could accommodate a buffet dinner for up to thirty-six. It is always a treasured event to be invited to The Outlook, to see Elizabeth's home and feel a part of the legacy.

The second and third floors of The Outlook are private, kept apart for the use of the chancellor's family. Gretchen Budig recalls that she loved living in the home with their three children. Their son, Chris, "had the most fun since he took over the third floor with all its little 'storage' rooms that were so small. I told him that they had to always be shut tight because they led into the underpinnings of the house. One time he forgot, and our cat went into the crawl space, and we didn't know it until we heard her meowing through the air vent in one of the upstairs bedrooms." Carol Shankel tells the story of her young daughter's job delivering the local newspaper. One morning when her supply was not delivered on time, she called to have the papers sent. When the delivery person would not believe that she lived at The Outlook, Carol had to vouch for her daughter's truthfulness!

This gracious home that was still able to host a chancellor with a lively young family is, at well over a hundred years old, a well-maintained and active symbol of the Watkins legacy.

Even the small cottage behind The Outlook, built with leftover stone, is still in service today. The sunny, inviting guest house in a park-like setting welcomes guests of the university. In the past, reservations were handled through the chancellor's office. Today, the Department of Student Housing manages the cottage and rents the facility to the university. The cottage is well maintained and has guest bookings into the next year.

For many years, graduate students or graduate married couples lived in the cottage to care for university guests, in return for free housing and tuition. The first couple to gain this happy assignment were KU's Distinguished Professor Emeritus Valentino Stella and his wife, Beth Roeder Stella, in the 1970s. At the time they were graduate students working on a PhD in pharmacy and a master's in piano, respectively. Beth remembers that their "duties included getting the bedroom ready for guests and providing a continental breakfast. . . . I kept the kitchen clean and tidy, so guests were never aware of us using it." The graduate student living quarters were in the lower level, a studio-size apartment, by the garage. Sometime later, Beth recalls, "the garage was turned into a proper apartment [with kitchen] so the accommodations eventually became quite nice by graduate student standards." She recalls a steady stream of visitors during their time as caretakers. "Guests ranged from people brought in to consult with the chancellor, board of regents, and guest speakers from various disciplines." Lawrence Chalmers was chancellor at the time, and the Stellas babysat the Chalmers's children while the parents attended university events.

The first building Elizabeth built alone was Watkins Scholarship Hall, in 1926. It underwent a major renovation in 2016 and has not missed a year of welcoming young residents into its small sheltered environment within the larger university. The hall was Elizabeth's unique idea, her "dream come true." Because it does not hold as many occupants as a modern dormitory would in a footprint of that size, rumors have surfaced from time to time that it would be razed. As Watkins Hall approaches its hundredth year of nurturing and caring for young women, it is impossible to believe it would or could be replaced.

The Lawrence Memorial Hospital was Elizabeth's next project, built in 1929. She also funded an expansion a few years later, but as the city grew, so did the need for more beds. In the spring of 1956 a south addition was completed with funds from the federal government through the Hill–Burton Act. Facilities for all departments of the hospital were included in this expansion, which brought the total number of beds to 146. In December 1969, another addition expanded the number of beds to 165. In August 1975, ground was broken for a new building that virtually replaced the old. Only the 1969 wing was retained, and the capacity was two hundred beds. The hospital Elizabeth built was demolished in 1999.

The last year that nurses lived in the nurses' home was 1963. After that, the home that Elizabeth had built for Lawrence Memorial Hospital in 1930 was used mainly for supervisory staff. It was razed along with the hospital in 1999.

Elizabeth's hospital for KU students, Watkins Memorial Hospital, was built in 1932. For forty-two years, it served students at its convenient campus location. In May 1974, a new student health center opened, the Watkins Health Center, built with funds from Elizabeth's gifts to the university and in tribute to her legacy. The former hospital, the first example of Art Deco architecture on campus, became the home of the School of Social Welfare. It was renamed Twente Hall, in honor of Esther Twente, the founder of the School of Social Welfare. As with all of Elizabeth's projects for the University of Kansas, the well-built Twente Hall still graces its location on campus; it is still useful and, therefore, true to Elizabeth's intent.

The sister to Watkins Hall, Miller Scholarship Hall, was built next, in 1937. As with Watkins Hall, Miller Hall was also updated with a major renovation in 2016 that has equipped it to serve as a home to young students for many years to come. Watkins and Miller are the centerpieces of KU's unique scholarship hall system. Elizabeth never completed her planned scholarship hall for men, but the ten other men's and women's scholarship residences on the KU campus were inspired by her "theory."

The last of Elizabeth's building projects, a nurses' home built in 1938 for the campus hospital, is simply named "Watkins Home" on the stone above its doorway. From 1974 until 1984, the building was used for community services, and it held a computer center for students during this time. In 1984, it became the Hall Center for the Humanities. When the Hall Center moved into a new home in 2005, the School of Social Welfare expanded into the Watkins Home. Twente Hall, now home of the School of Social Welfare, sits next to the Watkins Home, which is used for that school's faculty, graduate student offices, and conference rooms. The two buildings still share a linked purpose. Solidly built, the Watkins Home has served many needs for the university over the years.

Overall, the buildings constructed by Elizabeth Miller Watkins have stood the test of time. She learned from JB to choose quality materials and monitor the construction process closely. Mark Reiske, current university architect and director of KU Facilities Planning and Development, appreciates the fine quality of construction of all the Watkins buildings. During the 2016 renovation of Watkins and Miller Halls, engineers were amazed at the quality and durability of the original electrical wiring and craftsmanship. JB and Elizabeth both chose quality materials, as, for example, the carefully selected oak flooring and the long-lasting terrazzo floors in The Outlook. They closely supervised construction and pored over bills. With KU's careful maintenance, these well-preserved buildings have stayed true to Elizabeth's purposes. They have provided health and education to many and are an inspiration to others.

The Watkins legacy also includes the many trust funds or endowments that Elizabeth bestowed. The first listed in her will is a trust of $5,000.00 for the perpetual care and upkeep of the Watkins lot in Oak Hill Cemetery, by which Elizabeth ensured that this would not be a financial burden on the city.

The largest trust in Elizabeth's will, $250,000.00, was for the Watkins and Miller Scholarship Halls, a reflection of her emotional attachment to the halls that extended to its future residents. After her death in 1939, the funds were invested and the income was to be divided equally between the two halls and used "perpetually for maintenance, upkeep and operation." As of 2018, the Watkins and Miller Halls Trust had grown to $3.9 million. Following Elizabeth's instructions, a portion of the income from that trust is annually divided between the halls and used by the university for their upkeep and maintenance.

Lawrence Memorial Hospital received a trust of $100,000.00; to this day, the income from that trust is still invested and is used for the operation of the hospital.

The Watkins Memorial Hospital on the KU campus also received a trust of $175,000.00. It also is invested, and income from it is used for maintenance, upkeep, and operations.

Smaller gifts were made to Elizabeth's church, First Presbyterian, its Reverend Aszman, and numerous other charities, within Kansas and without.

Elizabeth's will names more than eighty individuals who received financial gifts. Names include family members, friends, business associates, and the present and former housemothers of Watkins and Miller Scholarship Halls. Larger amounts, many in the form of lifetime incomes, were specified for close relatives. She remembered longtime Watkins Bank employee T. C. Green with a gift of five years' salary. She left Dick Williams's wife, Mary, her ermine cape, and she left special bequests for the Williams children.

It is curious that her long pearl necklace from JB, known to be her favorite item of jewelry, is not mentioned in the will. Julius Marks of Marks Jewelry in Lawrence appraised the necklace on June 17, 1939: "59 genuine pearls, graduated platinum and diamond clasp, set with small marquis diamonds and four small round diamonds. Total weight of pearls approx. 240 grains. Valuation—$4800.00." That would be nearly $100,000 in 2022 dollars. The whereabouts of Elizabeth's favorite pearls are, to this day, a mystery. Her other jewelry was given to chosen individuals.

Elizabeth had allotted these gifts carefully. Her beloved Watkins Hall received a painting, *Sunset at Long Beach* by Richard Dey de Ribcowsky (1880–1936). Born in Bulgaria, Dey de Ribcowsky came to the United States in 1910 and settled in California in the 1920s. He exhibited his paintings in prominent California hotels, and Elizabeth undoubtedly purchased hers on one of her trips. The painting still hangs in Watkins Hall. Elizabeth bequeathed a tapestry to Miller Hall.

True to form, in her will Elizabeth listed instructions about how to invest the funds she left various groups. She named her executors: Dick Williams, her business manager, Raymond Rice, her attorney, and Judge Hugh Means. She also specified their salaries, with yearly limits not to be exceeded. She established that Dick Williams should have office space in Lawrence City Hall, the former Watkins Bank building, for five years, and she directed payment to be made for that. She remembered that it had taken her five years to settle JB's estate, and she provided a workspace for Dick while he settled hers.

The largest gift in Elizabeth's will was to the Kansas University Endowment Association (KUEA). All real estate she owned within the state of Kansas was given to that entity "to be held, managed, controlled and disposed of by it and the rents, profits and income therefrom and the proceeds of the sale thereof to be received, held, used and disbursed by" KUEA. Crops grown on over twenty-four thousand acres of Kansas farmland have yielded millions of dollars to finance a myriad of KUEA projects and programs. Elizabeth specified that the association should employ Dick Williams to oversee and manage her gifts for "as long as he cared to do so." This agreement was set separately from her will on December 18, 1930.

Judith Galas, in her research paper about Elizabeth Watkins, wrote, "At the time, her gift was the largest ever given for the benefit of a state university, and it formed the basis of an unrestricted fund that continues to support KU and the Endowment Association. Over the years, income from that fund has put Elizabeth's fingerprints all over K.U."

In a 1971 presentation to the Douglas County Historical Society, former KUEA head Irvin E. Youngberg outlined the Watkins gifts thirty-two years after Elizabeth's death: "Much of what has been done with the resources Mrs. Watkins gave is generally known in the Lawrence and University communities, but many things that daily touch the lives of students, staff and townspeople alike are less well known. For example, residents are reminded of the time of the day by the large bell in the Campanile, but few are aware that the bell, which tolls the hours, is a memorial to Mrs. Watkins' long-time friend, Dean Templin, was made possible by the Watkins legacy."

Youngberg went on to list other gifts from the Watkins Fund. The fund was the largest donor for construction of Danforth Chapel. In the 1950s it provided a grant to the School of Business for use in implementing the case study method. In 1952, a grant from the fund was used to start the university's study abroad program, which "literally carried the name of the University of Kansas around the world." The student union at the KU Medical Center in Kansas City was built with Watkins funds. Watkins monies paid for the feasibility study for the Greater University Fund; this new fund allowed KU alumni and friends to pool their resources and provide broad support for the university's needs. Stephenson, Pearson, and Sellards Scholarship Halls were partially paid for with Watkins Fund income. And Watkins–Berger Scholarships give high-achieving students recognition and support.

Elizabeth's benefactions extended to faculty as well as students, Youngberg noted. With the income KUEA received, it gave grants to faculty for research outside the continental United States. By 1956, the Watkins Staff Revolving Fund was established to provide interest-free short-term loans to faculty, as they waited for the state to reimburse them for travel and other expenses. Watkins Summer Staff Fellowships, set up in 1954, provided "grocery and rent money" to junior staff members, which allowed them to use their summers for independent research, to improve their qualifications as teachers, or to develop new curriculum. According to Youngberg, this program helped the university retain outstanding young faculty who otherwise might have been tempted by more financially appealing offers in other places.

Youngberg also noted the extensions of the physical campus made possible with the income from the Watkins farmlands. The campus of the KU Medical Center, based in Kansas City, Kansas, was able to double in size, giving the institution space to expand research, teaching, and hospital areas. Quick access to Watkins funds helped the university's School of Medicine land a US Public Health Communicable Diseases Center, with its specialists and staff.

After World War II, acquisition of the 212-acre Bisonte farm southwest of the Lawrence campus added much-needed room for expansion as the student body grew rapidly with the return of veterans. Small tracts to the east of campus were used to build new scholarship houses. In 1945, the Gowans tract, purchased with Watkins funds, was used to build Sunnyside, a faculty housing project. West campus has grown thanks to purchase of the sixty-acre Brown farm in 1946, with its signature stone barns. In all, nearly four hundred acres south and west of the initial campus were purchased to house a field house, intramural fields, and the large dormitories on "Daisy Hill," with space still available for future expansion. The campus of today would not have been possible without the additional land, all purchased with JB and Elizabeth Watkins's invested income.

In addition to the well-known Watkins bequests that benefit KU, the

Watkins influence extends even into the athletic life of the university. There is a link to Elizabeth's business manager. Dick Williams had begun working for the Watkins National Bank in 1915 after his graduation from KU, and then, when Elizabeth's nephew, heir apparent Frank V. Miller, died suddenly in 1923, Williams stepped in. He and his family became like family to Elizabeth. He was executive vice president of Watkins National Bank from 1925 until its merger with Lawrence National Bank in 1927 and was later instrumental in establishing Douglas County State Bank in 1952, where he served as president until his death in 1970. His early business experience with Elizabeth served him well.

To explain the link among Williams, Watkins, and KU Athletics, we look to the history of KUEA. Dick Williams managed the Watkins bequests to KUEA, both monetary funds and the Kansas farmland, beginning in 1939, after Elizabeth's death. In 1949, Dick organized KUEA's John H. Outland Fund to provide scholarship assistance to student athletes. His sons, Skipper and Odd, continued his work with KUEA and focused on athletics at KU.

The Outland Fund was later renamed the Williams Fund. Scott McMichael, a former director of the Williams Educational Fund, now assistant athletic director and senior director of development at the University of Colorado, Boulder, tells how the fund was renamed: "In the early 70's the Outland Fund name was changed to the Williams Educational Fund in honor of Dick, Skipper & Odd for their tremendous commitment and vision helping the Athletic Department move forward. . . . The Williams Fund continued to provide K.U. student-athletes the opportunity to not only compete at the highest level, but more importantly the ability to obtain a first class education." Education, the keystone of JB and Elizabeth's legacy, was still the goal.

With no end in sight, the legacy of Elizabeth and JB Watkins continues to benefit many, in many ways. Dale Seuferling, president of KUEA, gave this tribute to the lasting Watkins legacy:

More than 82 years after her death, the philanthropic legacy of Elizabeth Watkins endures at the University of Kansas. In addition to the many specific gifts contributed by Mrs. Watkins, perhaps her greatest legacy is her inspiration of others to advance KU through their own gifts.

Evidence of her philanthropy abounds, from iconic buildings that continue to grace Mount Oread to the endowments that fund so many initiatives, the University of Kansas would not be the university it is without the generosity of Elizabeth Watkins. In her lifetime, she made foundational gifts that continue to influence the Jayhawk experience for students, faculty, staff and more.

More than that, she modeled the behavior others would later embrace as they, too, made gifts to the university. As an example, Watkins gave 24,000 acres of Kansas farmland to the university through KU Endowment. Today, KU Endowment is the trustee to more than 50,000 acres across the state, with holdings in 50 Kansas counties. Without question, Elizabeth Watkins' generous act inspired and informed so many donors to follow her example.

Promising students with the motivation to succeed but not the means to pay for school, can thank Elizabeth Watkins for providing money to build the first scholarship halls at KU—Miller and Watkins Halls. Again, not only did Mrs. Watkins create a KU "first" with her gifts, but her foresight inspired donors to contribute ten more halls to create a vibrant scholarship hall community at KU.

In KU's history, Elizabeth Watkins was a pioneering philanthropist. It is therefore fitting that we honor those who have made provisions for KU in their estate plans by welcoming them into the society named in her honor—The Watkins Society.

Whether it was her giving while she was alive, or the provisions she made in her estate plans, Elizabeth Watkins' generosity shaped—and continues to shape—the University of Kansas we know today.

More importantly, her giving continues to inspire us all to give what we can to "build a greater university than the state alone can build."

Yes, Elizabeth wanted to build the university. We know from her actions and her words that helping young people get an education was her most fervent wish. Elizabeth's novel idea for scholarship halls must be considered one of her greatest legacies, certainly the one that was dearest to her. Thousands of young women and men were able to get an education, thanks to the financial help the scholarship halls provided.

The first of its kind in the nation, Watkins Hall proved to be a success, under Elizabeth's watchful eye. Unique to the University of Kansas, this system of housing began with Elizabeth's idea and her donation of Watkins and, later, Miller Scholarship Hall. KU now boasts twelve scholarship residences that offer affordable living for motivated and high-performing students.

As Don Alderson, former dean of men at KU, stated, "Watkins Hall started it all." He defined the "recipe" for success as "one part scholarship, one part work." In the scholarship hall system, especially, the legacy has stayed true to Elizabeth and JB's original intent: a hand up, not a handout. Other universities may have one scholarship house or two, but none have a robust scholarship hall community that matches KU and its twelve scholarship houses.

In further tribute to Elizabeth's contributions, KU's East Historic District gained national recognition on January 23, 2014. "Eight of the University of Kansas' scholarship halls, the chancellor's residence and the beloved Danforth Chapel [built largely with Watkins funds] are all part of a new historic district recently listed in the National Register of Historic Places." Announcing the news, Chancellor Bernadette Gray-Little said, "I can't tell you how many alumni have shared with me their fond memories of living in a scholarship hall, or of getting married in Danforth Chapel. These places are central to the lives of so many Jayhawks, and we're pleased to be able to preserve these buildings and landscapes so that current and future students can have similar experiences while at KU."

Watkins Hall and Miller Hall have each been called "an incubator" for leadership and "a hearth" for support and advice; the scholarship halls have led young women and men to lives of direction, passion, and motivation. Elizabeth's "dream come true" can perhaps be summed up in the words of Creta Carter Nichols, who lived in Watkins Hall from 1956 to 1958: "We Watkins women believed we were in charge of our own lives and that our futures depended on us. . . . We were in college because we had decided . . . to propel ourselves into a future of opportunity and challenge. . . . We believed that our lives, for the most part, depended on what

From two, now twelve

The long history of scholarship halls is built on generous private gifts, starting with two from Elizabeth Miller Watkins. She funded Watkins Scholarship Hall in 1926 and Miller Scholarship Hall in 1937, the first two halls of their kind in the country. Watkins was instrumental in the design and operation of this new type of housing. The scholarship hall community has since grown to 12, six for men and six for women. The halls, the years they opened, and the donors whose gifts made them possible:

Watkins Scholarship Hall, 1926

Battenfeld, 1940, men; Jesse and Margaret Battenfeld, in memory of their son, John. *Sellards,* 1952, women; *Pearson,* 1952, men; and *Grace Pearson,* 1955, men; J.R. and Gertrude Sellards Pearson, a 1901 KU alumna. *Stephenson,* 1952, men; partly funded by Grace Stephenson, in honor of her husband, Lyle Stephenson. *Douthart,* 1954, women; Burt Chronister, in memory of his wife, Ava Douthart Chronister, a 1901 graduate, and her sister Lela Douthart, an 1899 alumna. *K.K. Amini,* 1992, men; K.K. and Margaret Amini. *Margaret Amini,* 2000, women; K.K. and Margaret Amini. *Dennis E. Rieger,* 2005, women; Annette and Roger Rieger, in honor of Roger's brother. *Floyd H. and Kathryn Krehbiel,* 2008, men; Karl Krehbiel, in honor of his parents. He gave an additional $400,000 to establish a hall maintenance fund, as Watkins had done with the first two scholarship halls. *Crawford Community Center,* 2007, not a residence but a convenient place for all scholarship hall residents to study or hold meetings. Originally the home of KU Professor Reginald Strait and his wife, Juanita. She bequeathed it to KU Endowment, and Tom and Jann Rudkin funded its renovation; it's named for Jann's mother.

From two, now twelve—an overview of the scholarship hall community at KU that Elizabeth began with Watkins and Miller Scholarship Halls. (Kansas University Endowment Association, reprint of article in *KU Giving* magazine, Winter 2012, with thanks to Dale Seuferling)

we did with our innate gifts. But I will never forget that, in addition to our belief in ourselves, at Watkins we thrived in the atmosphere of support, appreciation, respect and encouragement we gave each other."

That atmosphere of respect and encouragement was facilitated by the forethought and care that Elizabeth Miller Watkins put into building her "dream come true." Her unusual architectural design with the seven small kitchens in the lower level of each hall provided the space for cooperative work in small groups, resulting in the effect she sought: a family atmosphere within the larger university. Although the seven small kitchens are still unique to Watkins and Miller Halls and are not duplicated in the newer scholarship halls, communal work is required as an essential component to life in each hall.

The support provided by the scholarship halls has been tested through the years. Eileen Griffith Bennett, who lived in Watkins Hall from 1940 to 1944, related that "there had been a great amount of talk of war in Europe. When we in Watkins Hall were gathered to hear President Roosevelt announce our declaration of war in 1941, it took on a new, horrible reality.... The Dean of Men called an all-student convocation at the University. He spoke of how much we were all going to be needed in the workforce in this country, and urged us to be serious students and graduate as early as possible." Events of the late 1960s and early 1970s—the Vietnam War, peace protests, the burning of the Kansas Union, Civil Rights marches—made campus life unstable, but incredibly interesting. The protective environment of Watkins and Miller Halls was especially important in unsettled times; as they gathered in the small kitchens, residents with close relationships could talk over current events.

The halls also provided diversity of experience. Residents learned to live and work cooperatively with others, perhaps very different from themselves, another valuable legacy facilitated by the design of the halls. Margery Lewis Wigner was a resident in Watkins Hall from 1938 to 1941. Her daughter, Betsy Wigner Holste, shared: "For my mother, living at the halls was a growing experience. She met people from varied backgrounds—like Herta Eichterschelmert. [Mother] wrote of getting to know her and understand what a rough life Herta and her family had led before coming to the United States. Herta had fled Europe before WWII because of Nazi persecution."

Elizabeth's scholarship hall idea helped young people who might otherwise not have been able to afford an education; living in the halls also helped them learn the tolerance that comes from communal living. Horizons were expanded as people with different religions and customs, people from different countries, lived together. As Lena Hayden Esterly, a former housemother at Watkins Hall, said of Elizabeth, "She knew what women need and gave wisely, generously and nobly." So wisely did she give these two scholarship halls that now the University of Kansas has twelve.

Throughout their lives, JB and Elizabeth shared common goals. Individually, and then together, they understood the importance of education. Their lives proved the value of attention to detail, careful planning, and exceptional work ethic. Their stewardship enabled intelligent and careful giving that has enhanced the lives of thousands of young people who, in turn, have spread that generosity of spirit all over the world.

These are the lasting legacies of JB and Elizabeth Watkins, who truly were partners for good.

~

"The Hedge"
The old lilac hedge still stands staunch and strong;
In Summer it straggles and sprangles along.
In Winter it catches the dead leaves and snow.
Its branches stringed harps to the fierce winds that blow;
But in April its fragrance is heavenly sweet,
And its bloom fairer pictures than most eyes e'er greet.
How wondrous like humans these lilac trees grow,
The straight and the crooked, the quick and the slow,
The smooth and the gnarled ones, the sturdy, the weak,
Some hugging the shadow, some sunshine to seek,
But when duty and law and occasion conspire
Both lilacs and humans achieve heart's desire,
Then here's to The Hedge! May its bloom never fail,
May it round out in vigor its century tale,
Bringing joy to the hearts of the freshman so gay,
And thoughts poignant sweet to old grads far away;
From all the old days there's no object more dear,
Binding THEN to the NOW linking There to the Here.
And I should be so happy, when time comes for rest,
To be chosen and guided to realms of the blest,
When Earth Winters pass in the change of the years,
And with Springtime comes April, half laughter, half tears,
From Heaven I'll surely look over the edge,
To perchance catch a glimpse of THE OLD LILAC HEDGE.
    Arvin S. Olin, died March 27, 1935

Arvin S. Olin was dean of education at KU from 1913–1915. A friend of Elizabeth's, this poem is preserved on her personal stationary.

Bibliography

Archival collections

Kansas City Public Library, Missouri Valley Special Collections, Kansas City, MO

Lawrence Public Library, Lawrence, KS

City Directory website, accessed through Lawrence Public Library: https://www.ancestryheritagequest.com/HQA/CityDirectories

Postma Postcard Collection: https://history.lplks.org/items/browse?collection=1&page=28

McNeese State University, Lake Charles, LA

J. B. Watkins Collection 1887–1905, 2.54 linear feet, Collection no. 43

Spencer Research Library, University of Kansas, Lawrence

Alumni Magazine: Shirley Ward Keeler, "Shock Troops of Housing" (January 1959); Chris Lazzarino, "Better to Give" no. 2 (2011): 23

Eighth Annual Catalogue of the Officers and Students of the University of Kansas, 1873–74, LD2677.U55, 1873–74

First Presbyterian Church records, RH C3667

Graduate Magazine: Fred Ellsworth, article about Watkins Hall and Elizabeth's philanthropy (December 1925); Scholarship Hall governance information (April 1937)

J. B. Watkins Papers, 627 linear feet, letters and business papers, RH MS1

Letters of Elizabeth Watkins, cataloged and indexed, RH MS 1

Nellie Barnes Papers, PP466

Opening of University Hospital. Pamphlet, University of Kansas Archives, Watkins Memorial Hospital, Building File, 0/22/97, 1932.

Watkins Museum of History, Lawrence, KS

Elizabeth Miller Watkins Scrapbook

"Friends Called Her Lizzie." Pamphlet. Friends of Watkins Museum, January 2002

Galas, Judith. Unpublished research paper on Elizabeth Watkins, 1998, Folder 3/25

Hodgson, Arthur. Letter, March 9, 1995. Folders 1/20–22

Janice Gartrell Scrapbook pages, Folder 4/3

Kitchen 8 Archives: newsletters and items pertaining to Watkins and Miller Halls, Kitchen 8 members, and Elizabeth Watkins

Meet Miller, pamphlet revised 1955, Folder 1/45

Memorandum on the J.B. Watkins Mortgage Company Records, Professor Malin to Robert Vosper, director of Libraries at University of Kansas, Folder 3/16

Wall, John. Interview by Monica Gambrell, September 14, 1993, Folder 2/47

Watkins, Jabez Bunting. *The True Money System of the United States*. New York: Press of Andrew H. Kellogg, 1896. (Photocopy) Folder 3/4

Newspapers

American Press (Lake Charles, LA)

Commercial Newspaper (Lake Charles, LA)

Daily Signal (Crowley, LA)

Daily Times-Record (Jennings, LA)

Findlay Jeffersonian (Findlay, OH)

Jeffersonian-Democrat (Brookville, PA)

Kansas City Gazette

Kansas City Star

Kansas Weekly Capital

Lawrence Daily Journal

Lawrence Daily Journal World

Lawrence Gazette

Lawrence Journal-World

New York Times

Newton Daily Republican (Newton, KS)

Philadelphia Daily News (Philadelphia, PA)

Republican Journal (Lawrence, KS)

Shreveport Journal (Shreveport, LA)

St. Landry Clarion (St. Landry, LA)

Sunday News and Tribune (Jefferson City, MO)

Times-Democrat (New Orleans, LA)

Topeka State Journal (Topeka, KS)

Town Talk (Alexandria, LA)

University Daily Kansan (University of Kansas, Lawrence)

Weekly Record (Lawrence, KS)

Weekly Town Talk (Alexandria, LA)

Western Home Journal (Lawrence, KS)

Interviews

Barlow and Streeter families, interviewed by Norma Hoagland

Beth Roederer Stella, interviewed by Norma Hoagland (email)

Carol Shankel, interviewed by Norma Hoagland (email)

Dale Seuferling, interviewed by Norma Hoagland (email)
Gretchen Budig, interviewed by Norma Hoagland (email)
Mark Reiske, interviewed by Norma Hoagland (email)
Nancy Helmstadter, interviewed by Mary Burchill
Scott McMichael, interviewed by Norma Hoagland (email)

Websites
"Benjamin Harrison," History.com, https://history.com/topics/us-presidents/ben
    jamin-harrison
Burns, Stanley, The Burns Archive, http://www.burnsarchive.com
Campus Heritage Plan, University of Kansas, fpd.ku.edu/campus-heritage-plan
City of Lake Charles, http://www. https://www.cityoflakecharles.com/
1870 Census, Ancestry.com, https://www.ancestry.com
Eleanor Roosevelt Papers, digital edition, https://erpapers.columbian.gwu.edu
    /online-editions
"Hot Springs, AR," Wikipedia, https://en.wikipedia.org/wiki/Hot_Springs,_Arkansas
"James Stewart Thomson," Political Graveyard.com, https://politicalgraveyard.com
    /bio/thomson.html
Jayhawker, University of Kansas yearbooks, www.e-yearbook.com/yearbooks/Kan
    sas_University_Jayhawker_yearbook/year/html
Lawrence Memorial Hospital website, https://www.lmh.org/foundation/history/
McCool, John, KU History, http://kuhistory.ku.edu/articles/25-rooms-riv-vu
Papers and Letters of JB Watkins and Elizabeth Miller Watkins (Spencer Research
    Library), https://archives.lib.ku.edu/repositories/3/archival_objects/102915
Printer's Row Publication Blog, https://www.portablepress.com
Punton Sanitarium, Preliminary Inventory of Neurological Hospital Association
    of Kansas City Records, 1935–1975, State Historical Society of Missouri, Kansas
    City Research Center, https://shsmo.org
"Richard Dey de Ribcowsky," Art in Embassies, https://art.state.gov/personnel/dey
    _de_ribcowsky/
Watkins Museum, online exhibit, https://www.watkinsmuseum.org/online-ex
    hibits/a-thing-of-beauty-the-story-of-the-watkins-building/
Wright, Marilyn, *Laurinburg Normal and Industrial Institute*, NCPedia, http://ncpe
    dia.org/laurinburg-normal-and-industrial-in

Other Sources
Hot Springs National Park, Arkansas, informational pamphlet. National Park Ser-
    vice, US Department of Interior, GPO:2019-407-308/82393, updated 2018.
KU Endowment Association. Morton County file, File 5346.

KU Office of the Chancellor. Welcome to the Outlook, pamphlet, 2021.

Leonard, Phil. *Lawrence Fire Department, Lawrence, Kansas, 1859–1976.* Full text available at https://assets.lawrenceks.org/fire-medical/files/LFD%20History%20 1859-1975%20(PL).pdf

National Archives. Civil War Pension File. Valentine Miller. Box #36035, Cert #249139.

Rankin, Robert. "An Idea That Grew." Paper read by Rankin before the Old and New Club on April 5, 1945. Author's collection.

Statements of former residents of Watkins and Miller Scholarship Halls, Kitchen 8 Archives, Watkins Museum of History, Folder 4/10 (unless otherwise noted)

Creta Carter Nichols, Watkins 1956–1958, Folder 4/6

Donna Holm Fisher, Watkins, 1946–1949, Folder 4/4

Doris Kent Fox, Watkins, 1935–1937

Eileen Griffith Bennett, Watkins, 1940–1944

Francis Strait Brown, Watkins, 1936–1938, Folder 4/5

Harriet Cowles Dyer, Watkins, 1926

Judy Johnson Niebaum, Miller, 1958–1961

Katherine Monroe Cook, Watkins, 1929–1933

Margery Lewis Wigner, Watkins, 1938–1941

Mary Ellen Roach Higgins, Watkins, 1938–1942

Pat Gardner Stein, Miller, 1953–1957

Ruth Green Saffel, Watkins, 1942–1946

Sarah Wohlrabe Shortall, Watkins 1972–1976

Susan Harshaw Kissinger, Watkins, 1936–1938

Books, Journals, and Other Published Sources

Armitage, Susan H., and Elizabeth Jameson, eds. *The Women's West.* Norman: University of Oklahoma Press, 1987.

B. Altman & Co. *Altman's Spring and Summer Fashions Catalog, 1915.* New York: Dover, 1995.

Barker, Jeffrey H., and Melissa Walker, eds. *Kansas Boy: The Memoir of A. J. Bolinger.* Lawrence: University Press of Kansas, 2021.

Bogue, Allan G. *Money at Interest: The Farm Mortgage on the Middle Border.* Lincoln: University of Nebraska Press, 1955.

Broadwater, Robert B. *The Battle of Perryville, 1862: Culmination of the Failed Kentucky Campaign.* Jefferson, NC: McFarland & Co., 1911.

Caldwell, E. F., comp. *A Souvenir History of Lawrence, Kansas, 1898: Containing*

Numerous Fine Half-Tone Illustrations and Descriptive Matter Reflective of the City and County. Kansas City, MO: Lawton & Burnap, 1898 (Lawrence, KS: House of Usher, 1985 [?] facsimile repr.).

Carson, Gerald. *The Cornflake Crusade*. New York: Rinehart, 1957.

Cheever, Susan. *Louisa May Alcott*. New York: Simon & Schuster, 2010.

Clarke, Mary Patterson. *The History of the First Methodist Episcopal Church of Lawrence, Kansas*. Kansas City, KS: Franklin Hudson Publishing, no date.

Connelly, William E., comp. *A Standard History of Kansas and Kansans*, 5 vols. Chicago: Lewis, 1918. Full text at HathiTrust digital library, https://hathitrust.org.

Cooper, Anderson. *Vanderbilt: The Rise and Fall of an American Dynasty*. New York: HarperCollins, 2021.

Cormier, Adley. *Lost Lake Charles*. Mt. Pleasant, SC: History Press, 2017.

Cutler, William G. *History of the State of Kansas*. Chicago: A.T. Andreas, 1883. http://www.Kancoll.org/books/cutler/douglas/douglas-co-p3.html.

Dary, David. *Lawrence, Douglas County, Kansas, an Informal History*. Lawrence, KS: Allen Books, 1982.

Edwards, Owen. "The Death of Colonel Ellsworth." *Smithsonian*, April 2011, https://www.smithsonianmag.com.

Flatow, Ira. *They All Laughed: From Light Bulbs to Lasers: The Fascinating Stories behind the Great Inventions That Have Changed Our Lives*. New York: Harper Perennial, 1993.

Frederiksen, D. M. "Mortgage Banking in America," *Journal of Political Economy* 2, no. 2 (March 1894): 203–234.

Griffin, Clifford S. *The University of Kansas: A History*. Lawrence: University Press of Kansas, 1974.

Haupt, Shirley. *Port of Lake Charles: A Vision for the Future*. Lake Charles, LA: Port of Lake Charles, 1998.

Hirsh, Jeff. *Manhattan Hotels 1880–1920*. Dover, NH: Arcadia, 1997.

Hoagland, Norma Decker, comp. *Watkins & Miller Halls: University of Kansas*. Lawrence, KS: Historic Mount Oread Friends, 2016.

Kiernan, Denise. *The Last Castle: The Epic Story of Love, Loss, and American Royalty in the Nation's Largest Home*. New York: Touchstone, 2017.

Lowry, R. E. *History of Preble County, Ohio: Her People, Industries and Institutions*. Owensboro, KY: Cook and McDowell, 1981.

McCollister, John. *The Baseball Book of Why: The Answers to Questions You've Always Wondered about from America's National Pastime*. Guilford, CT: Lyons, 2020.

McElhenie, Fred. *Making Do and Getting Through: KU Co-ops, Halls and Houses, 1919–1966*. Lawrence, KS: Historic Mount Oread Fund, 2006.

Nasaw, David. *Andrew Carnegie*. New York: Penguin, 2006.

Newcomb, Jack, ed. and comp. *A Thing of Beauty: The Story of the Watkins Building.* Watkins Community Museum, Lawrence, KS: 1988, rev. 1991.

Nofi, Albert A. *A Civil War Treasury.* New York: Da Capo, 1995.

Pratt, Fletcher. *Civil War in Pictures.* Garden City, New York: Garden City Books, 1957.

Preble County Historical Society. *A Pictorial History of the One-Room Schools of Preble County, Ohio.* Preble County, OH: Preble County Historical Society, no date.

Rayne, Mrs. M. L. *What Can a Woman Do or Her Position in the Business and Literary World.* Detroit, MI: F.B. Dickerson & Co., 1884.

Riney-Kehrberg, Pamela, ed. *The Routledge History of Rural America.* New York: Routledge, 2016.

Rowe, Elfriede Fischer. *Wonderful Old Lawrence.* Lawrence, KS: World Company, 1971.

———. *More Wonderful Old Lawrence.* Lawrence, KS: House of Usher, 1981.

Sain-Baird, Jessica, and Charles Higginson. "The Lady Bountiful." *KU Giving Magazine* 4, no. 3 (summer 2011): 12–17. (See inset "Whence the Watkins Wealth," p. 15.)

Scott, Emory Frank. *One Hundred Years of Lawrence Theatre.* Lawrence, KS: House of Usher, 1979.

Silver, Marisa. *Mary Coin.* New York: Blue Rider, 2013.

Skocpol, Theda. *Protecting Soldiers and Mothers: The Political Origins of Social Policy in the United States.* Cambridge, MA: Belknap Press of Harvard University Press, 1992.

Stuckey, Clay W. *An Illustrated Gazetteer of Limestone Mills in Owen, Monroe and Lawrence Counties in 1950.* Self-published, 1999; rev. ed., Bedford, IN: Lawrence County Historical Genealogical Society, 2016.

Taft, Robert. *Across the Years on Mt. Oread 1866–1941: An Informal and Pictorial History of the University of Kansas.* Lawrence: University of Kansas Press, 1941.

———. *The Outlook.* Lawrence: University of Kansas Press, 1955.

University of Kansas. *Watkins Hall Residence for Women.* Topeka, KS: State Printer, 1926.

Webb, Bernice Larson. *The Basketball Man: James Naismith.* Lawrence: University Press of Kansas, 1973.

Weichert, Sandra Swanson. *Historic Mount Oread: A Catalog of KU's Landmarks.* Lawrence, KS: Historic Mount Oread Fund, 1999.

We Unitarians: An Account of Unitarianism in Lawrence, Kansas 1854–1994. Lawrence, KS: Self-published, 1995.

Index

Entries in italics refer to photographs. Entries followed by *n* refer to notes.